turnbacktime
BBC

THE HIGH
STREET

turnback time
BBC

THE HIGH STREET

100 YEARS OF BRITISH LIFE THROUGH THE SHOP WINDOW

PHILIP WILKINSON

Quercus

CONTENTS

INTRODUCTION 6

THE BIRTH OF THE HIGH STREET 10

THE VICTORIAN HIGH STREET 20
1870–1901

THE EDWARDIAN HIGH STREET 62
1901–1917

THE INTERWAR HIGH STREET 100
1918–1939

THE WARTIME HIGH STREET 140
1939–1945

THE POST-WAR HIGH STREET 176
1945–1969

THE 1970S HIGH STREET 214
1970–1979

THE FUTURE OF THE HIGH STREET 250

YOUR HIGH STREET'S STORY 256

THE SHOPKEEPERS 266

INDEX 268

PICTURE CREDITS 272

THE MAKING OF... THE HIGH STREET

In the summer of 2010, BBC One invited seven shopkeepers and their families to take part in an extraordinary living history experiment – to run four shops exactly as they would have been in six key eras of British history, from the boom years of the High Street in the 1870s through a century of highs, lows and profound changes that paved the way for how we shop today.

Over a period of six weeks, a group of modern day butchers, bakers, caterers and retailers left their lives and livelihoods behind to trade their way through one hundred years of history in the picturesque but neglected market square of Shepton Mallet, Somerset. As they journeyed through time, their challenge was to run these businesses according to the rules and regulations of the day, and to convince the residents of Shepton Mallet to love their small shops once more.

The shopkeepers had to deal with whatever history threw at them, from hand-making their own Victorian produce to horse-drawn deliveries, 1940s rationing to the arrival of the 1970s supermarket, in order to discover if the past holds the clues to the future of the great British High Street. Throughout their remarkable journey, the shopkeepers and the town saw first-hand what we have lost and gained, and found out whether they could bring back Shepton Mallet's High Street and make it thrive.

INTRODUCTION

PEOPLE USED TO CALL BRITAIN a nation of shopkeepers, but we have become besotted with out-of-town malls, superstores and online shopping. Over the past 150 years or so the High Street has changed out of all recognition. This book looks at what we have lost along the way, and what we have gained too. Chronicling the changes on the High Street from the Victorian period onwards, it charts the route from personal service to self-service, from make do and mend to the disposable society, from the customer is always right to the customer wants it now. It's an exciting journey, showing how both retailers and their customers adapted to both good times and bad during a century and a half of change on the shopping streets of Britain.

THE HEART OF THE NATION

Several people, including Napoleon and the Scottish philosopher Adam Smith, have regarded the British as a nation of shopkeepers. The phrase was originally meant to be disparaging – indicating a people obsessed by the trivial concerns of buying and selling on a small scale. But it means far more than this because it refers to the way in which Britain has long placed shopping at the heart of the national culture. And for hundreds of years, the main place where we have bought life's essentials and its little luxuries, from bread to beef, buckets to baubles, has been the High Street.

The High Street is a practical place. It employs lots of people, who sell the food and household goods that we need to survive. It's also a place where people go for fun, to relax in a restaurant, to browse in boutiques and bookshops, to meet friends and to buy presents. Those who work there spend most of their lives there – and traditional shopkeepers lived above the shop too. But with the rise of Internet shopping and out of town retail centres, we are spending less time on the High Street and it is no longer such a focal point at the heart of our towns and cities.

Every town has a High Street, and it's a street that sums up the town – its character, its history and the needs, likes and dislikes of the local people. Shopping streets can be hugely varied. The Georgian sophistication of Bath, the long history of York or Chester, and the Victorian grandeur of Leeds or Newcastle are all reflected in the architecture and style of their shopping streets. In smaller towns, shopping streets are often distinctive because they contain small businesses, a local bakery, say, or a butcher's shop, that have been run by the same family for many generations. These businesses might also stock produce sourced nearby – local cheese or meat, fruit grown in the region – and so be key players in making their area distinctive and special.

But the High Street is also home to the chain stores. They make the place less distinctive, but also bring in custom. Chains such as Boots and Marks & Spencer Ltd have had a long presence in British towns. Even if some people complain that they detract from the local distinctiveness of the High Street, many of these shops are cherished and have been for generations. There is an outcry when one of them is forced out of business, as happened to Woolworth's in 2008–9. People want both shops like these and the High Street in general to do well, because a healthy High Street usually means a prosperous town, and economists scrutinise the results of our retailers in hopeful search for signs that the economy is on the upturn. Understand the High Street and you can grasp what makes us and our towns tick.

TIMES OF CHANGE

This book describes a gradual process of change in Britain's High Streets, showing what it was like for both shopkeepers and customers in six different periods: Victorian, Edwardian, interwar, the Second World War, post-war and the 1970s. It's a fascinating story, showing how such basics as how we buy our daily bread or weekly joint of beef have changed over the years, how shops have been transformed from the small businesses of the Victorians to today's supermarkets and how the skills of retailers and the expectations of customers have altered almost beyond recognition.

Along the way their proprietors had to cope with dramatic upheavals that turned the world, and especially the world of retailing, upside down:

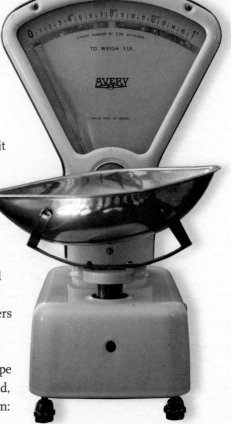

the two world wars, the depression of the late 1920s and early 1930s, the huge social transformations of the 1960s and so on. Responding to such changes was a huge challenge, but retailing emerged renewed and refreshed each time. And change happened in the good times too, because even when things were going well, retailers felt the need to reinvent themselves constantly, to cope with burgeoning competition and to convince customers that what they offered was the latest and the best.

THE SIX AGES OF SHOPPING

Each of the eras covered in this book made some special contribution to retailing, and these contributions are interesting both in their own right and because they are often things that have been lost, or obscured, in shopkeeping today. We learn a lot from them, and at a time when retailing faces yet more difficulties and crises, it is worth learning everything we can.

In the Victorian era, retailing was about craft skills that were learned, painstakingly, over a long period of time. Shopkeepers had apprentices, and the skills they learned were taken very seriously. The grocer had to know how to blend tea, grind coffee and cure and slice bacon; bakers made their own bread; ironmongers actually made many of the metal items they sold in their shops, from simple buckets to intricate fire grates and ranges. So even if Victorian shops were sometimes dingy and unhygienic, their owners' skills were prized. Customers could ask for goods to be made or mixed individually, and could speak directly to the person who baked their bread or made their kitchen utensils. Many of today's consumers, used to buying bread made in a distant factory or cutlery manufactured in China, have lost a sense of where goods are produced.

For the Edwardians, a love of luxury drove some of their most successful retailers. It was an age of elegance and, for the rich, extravagance, but it was also the prelude to the First World War, when many had to endure shortages and deprivation. It was impressive how Edwardian shopkeepers managed to service Britain's diverse population with both cheap bazaars and lavish department stores, high-class bakers and cheap grocers.

The interwar years showed how retailers could take the initiative and adopt new ideas to keep their businesses profitable. Delivery vans and dough-mixing machines, new products like the wireless and new fashions in shop design kept the High Street on its toes. But those working in the most successful shops held on to what was best in their traditional values, above all giving good service and putting the customer first. This often proved a winning combination that got shops through the tough times of the Great Depression.

During the Second World War the High Street showed more than at any other time how retailing could adapt quickly in a crisis. Dealing with rationing, making the best of meagre stocks, handing out advice about new recipes and ways of 'making do and mending' – all these things helped make people's lives bearable in wartime. Shop owners and customers alike discovered that even the deepest crisis could create opportunities.

There was a mixture of optimism and real hardship in the post-war era. The huge rebuilding programme gave many towns entirely new shopping streets – and often new ways of shopping as more and more businesses adopted self-service. New cultural influences, from America and from the young, brought new styles in clothes, music, even food. Retailers were learning quickly once more.

The same went for the 1970s, when the changes of that decade – the huge expansion in supermarket shopping, the beginnings of out-of-town retailing, the widening gulf between small shops and multiples – are still having an impact 30 years on. And these developments are especially important now, because Britain's shops face still more changes and challenges. The recent global economic crisis, the growth of out-of-town shopping, green challenges to consumerism and the meteoric rise of Internet trading have all put pressures on the High Street. Understanding the High Street's history and its endless past transformations can help us to see how it might adapt in the future.

Below Service with a smile. At its best the British High Street brings together good business skills and a rapport with the customers.

Chapter One

THE BIRTH OF THE GREAT BRITISH HIGH STREET

TO UNDERSTAND THE STORY of the High Street,
it's worth looking at its early history, to discover how shops
began in the first place. This is a fascinating story, taking us
back almost a thousand years, to a time when there
were hardly any shops at all.

In the Middle Ages most people did not need to shop as much as we do. Country people grew most of their own vegetables and crops and kept animals for milk and meat. In towns some people also had the space to grow food, but many bought their provisions at the local market, where country people came, both to sell their wares and to buy the things they needed but could not produce themselves. Medieval markets were special because the right to hold a market was granted by the monarch in a document called a charter. This would lay down the place where the market was to be held and on which day (or days) of the week. The right to hold the market was vested in the lord of the manor, who would charge traders for the privilege of setting up a stall in the market place.

Many market charters go back hundreds of years. Some were even granted by William the Conqueror to his most trusted lords, giving them the right to hold a market on a certain day in a particular town, and in some places it is still market day on the day of the week set down in a charter of the 11th or 12th century. Markets attracted custom, and a town that held a market would expand as more people – both potential market traders and customers – moved there. So towns grew up around markets, and one definition of a town is a place that has a market.

MARKET DAY

For traders market time was when they did most of their business. For shoppers it was also a special day, a chance for them to escape the drudgery of their everyday lives and meet their friends. And so the lively, colourful, holiday-like atmosphere of markets that we know today, with lots of noise and banter, almost certainly dates back to their earliest days.

Early market traders sold their goods from simple stalls, which were quite similar to the market stalls of today. These were arranged in rows and had a demountable wooden frame that supported a table for the goods and a cover to keep both stock and trader dry. Some of these rows of stalls became permanent structures, and traders such as fishmongers and butchers preferred these, perhaps because if they were allotted their own permanent stall they knew that it was clean. These rows of permanent stalls were still fairly crude structures, made of wood. They were called 'shambles' (from an Old English word for a table) and the only surviving shambles – a small group of stalls from what would have been a much larger one – are in the market place at Shepton Mallet in Somerset.

Markets soon developed more permanent architecture. Many markets had a market cross, to remind early traders that God was watching over them and that their deals should be fair. Sometimes the cross topped a stone building – often octagonal and intricately carved – where customers and traders could sit or shelter from the rain. Some stunning Medieval market crosses remain – Chichester in West Sussex and Salisbury and Malmesbury, both in Wiltshire, all have good examples.

Most of the stallholders in the early markets sold food. There were farmers who would bring in their produce – meat, cheese and eggs – and, in towns not

too far from the coast, fishmongers who would offer the latest catch. Parts of the market might also be set aside for livestock, where farmers could bring stock they wanted to sell and haggle with their colleagues. Some of these later developed into specialist livestock markets.

As well as markets, there were fairs. These were mega-markets, annual events to which traders would come from much farther afield. They sold everything – cloth, fleeces and gloves, carved wooden ornaments and intricate metalwork, fine wines, and herbs and spices. If market day was a holiday, a Medieval fair was a true festival of buying and selling.

FROM WORKSHOP TO SHOP

When people came to town for the market, they would also look further than the stalls themselves. Most towns had traders – craftsmen especially – who needed a permanent base. On market day the workshops of carpenters and metalworkers, leatherworkers and potters would be thrown open so that buyers could purchase goods or commission a craftsman to make something. And so the workshop, a place where things are made, became the shop, where things are sold – although there would have been no shop window and little in the way of a display of goods.

To begin with these artisans and workshop-keepers were a cut above the market traders. In the Middle Ages, to trade from a shop in this way, a person had to be a freeman or citizen; in other words, to have some standing in the town. Most were not rich, but their trade or skill gave them status and they were proud of their craft. Some of their neighbours, though, might be rich merchants with large town houses that doubled as business premises. So the ground floor

of a merchant's town house might consist of a generous storage area in which stock could both be kept and shown to visiting customers. Above the storage area, or sometimes behind it, the merchant and his family would have their living quarters.

FROM STALL TO SHOP

Although they did not usually aspire to the rich kind of house enjoyed by merchants, many market traders also saw the attraction of having a base in town where customers could come every day. So in some places rows of stalls gradually became more permanent, evolving over the years into shops. These first-generation shops were often crammed into a very tight space and the streets were very narrow because they originally made up the space between the stalls in a market place. The 16th-century London historian John Stow, in his *A Survey of London*, described how Fish Street in the capital evolved in this way:

> …*these houses, now possessed by fishmongers, were at the first but moveable boards, or stalls, set out on market-days, to show their fish there to be sold; but procuring licence to set up sheds, they grew to shops, and by little and little to tall houses, of three or four storeys in height, and are now called Fish Street.*

So the fishmongers acquired permanent premises, with storage space and somewhere to live above the shop, and London acquired another street, albeit a cramped one with buildings that lacked open space behind them. It is significant that it was the fishmongers that Stow picked out. Many of these early rows of shops were occupied by fishmongers or butchers, the first kinds of traders to have shambles.

This move from market stalls to shops on the same site happened in many towns. The evidence for it is quite easy to spot – cramped narrow streets running next to a market place are the clearest sign. Salisbury has several such streets, and their names confirm this transition – they include Butcher Row, Fish Row and Oatmeal Row. The narrow streets in Ludlow in Shropshire and the picturesque Shambles in York share a similar history.

These shops on the sites of shambles were probably built in the late Middle Ages, in the 15th or 16th century. Shops in those days did not look quite like the ones we know today. Glass was still very expensive and these shops did not have a shop window. Instead, much of the front was taken up by a large wooden shutter, hinged along the bottom. At opening time this was opened downwards, so that it stuck out into the street, where it was held flat on a trestle, forming a kind of table. The shopkeeper could then arrange his goods on it, and this display would entice customers just as effectively as a modern shop window.

SHOP WINDOWS

In the late 17th century, London led the trend towards a new kind of shop. After the Great Fire of London in 1666, most of the city was rebuilt along similar lines to before. Traders wanted to keep their original sites so that people would know where to find them, and architects like Sir Christopher Wren were disappointed when their proposals to replan the city went for nothing. But there were changes. Samuel Pepys, a keen observer of 17th-century life, noticed one important development in 1667: 'I walked in the Exchange, which is now made pretty, by having windows and doors before all their shops to keep out the cold.' Glass windows had arrived, and shopping could be done in comfort.

So, by the 18th century, shops had started to become more like the ones we know today. Many had windows – not of plate glass, but of many small panes – and their frontages were decorated with a host of knowing architectural details. Features such as columns and pilasters were borrowed from the vocabulary of classical architecture, so that the most upmarket shops became virtual temples of commerce. Gilding and polished mirrors were used too, to reflect the light of candles and to make shops look rich and inviting.

The interiors of these new shops were proper indoor spaces, quite unlike the half-inside, half-outside impression given by the Medieval and Tudor shop. They were often beautifully fitted out, with fine furniture and well-made shelves, drawers and counters, as if to convey a sense of luxury. One observer, André Rouquet, vividly described this new opulence in the shops of London:

> The London shops of every kind, make a most brilliant and most agreeable show, which infinitely contributes to the decoration of this great city. Everything is rubb'd clean and neat; every thing is inclosed in large glass shew glasses, whose frames, as well as all the wainscot in the shop, are generally fresh painted, which is productive of an air of wealth and elegance that we do not see in any other city.

The goods on offer were more varied, too, because in the 18th century Britain began to become a centre for industry. While it was not yet perhaps the workshop of the world that it would become in the next century, there was still a widening choice of consumer goods, from fabrics to jewellery. And as the century went on, choice and variety increased still further, fuelled by Britain's steadily growing industry and by imports from the empire.

The glittering variety of Britain's shops in the mid-18th century has led some historians to suggest there was a retailing revolution in this period. This, they argue, is the era in which we became consumers, spending our money not just on food and the essentials of survival, but also and increasingly on luxuries and items of display. This was when, it is said, we began to define ourselves by the kinds of possessions that we owned.

Other historians have questioned this idea, pointing out that we know so little about earlier shops and what they sold that it is implausible to talk about such a revolution. Yet there was an industrial revolution taking place, and this was not solely about building steam engines and canals. It is likely that there was a big change in retailing and consuming in the 18th century, especially for the people from the middle and upper classes who had plenty of disposable income. The shops of the 18th century, with their glass windows, effective lighting and rich displays, sparkled as never before, and customers responded with enthusiasm.

CLASS DISTINCTIONS

Georgian shops were a far cry from the brash fronts put up on today's High Streets, and outside London and the large cities the picture was very different. For a start, many people in the country still did not need to go shopping for most of their needs. If they belonged to the upper classes they had farms to produce their own foods; poorer people grew food in their gardens, kept a pig, made their own clothes and got by with very basic possessions. If they did need to supplement what they grew with extra food, they mostly went to the market, or to a small local general store, and bought the cheapest available.

The middle classes were more likely to go to the 'high-class' shops on the High Street. It was mostly they who would patronise established traders, such the local grocer, who called himself a 'high-class' tradesman and saw himself as a skilled craftsman, knowledgeable about blending teas and drying fruit. The grocer was a purveyor of mainly imported items – such as sugar, tea, coffee and spices – many of which carried trade tariffs and so were expensive. These were foodstuffs above all bought by the middle classes. The middle-class shopper might also call at the baker and confectioner, who baked his own stock behind the shop, or the butcher, both of whom were also craft traders, while the lower classes baked their own bread and relied for meat on the pig kept behind the cottage.

So in the early 19th century the more upmarket shopping was done in shops on the High Street while the poor resorted to market stalls. High-class grocers, butchers and bakers prided themselves on the quality of their goods. They often did well and rose to prominence in the community as councillors, churchwardens or members of other influential local groups.

CITIES AND SHOPS

Around the middle of the 19th century this pattern began to change. As Britain became increasingly industrial, more and more people moved to the cities to take up jobs in factories. They lived in small, cramped houses and had neither the space nor the time to grow their own food. They needed basic shops offering good value.

They were helped by several developments. Trade barriers and tariffs had mostly disappeared by the 1860s, bringing a variety of imported goods into the

country at much lower prices than before. Expanding industries at home also made more goods available. The new transport links, especially the railways, carried all this merchandise around, and a new breed of wholesalers sold it to the retailers. Above all, it became fashionable to consume – to fill the home with ornaments and acquire fashionable items, from Staffordshire dogs to pianos. People liked to have more than one suit of clothes, including special clothes for 'Sunday best'.

The fashion for this kind of consumerism gathered momentum as the Victorian period went on. By the late 19th century Britain's industry was among the most successful and productive in the world and the country was at the centre of a vast empire. Products flowed around the country, both from abroad and from booming manufacturing centres such as Birmingham, a city that became known as the workshop of the world. The profusion of goods on offer was famously displayed in the Great Exhibition at the Crystal Palace in London in 1851.

So by 1870, at the height of this explosion of retail activity, the High Street began to look a little more like the High Street of modern times. True, the Victorian High Street was more chaotic than our own. Displays spilled out of shops over the pavements, signage was often colourfully varied and shoppers had to contend with mud spattered by carts and carriages and with importunate beggars. The shops themselves were very diverse, ranging from glittering emporia aimed at the rich to dingy food shops supplying fare of variable quality and frequented by those with little money. Amid this variety and chaos, the story of the modern High Street begins.

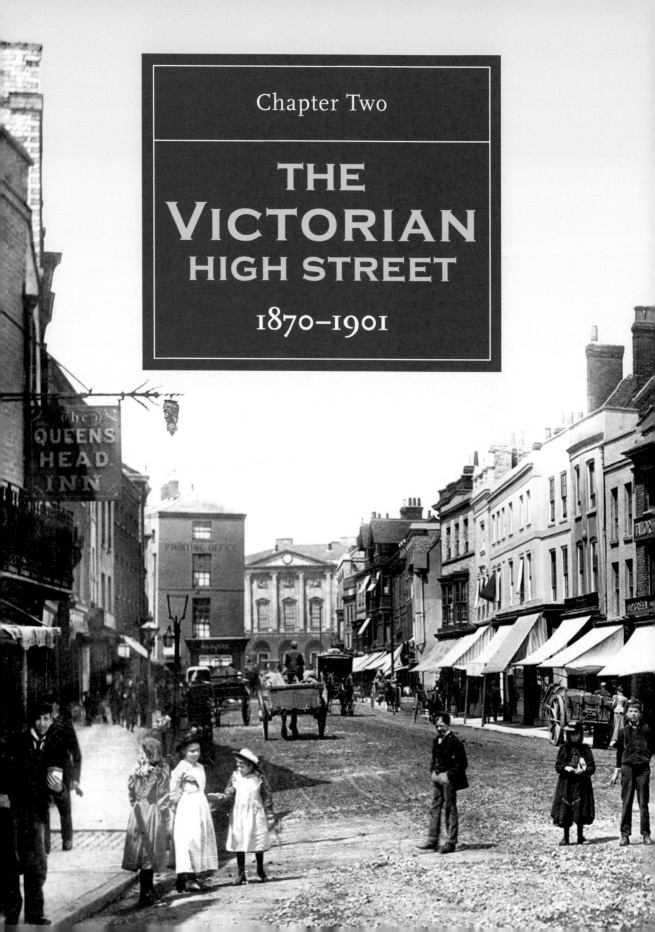

Chapter Two

THE VICTORIAN HIGH STREET

1870–1901

THE VICTORIAN HIGH STREET was full of shops, full of shoppers and full of life. Britain's wealth from trade and the country's enormous empire brought prosperity to towns and cities, and a huge range of traders set up shop, from butchers and bakers to ironmongers selling a bewildering variety of items and photographers taking people's portraits.

During Queen Victoria's reign Britain was changing fast. In the century before she came to the throne, two developments had changed the course of the history of Britain and the world. First, Britain had acquired an empire of global proportions. A combination of bravery in exploration, meticulous organisation and sheer acquisitiveness had put vast tracts of North America, Africa, Asia and Australia under British rule. Second, the Industrial Revolution arrived. Britain's mines and factories hummed with activity, and people flocked to the ever-expanding towns and cities to find work.

The combination of empire and industry bore rich fruit in the Victorian era, when more and more factories were built. Raw materials such as cotton flooded into Britain and were processed into fabrics in British mills. These then were sent back out again to find ready markets across the empire. Britain became the wealthiest of all nations and by the 1880s was responsible for around a quarter of total world trade.

This frenzied industrial activity, together with the trade links provided by the empire, had a huge impact on both shops and shoppers. You could buy almost

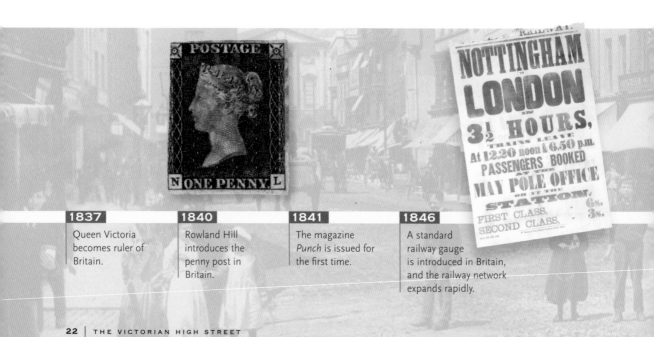

1837
Queen Victoria becomes ruler of Britain.

1840
Rowland Hill introduces the penny post in Britain.

1841
The magazine *Punch* is issued for the first time.

1846
A standard railway gauge is introduced in Britain, and the railway network expands rapidly.

anything in Britain – especially in the big cities where the rich congregated and shops expanded to meet the demand. In smaller country towns there were fewer shops, with narrower ranges of goods, but even here there was change. Commodities such as tea and sugar, both very costly in the 18th century, became more widely available as supplies were shipped in bulk from India. And so the power of the empire was felt even in grocers' shops and in drawing rooms in the remotest of country locations.

THE TRANSPORT REVOLUTION

Victorian shops could stock a range of goods from outside their local area because of a revolution in transport. Global transportation of goods was not a major problem. Vast distances were covered by Britain's ships, and the main ports had docks with long rows of warehouses to take their cargoes. But how did the goods get from warehouses in Liverpool or London to shops in Ely or Exeter?

The 18th century had answered the question with canals, but canal transport was slow. The real answer was the railways. Unlike barges or carts, they were fast, and the mines provided ample coal for their fuel. Building track, stations, tunnels, viaducts and all the other parts of the railway infrastructure was costly and time-consuming. But there were profits to be made and soon businessmen were investing in this new form of transport. Soon after Victoria came to the throne in 1837, a railway boom was under way. Railways, sparse in the 1830s, multiplied in the following decade, and by the 1870s there was an intricate network of railway lines – main arteries connecting large cities, and branch lines leading to smaller towns.

Railways transformed what people could buy. In former centuries most of the goods in shops and on market stalls were produced locally. Now even food and drink could be moved around at speed and pies from Melton Mowbray,

1851
The Great Exhibition is held in the Crystal Palace, London.

1859
Charles Darwin publishes *On the Origin of Species by Natural Selection*.

1861
Albert, Prince Consort, dies.

1863
London's Metropolitan Railway, the first underground line, is opened.

1867
Joseph Lister describes the practice of antiseptic surgery.

cheese from Cheddar and beer from Burton-on-Trent found markets far beyond their local regions. It was the beginning of a major change in the way we buy food, opening up consumer choice. Food retailing has never looked back.

GOOD FOOD, BAD FOOD

But it has never been easy to make a lot of money selling food on a small scale. Many shopkeepers were tempted to rest a discreet hand on their scales so that they gave short weight, or, in an age long before sell-by dates, to palm off goods that were far beyond their best. But some people went further, adding cheap additional ingredients, often far from healthy ones at that, to their food to bulk it up. The 19th century was a great age of food adulteration. The things that were mixed into foodstuffs beggar belief. Alum was added to flour, copper sulphate to pickles and preserves, iron sulphate to tea and a range of chemicals to chocolate. Many foods also had dangerous substances added to make them look more appetising: copper compounds were sometimes stirred into butter to improve its colour, while there were reports of Gloucester cheese 'enhanced' with red lead.

A *Punch* cartoon of 1855 summed it up. A girl stands at a grocer's counter with an order from her mother: 'Mother says, will you let her have a quarter of a pound [0.1 kg] of your best tea to kill the rats with, and an ounce [28 g] of chocolate to get rid of the black beadles [i.e. beetles].' It all made the watering of milk and the recycling of used tea leaves, both also common, look relatively innocuous.

The government, at first reluctant to interfere with the way people did business, eventually passed a number of Pure Food Acts, the first in 1860. But the law was aimed squarely at the producers of adulterated foods. Shopkeepers were not liable, and the purchase of food remained fraught with hazards.

1870
The Education Act introduces free elementary education for children.

1871
Bank Holidays are introduced in England and Wales.

1875
The Public Health Act gives local authorities responsibility for sanitation and water supply.

1877
Queen Victoria is proclaimed Empress of India.

1878
The first electric street lighting is installed in London.

FASHION AND TASTE

The revolution in consumer choice and the ready availability of all kinds of goods meant that the market was full of decorative items that the Victorians liked to cram into their houses. From photographs in frames to pottery dogs, fire irons to foot stools, they filled their homes as never before: Victorian clutter was born. It looks old-fashioned now in the age of high tech and minimalist design, but in the 19th century, items such as portrait photographs and electro-plated toasting forks represented new technology, and the Victorians were fascinated by the latest inventions.

But they also had a strong traditionalist streak. The favourite Victorian style of architecture was Gothic, the pointed-arched style of the Medieval cathedrals. They loved this so much that Gothic arches appeared on everything – not just on buildings like schools, town halls and factories, but also on bookcases, chairs and picture frames. The Victorian love of craftsmanship and intricacy was fulfilled by items such as finely carved Gothic-style furniture, even if some of the mouldings were carved by machine.

Towards the end of the century more sophisticated shoppers, influenced by the pared-down designs and hand-crafted furniture of the Arts and Crafts movement that had begun in the 1860s, threw out the clutter. But the white walls and airy interiors of Arts and Crafts architects such as C.F.A. Voysey and M.H. Baillie Scott, although influential on the design-conscious middle classes, passed most ordinary Victorians by and people clung to their love of clutter, innovation and ever-increasing choice. Most Victorian shopkeepers were happy to carry on supplying their needs.

Natural History Museum, London

1879
Australian frozen meat goes on sale in Britain for the first time.

1881
The Natural History Museum, London, is opened.

1885
Karl Benz builds the first motor car.

1888
J.B. Dunlop develops the pneumatic tyre.

1897
Queen Victoria's Diamond Jubilee is celebrated.

SETTING
UP SHOP

Stocked up with a rich mixture of local and imported goods and offering a warm welcome to eager customers, Victorian shopkeepers looked forward to turning a handsome profit. Many were food retailers, such as butchers, bakers and grocers, but there were also traders such as ironmongers, who offered everything from the most utilitarian tools and utensils to fancy lamps and cutlery, dealers in crockery and glassware, drapers and retailers of leather goods. All hoped to persuade shoppers to put something extra in their basket.

Many shopkeepers were successful, but the route to prosperity was rarely smooth. There was plenty of competition. Some successful businesses opened shops in several towns, and local traders for the first time had to face stiff competition from owners of several shops, the ancestors of today's supermarket owners. For many shopkeepers, though, the challenge came not from these 'multiples', such as Lipton's or Sainsbury's, but from fellow local businesses, especially market traders. Street markets had been the main shopping centres of earlier centuries and they were still a useful source of goods for the Victorian shopper. Their keen prices and regularly replenished stocks of basic household items made them the shopping destinations of choice for anyone on a tight budget – and that meant most working-class households.

Housewives liked the fact that at market stalls they could buy meat, eggs and vegetables direct from the farmer or grower, and often fish too. For Victorian shopkeepers it was often a case of 'if you can't beat them, join them', and many took a stall on market day to give their business an extra chance to

Opposite The Victorian ironmonger's not only supplied metalwork and tools, but everyday household essentials.

make a sale. So in traditional market towns, markets continued to thrive, while in recently expanded Victorian cities the authorities built new market halls where stallholders could trade in the dry.

The continuing popularity of markets meant that there was something of a class division in shopping, with the rich patronising the comfortable and more expensive shops and poorer people shopping in the market. But in the Victorian period this distinction was breaking down. The greater variety of shops, some selling cheap goods brought in from afar on the railway, encouraged this change. So too did better marketing by shopkeepers as they realised the power of alluring shop fronts and ingenious advertising.

So, although the Victorians were highly class-conscious, there were signs that the class barriers on the High Street were beginning to blur as the 19th century progressed. Shopkeepers saw the expanding market, embracing rich and poor alike, as an opportunity and, from grocer to ironmonger, haberdasher to milliner, shops burgeoned and counters groaned with goods.

THE VICTORIAN GROCER

By the end of the Victorian era the grocer was the linchpin of the High Street. Grocers sold a range of foods and household goods. But it had not always been like this. Grocers began as dealers in various kinds of produce, including teas, coffees, sugar, dried fruits and spices, many of which were imported from overseas. They bought these items in bulk (or in 'gross', hence the word 'grocer') and weighed out the quantities their customers required.

Dealing in these kinds of items meant that a Victorian grocer had to have both a different set of skills and a different range of equipment from a modern food retailer. He needed a variety of paper bags, cartons and labels – as well as business cards and printed stationery for bills and letters, which meant his outlay at the printer and stationer's alone could be substantial. And he needed equipment such as scales, barrels, casks, jars and furniture in which to keep his stock, plus a hand cart or a horse and cart for deliveries.

Most of the items sold by the grocers in the 17th and 18th centuries were seen as luxury items and so their customers were those with higher incomes – the middle classes and above. Poorer people were likely to have a much more restricted diet, and many grew their own food. They did not need to visit the grocer to supply their basic fare of vegetables, bacon and bread, so grocers served mostly the carriage trade.

But the Industrial Revolution changed the food market. In the 19th century, increasing numbers of people worked in factories and lived in small houses in towns and cities. Most of them did not have gardens to grow food in and if they did have a garden they had little time to tend it. What they needed was a one-stop general store for food and basic household items. So during the Victorian age the role of the grocer began to change. Low import duties reduced the prices of goods brought in from abroad. Increasingly, grocers supplied not just the rich but everyone with basic food products, both imported goods, such as sugar and tea, and home-produced items such as cheese, milk, jam and butter. Because records are scarce, it is hard to say exactly when this change took place, but it started between the 1830s and the 1860s, over which time the number of

THE DAIRY AND ITS PRODUCTS

The milk, cream, butter and cheese sold by Victorian grocers was mostly produced by hand on dairy farms and delivered regularly to the shopkeeper, who would sell some on the premises and deliver some to customers' homes by cart. Before the introduction of milk bottles towards the end of the 19th century, milk was carried around in churns and measured out in jugs. In the Victorian dairy, the milk from the cows was collected and left to settle in large bowls. The cream settling on the top could be skimmed off for sale separately or for other uses.

LEFT *The proprietor and his staff stand in front of Bishop & Son's dairy, London, in about 1900. Delivery carts are at the ready.*

MAKING BUTTER

One of the main dairy products derived from cream was butter, which was widely used in the days before margarine or spreads made from vegetable oils became common. Butter was made by first letting the cream sour, then churning it vigorously, a process that took at least half an hour. By the end of the churning process the buttermilk had separated from the rest of the cream; this liquid was removed, leaving 'grains' of butter almost ready. The grains of butter were then kneaded and worked together with a pair of wooden boards known as scotch hands, creating a solid mass of butter and eliminating any remaining buttermilk. A little salt could be added to enhance the taste before the butter was cut into blocks ready for sale. The buttermilk could be drunk or used in baking.

ABOVE *Butter churn*

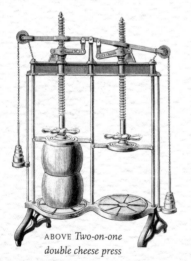

ABOVE *Two-on-one double cheese press*

MAKING CHEESE

Cheese was made in various ways according to local fashion and its quality and taste varied according to the materials used. Cheese could be made of whole milk, as in Cheshire; of milk and cream, as in Stilton; of a mixture of new milk and skimmed milk, as in Gloucestershire; or of skimmed milk only, as in Suffolk. In each case the key first stage in cheese making was to separate the solid curds of the milk from the liquid whey. This was usually done by adding rennet, which is derived from curdled milk from a calf's stomach. The curds could be compressed in a press to squeeze out more whey or kneaded together to make solid cheese. Some cheese makers added natural colouring such as arnatto, turmeric or marigold to enhance the appearance. Some cheeses were allowed to age, which improved the flavour.

groceries and general food stores in London seems to have increased fivefold. Other towns were probably not far behind.

Not all grocers made this change. Some were reluctant to give up their luxury goods and rich customers, and carried on as 'high-class' grocers. Others took the plunge by selling a wider range of cheaper stock, including new products such as condensed milk and margarine, to all comers. But it could be a risky business. The poor often asked for credit from their grocer, and when times became hard and people lost their jobs or had to take a cut in wages, these bills were not paid. Not surprisingly, many grocers went bankrupt.

All these changes meant that the grocer was the exception to the rule that Victorian food shopkeepers were specialists. Grocers stocked a wide range of foods, from teas to dairy products. Although some goods, such as branded sauces, jams and pickles, were supplied ready bottled by the manufacturer, grocers had to pack most of the goods themselves. They would buy tea, for example, in large wooden chests, weighing and bagging the amount the customer requested.

But the Victorian grocer's job was about much more than weighing and bagging. He had to be able to grind coffee, mix herbs and spices, cut and grind sugar, blend tea, and cut, cure and slice bacon. To achieve skills like these, grocers had to serve a long apprenticeship, during which time they got to know most of what there was to know about the stock. The experienced grocer would be able to offer advice about ingredients, blends of tea or coffee and different types of cheese.

Regular customers, shopping daily in the era before refrigerators, would come to value the advice of a good grocer, and the bond between shopkeeper and customer became much closer than it usually is today.

TRANSPORT AND PROCESSING

Many items in the grocer's shop travelled long distances to reach the High Street. Tea chests and big sacks of sugar, boxes of raisins and sacks of flour were both heavy and bulky. Since many of these items originated abroad, they had to be brought from the docks by train. All this added a considerable cost to the price of goods the grocer sold.

Change did not stop in the 1860s. More and more processed foods came in, and grocers were expected to offer them. If you wanted dried peas or biscuits, the grocer was your port of call. All kinds of processed products, such as Colman's mustard, Fry's cocoa and Cadbury's chocolate, were also soon to be found on the grocer's shelves.

Below Milk was delivered using a small hand cart carrying the milk churn and a range of measures. There would also be room for other dairy products such as butter.

In country areas, where a village might have just one or two shops, the local grocer found himself taking on all kinds of additional duties. Some combined the trades of, say, grocer and ironmonger, or grocer and baker. In an age before supermarkets, the rural grocer was the nearest thing to a 'one-stop' food shop.

QUALITY AND MARKETING

In a town with a thriving High Street and plenty of specialist shops, the grocer was the key retailer for food and general provisions, and often there was enough trade for more than one grocer. Because customers could buy from another grocer, or from market stalls or travelling food sellers, the canny grocer would strive to stand out from his competitors. One approach was to emphasise the traditional virtues of the food retailer, such as quality of stock and spotless premises. This was the strategy adopted by one of the most successful Victorian grocers, London's John Sainsbury. John, son of a hardware seller and grocer,

Below A Victorian advertisement for a South London branch of the 'Provision Merchant' Sainsbury's shows a high-class shop packed full with enticing goods.

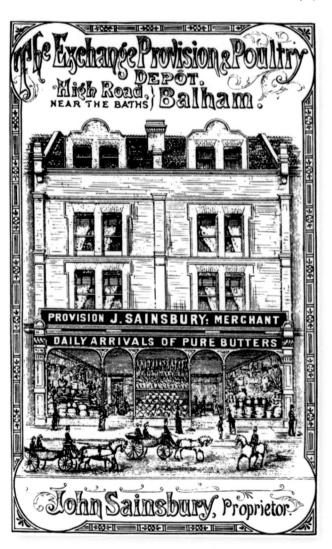

married his sweetheart Mary Ann, daughter of a grocer, in 1869. In that same year they started a small dairy produce shop in Drury Lane, selling food of the best quality in a clean and tidy setting. The Sainsbury business was a success because, at a time when food adulteration was still common and streets and street stalls were dirty and unappealing, their shop stood out from the crowd. Before long they opened more stores, developing each branch carefully and insisting on the same approach to quality and hygiene.

At around the same time another famous grocer, Thomas Lipton, was opening his first shop. Lipton too was the son of a shopkeeper, this time in Glasgow, but like many in the Victorian period he planned to make his fortune in America. He sailed to the USA in 1865, but failed to find well-paid work. He went from one job to another, ending up as a clerk in a department store before returning to Britain. Back home, he thought he could succeed in business by applying American principles to the grocery trade. So in 1871 he opened a small shop and, with

CURRENCY BEFORE DECIMALISATION

In the Victorian period (and until 1971) the British pound was divided into 20 shillings, each of which was worth 12 old pennies (5p). The low-value coins were made of copper in the early part of the period but later were made of bronze. They were colloquially known as 'coppers' and included the penny, halfpenny and farthing (quarter penny). Higher-value silver coins included threepenny and sixpenny pieces, the shilling and the two-shilling piece. There was also a crown, worth five shillings, and a half-crown, worth two shillings and sixpence. The pound bought much more in the mid-Victorian era than it does today. In the late 1860s, for example, a labourer might be paid around one pound a week, a skilled artisan just under two pounds and a senior clerk three pounds. Most of the labourers' and skilled workers' wages would have gone on rent, food and coal, with little left even for such items as clothes.

| Farthing | Penny | Sixpence | Shilling | Half-crown |

a mixture of financial acumen, determination and clever marketing, made a go of it. Like Sainsbury, he soon added more stores to his empire.

Marketing was a major key to Lipton's success. Perhaps as a result of his time in the USA, he knew how to make a big impact. In 1881, for example, he bought the largest cheese that had ever been made. This enormous cheese was said to contain the milk of 800 cows and it was claimed that no fewer than 200 dairymaids had laboured to produce it. Lipton put the cheese on display on Christmas Eve, making it known that coins had been concealed in it. Predictably, there was a stampede to buy a slice, and the police had to be called in to restrain the crowds. The entire monster cheese had long since disappeared when Lipton closed for business that evening. From then on, Lipton offered a giant cheese every Christmas and as a result always got plenty of publicity. Branches of Lipton's had opened across the country by the late-Victorian period, when they also began to gain a reputation for the high quality of their tea.

The small-town grocer could not hope to compete with the likes of Lipton and Sainsbury, both men on the verge of creating big business empires. But they could learn a lot from their success. For example, both Lipton and Sainsbury were good at using display, in the context of comfortable, well-presented shops, to bring in custom. And any Victorian grocer could see that a clean, attractive, well-ordered display of goods would win over shoppers.

Overleaf Many now-famous brands originated in the 19th century. Victorian entrepreneurs were good at coming up with new products and devising inventive ways of marketing them. Their advertisements made use of bold graphics, appealing characters and animals, and modern colour printing. Many advertisements were also turned into enamel signs for use outside.

SUNLIGHT SOAP

"THIS IS THE WAY WE WASH THE CLOTHES."

From the Painting by
G.D. LESLIE R.A.
Exhibited in the Royal Academy London,
1887.

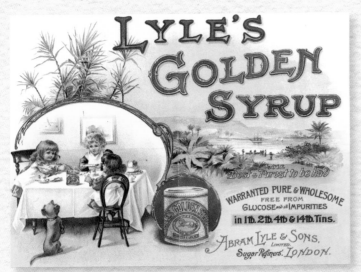

DESIGN AND DISPLAY VICTORIAN-STYLE

Although Victorian clutter still ruled, it became a little more ordered and even eye-catching as grocers learned the techniques of presentation, arranging their goods carefully on their shelves. The atmosphere inside the shops changed too, as many grocers emulated Sainsbury's style. There might still be open windows so that customers could see and even buy the stock from the street. But shopkeepers wanted to attract buyers inside, where they could be tempted by the enticing array of stock and the appetising scents of everything from bacon to freshly ground coffee.

Opposite Hudson Brothers, grocers of Ludgate Hill, London, had a large shop with rich wooden and tiled counters and stock arranged on wall shelves behind. These shelves were the main display area – the shop window was left uncluttered to give a clear view into the shop.

Following the example of Sainsbury, a hygienic but also welcoming environment was created. There were bentwood chairs for customers to sit on and be served in comfort. Most of the surfaces were tiled, for easy cleaning. The countertops might be of marble, combining an air of richness with cleanliness. Shops like this were pleasant places to visit, and, as their proprietors well knew, the more agreeable they were the more goods their customers would be likely to buy.

Huge strides in shop-front design helped the Victorian grocer display his goods with flair. The biggest advance was in the use of large panes of glass. Pioneering glass manufacturers Chance Brothers of Birmingham had begun producing sheets of glass measuring 4 feet by 3 feet in the 1830s. Soon even larger panes were available: ideal for use as crystal-clear shop windows. The eye-catching ways in which glass could be used in building were given huge publicity at the Great Exhibition held in London's Hyde Park in 1851 in the Crystal Palace, a vast building made almost entirely out of glass and metal. By the 1870s shop windows were making maximum use of big sheets of glass and shopkeepers' displays could be seen better than ever before.

These generous panes of glass were set in slender frames so that the greatest possible area of the shop front consisted of window. In this way the goods received optimum exposure and the passer-by was given an alluring glimpse of the shop's interior. Some frames were made of cast iron, which could be formed into all kinds of elegant shapes – especially popular were twisted columns and ornate mouldings. An iron frame and plate-glass windows were the latest technology in Victorian shop-building, and often showed that a shop was the most up-to-date on the street.

Charles Dickens summed up the new fashion in shop design in *Sketches by Boz*, published in periodical form in 1836–7 and as a book in 1839:

> *Six or eight years ago, the epidemic began to display itself among the linen-drapers and haberdashers. The primary symptoms were an inordinate love of plate-glass, and a passion for gas-lights and gilding. The disease gradually progressed, and at last attained a fearful height. Quiet, dusty old shops in different parts of town were pulled down; spacious premises with stuccoed fronts and gold letters were erected instead; floors were covered with Turkey carpets, roofs supported by massive pillars; doors knocked into windows, a dozen squares of glass into one; one shopman into a dozen . . .*

Dickens goes on to describe how the fashion abated, reappeared among the hosiers, abated once more, then revived among the chemists, and so on along the High Street. Fashionable streets were full of such glittering windows. But not every grocer could afford such lavish upgrades to their premises. Many local shops, especially in small towns where there was little competition, still had gloomy, rather poky premises, ill-lit and cluttered, which had not seen a lick of paint for years.

THE IRONMONGER

Above Holding a
two-handed saw, one
of the tools he would
be expected both to
make and repair, the
Victorian ironmonger
stands proudly in front
of his shop. From bird
cages to baths, much
of his vast selection
of stock was made
on the premises.

The Victorian ironmonger was first and foremost a dealer in metal goods. But in addition his stock embraced everything from wood wares and bedsteads to farm equipment and the kinds of items that today would be found in hardware shops, DIY stores, builder's suppliers' yards, and much more besides.

The range of goods was so vast that even the most organised of shopkeepers must have had trouble keeping track of them all. There was an array of small items for the home, such as pots, pans, kettles, urns, cutlery, candlesticks, fire irons and trays. All the rich variety of Victorian kitchen equipment, including cooking utensils and serving dishes, metal jelly moulds, cake and bread tins and metal dish covers, was sold by the ironmonger too. Many of these articles came from manufacturers that were nationally famous: shears from Wilkinson's, patent storage jars from Kilner Brothers and scales from Avery. Large domestic items were also stocked, such as mangles and other laundry equipment, and galvanised bath tubs of various designs.

A large part of the stock consisted of tools for every trade from carpenter to plumber – saws, chisels, hammers, planes, knives of various types, spanners and wrenches and so on. Nails, screws and nuts and bolts were also sold, in a huge range of types and sizes. The ironmonger had to be an expert in the needs of every trade and would be expected to supply the right tools for every job. Then there were larger implements for the farm, from seed drills to ploughs. And the stock list could also extend to fencing wire and railings, lawnmowers and stoves. As if all this were not enough, the ironmonger stocked many consumable commodities – oil, paraffin, glue, candles, linseed oil, paints (the colours mixed to order) and the like. All these gave the ironmonger's shop its characteristic smell – a mixture of oil and wood, laced with a metallic tang – that must have evoked in the customer's mind an Aladdin's cave of choice.

STOCK VERSUS SPECIALISATION

Many of these items were not kept in the front of the shop, but were stored at the rear of the premises. Here outsize goods, such as tin baths and farm implements, were housed in stockrooms that were often vast, dark and unheated. One of the challenges for a new apprentice starting work for an ironmonger was knowing where to lay hands on such items, especially when it was cold.

With a potential range of stock as wide as this, some ironmongers in bigger towns and cities chose to specialise. A number drew most of their custom from the building trade and in the following century became the first builders' merchants. Others called themselves 'furnishing ironmongers' and pitched their stock more squarely at the domestic market. Still others concentrated on farm equipment. But most, especially in the country, were generalists. They met the needs of all kinds of customers from a vast stockroom, and knew where to buy in items not held as regular stock because they were only occasional purchases. To locate such items, they used catalogues produced

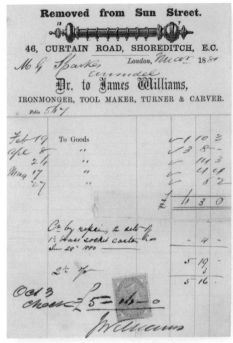

Above A bill from the 1880s shows the range of one London ironmonger, James Williams. As well as making tools and other metal goods, he also worked in wood, turning chair legs and doing carved work.

Left As well as tools and other iron items, ironmongers also dealt in brass wares. Shiny door furniture such as lion knockers and hinges looked good on town doors, while horse brasses in a range of patterns appealed to country customers.

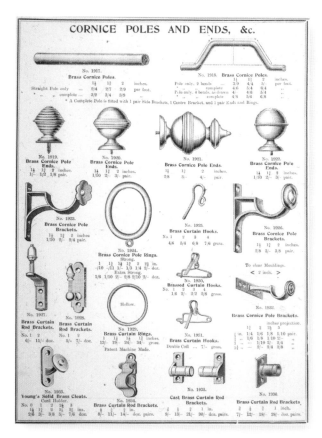

Above The Victorians loved ornate design, and ironmongers' catalogues contained a vast number of different variations on the poles, brackets, finials and other items used to hang curtains. Each was produced in a range of sizes.

Previous page Foundrymen working for James Hews, ironmonger of Maidenhead, stand in the yard at the foundry. Iron pipes and other components are stacked in the background.

by the large manufacturers of metal goods. The catalogues, often illustrated with engravings, showed items ranging from knife cleaners to safes in a choice of styles and sizes. With a huge railway network, plus local carriers and their carts, the customer did not have to wait long for a delivery.

HAND WORK

Victorian ironmongers were metalworkers as well as salesmen. The size of the workshop and the range of goods they could make varied, but in a country town where there were no alternative suppliers the ironmonger often made many of the goods on the premises. Pots, pans and kettles made out of sheet metal were key items, as were milk churns in rural areas. Objects like these were always in demand and not difficult for a skilled metalworker to make, although some ironmongers preferred to buy in more complex components, such as kettle spouts and handles, and attach these to bodies they had made in the workshop.

There were mending jobs too. In the Victorian period people expected goods to last, and if a tank sprung a hole or a bucket handle wore out or came adrift, they would take the item to the ironmonger for repair. Often a customer would bring in an item made by the shopkeeper or a member of the shopkeeper's family. Both owner and tradesman had a respect for such items, and the ironmonger would want to return a broken bucket or spade as good as new.

Most of this kind of metalwork could be done at the forge, where there were hammers, anvils and a fire to heat the metal so that it could be beaten into shape. Sometimes if an ironmonger had a forge, the business also offered a shoeing service for horses, although in Victorian times many blacksmiths and farriers did this work.

Some ironmongers took on even heavier and more challenging manufacturing jobs. These could require a foundry, a special workshop for making castings. The work entailed pouring molten metal into moulds to make a variety of items, from parts of tools to grates and fireplaces. Large castings, which required lots of space and a high degree of skill, were usually done at dedicated foundries in big towns and cities. But many a rural ironmonger ran a small foundry, supplying farmers with implements and perhaps producing small decorative cast-iron items to make the shop's stock more attractive. For an ironmonger with the right practical skills casting could be a sizeable and profitable part of the business.

SERVICES FOR THE HOME

The practical skills of the ironmonger often took him away from the shop to work in a customer's home. Victorian houses were mostly heated by coal and wood, which were burned in beautiful cast-iron fireplaces and stoves of the kinds that are prized by estate agents today but were seen by the Victorians as everyday items. Cooking was done on a coal-fired range – a combination of stove, oven and water heater – that was also made of iron. Naturally these metal products were supplied by the ironmonger, who would also install and maintain them. So a customer who wanted a new fireplace, stove or range would take the ironmonger's advice on the best one for the job and ask him to fit it.

Ironmongers also installed the systems of bells that the Victorian middle and upper classes used to communicate with their staff. These systems could be highly complex, with, for example, one bell for the butler's pantry, another for the maid, yet another for the housekeeper, and bell pushes or handles in every room. Both the controls and the bells were sold by specialist firms, but linking them together called for the installation of vast lengths of wire, and wire was the province of the ironmonger.

This was a time when technological change was moving faster than ever before, and the ironmonger's was often the place people went to find the latest developments. Various gas appliances, for example, from cookers to fires, first appeared during the 19th century. So did stalwarts of the Victorian home such as the sewing machine and the knife-cleaning machine. The century also ushered in the lawnmower and the humble carpet-sweeper. This last was an early hint that labour-saving devices would become more and more important in the home as the era of the large middle-class household with a small army of servants drew to an end.

Left When working at the forge, the fire had to be kept going strong so that there was always a source of heat. A skilled craftsman knew exactly when the metal was hot enough to beat it into shape.

CANDLE-MAKING

In the late-19th century there was no electric lighting but many people used oil lamps to light their main rooms. However, candles were still much used where there was no oil lamp and especially where quick, portable light was needed indoors – for example when going upstairs to bed. So every household needed a supply of candles, and ironmongers often made their own. The basic raw material was either beeswax or tallow, a substance made from rendered animal fat. The process of making a candle involved suspending the wick and dipping it into melted tallow or beeswax several times, gradually building up sufficient thickness.

MAKING BEESWAX CANDLES

The beeswax was put into a container and heated gently so that it melted. It was essential to use a gentle heat, stirring the wax regularly – if it got too hot the wax could ignite. The wax

was then strained through a linen bag and remelted, then cast into 'cakes'.

A quantity of beeswax was melted in a large vessel called a kettle. Above the kettle was suspended a metal hoop, which was fixed in such a way that it could be rotated above the molten wax. The ironmonger attached a number of cotton wicks to the hoop, turning the hoop so that one wick was positioned directly above the kettle. The ironmonger then took a spoon and poured molten wax slowly on to the wick. The hoop would then be turned and the next wick coated, and the process repeated until each wick was covered by one layer of wax. By the time all the wicks were coated the wax on the first wick had set and the process could be repeated by adding another layer of wax, making sure that the wax was not so hot that it would melt the previous layer. The wax was built up in layers until the candles were thick enough. When the candles had cooled, they were placed in a tank of warm water to soften them slightly, then rolled to an even shape and polished. Finally the ends were cut off neatly.

ABOVE *Ironmongers used a circular frame or hoop to hang the wicks when making beeswax candles. The hoop was the right shape for the round kettle in which the wax was heated.*

MAKING TALLOW CANDLES

Tallow was made by boiling chunks of beef suet in water until the water evaporated. The fat was then strained, because to burn without producing a smelly flame, tallow for candles had to be as pure as possible. Tallow candles were made by melting tallow in a vessel and dipping cotton wicks into the fat. After the first dip, some fat would adhere to the candle; this was then allowed to cool before another dipping, and the process was repeated to build up the fat in layers around the wick.

LEFT AND BELOW *With the wicks arranged carefully (left), the frame is ready to lower into the tallow. As the wicks are lowered (below), a little tallow sticks to each one.*

ABOVE AND RIGHT *Frames of half-made candles are hung on a wheel-like rack (above) to give the tallow time to set. After repeated dippings (right), the tallow builds up.*

Most Victorian towns had no gas-fire showroom, sewing-machine stockist or other traders specialising in the new technologies, so the ironmonger was the main source of all these new inventions. There was an air of excitement about these shops as the latest gadget came in and those with enough money hurried to try it out. Although to modern eyes a Victorian ironmonger's would seem to be crammed with often baffling bygones, to shoppers in the 19th century it was an exciting place, full of wonders and new possibilities.

PRESENTATION

The variety of the 19th-century ironmonger's business was summed up in the way some ironmongers described the services they offered. For example, an Oxford ironmonger, George Wyatt, traded from impressive premises in St Giles, not far from the centre of the city. He described his business in the late-Victorian period as 'Gas & water fitters, ironmongers, bell-hangers, and electricians, fishing tackle warehouse, agents of Scottish Union Insurance Co'. George Wyatt must have been able to master, or at least oversee, a remarkable range of activities. So, too, must his wife, for after George's death she seems to have carried on as an ironmonger, perhaps until their son was able to take an active part in the business, which later became George Wyatt and Son.

Below Cornish seedsmen Trevithick & Mabbott also traded as agricultural ironmongers, selling steel tools and farm gates along with seeds, flour and coal. Like many ironmongers, they also acted as insurance agents.

24   Rodda's Penzance Almanack, 1891.

TREVITHICK & MABBOTT,
MANURE, COAL, CORN,
FLOUR AND SEED MERCHANTS,
INSURANCE AGENTS,
Bone Crushers, &c.,
ARE SELLING FIRST-CLASS
HOUSE COAL,
PARLOUR COAL,
FIRE-LIGHTERS, FIREWOOD
(In Sticks or Blocks, Hard or Soft),
STEEL SHOVELS, HILTS,
FARM GATES
OF ALL SUITABLE LENGTHS,
COARSE FISHERY SALT
Agricultural Salt,
OATS, BARLEY, BRAN, SHARPS, THIRDS,
HAY, REED, &c., &c.;
FLOUR OF THE FINEST QUALITY,
Reliable Farm and Garden Seeds.
TRY THE BIBBY FEEDING MEALS
Good value offered, and special quotations for large quantities.

While George Wyatt had a stone-built shop front in the Gothic style – no doubt seen as a fitting companion to Oxford's graceful college architecture – many ironmongers took a different approach. Some had a quite plain wooden-framed shop window. They knew very well that an ironmonger's stock is what makes the first impression, and more often than not piled their goods on to the pavement, attracting passers-by with displays of baths, baskets and brooms. The shop front disappeared behind such an array, and no one cared if it was plain.

There was another style, though, that drew on the Victorian love of ornate metalwork – an iron shop front. Iron uprights and girders had been increasingly used in the building trade since the beginning of the Industrial Revolution in the 18th century. To begin with, iron was seen as a utilitarian building material, best suited to the construction of factories and warehouses, where it was prized because it was fireproof and because pieces of the same size and shape could be cast, making modular

building possible. But by the Victorian period iron was also being valued for its decorative qualities. You could cast decorative columns and capitals with floral decoration in iron, and an iron shop front could be made up of a series of slender iron arches, each framing a plate-glass window. A frontage like this made a perfect setting for an ironmonger's business. A good example is a surviving iron shop front at Witney, Oxfordshire, originally made for the ironmonger Thomas Clark and Son. The columns have spiral decoration running down them, and there are ornate capitals and other fancy details. Along the top runs an intricately decorated fascia that also contains a folding awning – a beautiful piece of Victorian design that must have mirrored the style of the shop's contents when it was first built in around 1870.

This kind of front reminds us that Victorian shops could be just as much about glamour and attracting the eye as their modern equivalents. Although ironmongers were the most practical and hands-on of Victorian shopkeepers, they still needed to attract business. So, amid the nails and tools, were also displays of electro-plated dishes and gleaming cutlery that were designed to entrance the Victorian housewife as she looked for something to lend an air of distinction to her sideboard or dining table.

Above A Victorian photograph of an ironmonger's shop in Weston-super-Mare shows a beautiful cast-iron shop front with slender columns between the panes of glass. The proprietor has used an area of pavement to extend the display of stock outside.

PAT a cake, pat a cake, baker's man, ❧ Prick it, and bake it, and mark it with B,
Prick it, and bake it as fast as you can; ❧ And put it in the oven for baby and me.

THE BAKER

Above This illustration
for a nursery rhyme
shows clearly how one
baker shaped loaves
by hand while another
loaded them into the
oven using the long-
handled peel.

One of the most regularly visited of all Victorian shops was the baker's. Their main product was known as 'daily bread' for a good reason: bread was one of the most important items in the Victorian diet, and the poorer you were the more of it you ate. So the bakery was a vital shop on the Victorian High Street, and everyone knew the baker.

Most Victorian bakers inherited their trade from the previous generation and learned on the job in the bakery. There had been an apprenticeship system, but this fell into disuse in the early 19th century and more and more bakers took on cheap labour without the mutual commitment of an apprenticeship. In the country, though, the bakery might well be staffed by just the baker himself, his wife and his family. Their work was very like the work of the previous generation from which they had learned the business, and that of many generations before them, for bread-baking had not greatly changed since the Middle Ages. It was heavy work in a hot environment full of flour dust. The onerous task of mixing and kneading the dough in particular required plenty of upper-body strength and was usually seen as a man's job.

This work took place around the main feature of the bakery – the oven. A Victorian bakery oven was a substantial brick structure built into the bakery. Although old stone country cottages and farmhouses sometimes had integral ovens, most households did not have an oven at all. Many housewives who wanted to make their own bread came to an arrangement with the local baker, mixing their own dough and taking it to the baker to put in his oven. In working-class areas people even brought their Sunday roast to be cooked in the bakery's large oven.

Inside the Victorian bakery

Baking involved a regular routine at the bakery, with the workers starting when it was still dark, so that customers could put fresh bread on the table in the morning. The first task was to mix the dough, a blend of wheat flour, yeast, water and salt. The mixing was done in a wooden trough, and when the baker had worked the ingredients to an even consistency free of lumps, the mix was left for 12 hours before more flour and salt were mixed in and the whole lot was left to rise. The resulting risen dough was cut and shaped into loaf-sized pieces.

Meanwhile, the oven was made ready. Victorian bakers used a brick-built oven called a side-flue oven. This had a tiled floor with room for around 150 'quatern' loaves (loaves weighing just under 2 kg) and a solid metal door. To one side was the furnace, which had a short flue leading straight into the oven. When the fire was lit, hot air would pass rapidly into the oven, heating it, and escape through a funnel-like chimney at the top. The baker would light the fire, feed it with coal and wait until the embers were becoming cinders. By this time the oven would be hot and the smoke would have died down. After cleaning the interior of the oven the baker threw a little flour on to the oven floor; if the flour blackened but did not catch fire, the oven was at the right temperature and the loaves could be put in.

When the baker was sure that the oven had reached the right temperature, he fed in the loaves one by one. To do this he used a long-handled, shovel-like

Below A group of bakers from Steeple Aston, Oxfordshire, together with a young family member eager to learn the trade, stand by their oven. The loaves they hold – the rounded cob and 'two-storey' cottage loaf – were popular in the 1890s.

implement called a peel, a tool that can be seen on woodcuts of bakeries dating back to the Middle Ages. The larger loaves were added first, so that they would spend longer in the oven and benefit from the hotter area at the back. When the oven was full, the door was closed and the batch left to bake for around two hours.

ADULTERATED BREAD

By using the baker's oven, families who had the time, space and energy to mix their own dough hoped to get around that persistent hazard of life in Victorian England, adulterated food. However, they still had to buy their own flour, and this ingredient was one of the most prone of all to adulteration. Indeed bakers were some of the most culpable of all traders when it came to this notorious problem. Reforming physician Arthur Hill Hassall was a highly influential campaigner against the practice of food adulteration, and in the early 1850s he set about defining the size of the problem by analysing thousands of food products. When he turned to bread his findings were astonishing: every single loaf he and his team analysed contained alum, which was added to flour in order to bulk it out in the same way in which dairymen were accused of adding water to milk. Hassall's findings were published in *The Lancet* and were widely publicised. Although the precise effects of alum in bread were not defined, some physicians were convinced that the chemical inhibited the bone-hardening power of wheat, possibly causing rickets, a disease that was widespread in Victorian Britain. There were other possible causes of rickets, but whether or not alum was involved it was clearly not contributing to the nutritional quality of the Victorians' daily bread.

In spite of the evidence that ingredients such as alum damaged people's health, the government was at first reluctant to bring in laws that would penalise retailers too heavily for food adulteration. The prevailing opinion seems to have been that the market would solve the problem –

Below To overcome fears of adulterated bread, some firms advertised loaves made with good-quality pure flour, as recommended by doctors and in the press. Customers were encouraged to check the colour and texture of any loaf before buying.

YOUR SECURITY IS IN THE NAME.

The Thoughtful Housekeeper
will carefully examine
THE FAMILY BREAD.

To be SURE of getting the RIGHT ARTICLE recommended by the
Doctors' Manifesto
and by the editorial articles published in the "Daily Mail"
ASK YOUR BAKER for
BROWN'S

D M
(DOCTORS') (MANIFESTO)

STANDARD BREAD

Made from the genuine 80 per cent. D.M. STANDARD FLOUR supplied by Charles Brown and Company, the old established millers of London and Croydon.

Here is an actual reproduction printed in Colour to show the careful Housekeeper just what the STANDARD BREAD should look like.

NOTICE THE COLOUR

It contains all the GERM and the SEMOLINA as instituted by Nature, who knew the right proportion for the benefit of health.

NOTICE ALSO THE TEXTURE, which should be even throughout.

ASK FOR "BROWN'S" D.M. And so get the GENUINE ARTICLE.

(SEE OVER)

THE FAVOURITE LOAF

T he Victorians ate various kinds of bread, but they especially liked white bread, which is made with flour from which the wheatgerm and bran have been removed. Since these elements contain an important part of the flour's nutritional content – most of the vitamins, for example – white bread is less good for you than brown, but the Victorians preferred its refined white quality. They were not alone. White bread had been produced for thousands of years – both the ancient Greeks and the Romans loved it, for example – but it had a particular popularity in the 19th century.

Mrs Beeton, author of the Victorian bible of household management, explained how white flour was made and knew about its poor nutritional quality:

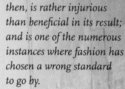

In order to render it white, [the flour] undergoes a process called 'bolting.' It is passed through a series of fine sieves, which separate the coarser parts, leaving behind fine white flour,—the 'fine firsts' of the corn-dealer. The process of bolting, as just described, tends to deprive flour of its gluten, the coarser and darker portion containing much of that substance; while the lighter part is peculiarly rich in starch. Bran contains a large proportion of gluten; hence it will be seen why brown bread is so much more nutritious than white; in fact, we may lay it down as a general rule, that the whiter the bread the less nourishment it contains. Majendie proved this by feeding a dog for forty days with white wheaten bread, at the end of which time he died; while another dog, fed on brown bread made with flour mixed with bran, lived without any disturbance of his health. The 'bolting' process, then, is rather injurious than beneficial in its result; and is one of the numerous instances where fashion has chosen a wrong standard to go by.

If Mrs Beeton knew of the drawbacks of white bread, countless Victorians must have known too. But they liked white bread and ignored her advice. White flour was available in large quantities thanks to the introduction in around 1880 of mechanical roller-milling, and white loaves were eaten by the million.

NIGEL DEVLIN
Baker

It's tremendously hard work. Carrying this through for six days is not a problem. Carrying it through for six months or even six years - what an endless, thankless task it must have been.

......

For five days we've been working hard, sweating profusely, drinking water like there's no tomorrow - I must have drunk gallons of the stuff. But the sheer hell of trying to keep clean, of trying to stay reasonably hygienic! Not being able to wash your hair is one thing, but actually smelling like the Victorians must have smelt is an experience you don't really want to repeat.

......

But the week's got better and today was no different. Today I was given two apprentices - I couldn't believe my luck. Having two young lads who were keen to work has made my life considerably better. It's actually been a pleasure to be at work today - it's the first time I can say that.

......

There is a huge sense of comradeship and working together that we've built up, even in this very short period. There's a sense that we need to be together to be strong. If that was true in Victorian times, as I'm sure it was, it must have been a wonderful feeling that you were part of something bigger. It's a sense of comradeship that, as we well know, is missing today.

customers would choose shops selling better-quality unadulterated goods, while dishonest traders would either mend their ways or go out of business. The argument ran that the *laissez-faire* economy, which had brought such prosperity to Victorian England, would sort it out. But it did not work out like that. The poor had little choice about where they bought the bread that made up such a large part of their diet. They would simply go to the baker whose prices were lowest, and these were often achieved by the heaviest adulteration. And in the country people often had little or no choice, for in a village or small town there might be only one baker.

So from the 1860s the government took more decisive action, introducing a series of laws making it illegal to sell adulterated foods and providing for an inspection service to detect the law-breakers. The 1872 Adulteration of Food, Drink, and Drugs Act, for example, made it illegal to sell foods containing ingredients simply intended to add weight or bulk, unless their use was openly declared. The new laws also encouraged local authorities to appoint food inspectors, controlled by the police, to make sure the law was adhered to. But the appointment of inspectors was not compulsory and the fines imposed on those selling adulterated foods were not heavy. So in some areas, especially those where there were no inspectors, the problem of bad bread and other adulterated foods continued through the final decades of the century. Gradually, however, the laws were tightened further and more inspectors were appointed, and as the century drew to a close the problem of bread made with alum went away.

Below Huntley & Palmers of Reading were famous for their ornate biscuit tins, with new designs coming out in time for Christmas. Their biscuits were sold all over the British Empire.

New lines and new machines

Bread made up the most important part of the baker's business. But an enterprising baker would also manufacture cakes and biscuits. These were far more labour-intensive, but could bring in extra profit, so if the baker had the staff, someone in the bakery would learn the necessary skills of mixing, rolling, cutting and decorating. However, rolling and cutting out thousands of biscuits took a lot of work and by the 1840s there were machines for doing this. Biscuit-making became a mechanised business, and as the century went on, was more and more the preserve of specialist manufacturers such as Huntley & Palmers of Reading and J.D. Carr of Carlisle. By packing their biscuits in airtight boxes and tins they could send their wares all over the country (and indeed the world), and soon biscuits were part of the stock in trade of the grocer as well as the baker.

Most Victorian bakers did without modern technology. There were various attempts to create a mechanical dough mixer, to cut down the effort that went into the most laborious part of the bread-making process. For example, baker Ebenezer Stevens patented a dough mixer in 1858 that was powered by a steam engine outside the bakery. Stevens built such a mixer for his premises in Islington, North London, and later in the century some larger bakers bought mixers made by a German firm, Werner & Pfleiderer. But installing a steam engine for this kind of machine required a big investment and lots of space, so it was not practical for most bakers, who carried on using the ancient craft skills they had learned from their parents.

MEAT TO PLEASE YOU

Most High Streets of any size had more than one butcher, and customers generally had their favourite. Many butchers were also specialists, so many people went to one shop for beef, to another for pork. Pork butchers were popular, and a pig was said to be an excellent investment for a butcher, since you could use virtually every part of it – 'everything but the tail and the grunt', as the saying went. As well as the pork itself, in a variety of joints from spare ribs to legs, the pig produced gammon, ham and bacon. The liver was eaten and other entrails were chopped up to make faggots or a herb-flavoured meat loaf known as haslet. Pork sausages, made with the aid of the recently invented sausage machine, were another delicacy – their shape, size, meat content and, above all, seasoning, varying according to local fashion.

The actual pigs varied from one locality to another, too, affording different local flavours. There were red-gold-haired Tamworths, closely related to the ancient indigenous Old English Forest pig; Gloucestershire Old Spots, tough, outdoor pigs producing tasty pork; Dorset Gold Tips, named for the golden ends of their hairs; Long White Lop-Eareds, now known simply as Lops; Lincolnshire Curly-Coats, the last pig breed to disappear in Britain; and many more. Some of these breeds have been revived, so that we can again begin to understand the variety of meat that was available across the country.

Below Pearce's Beef Steak Puddings were already very popular in 1891 when the poster shown here was printed. Could 6,760 customers be wrong?

SMALL IS BEAUTIFUL

The late-Victorian period was not a bad time to be a butcher. The population was rising and, on the whole, meat consumption was on the increase too. According to one study, average annual meat consumption in the 1830s was around 87 pounds (39.5 kg) per head, while by the 1870s it had risen to 110 pounds (49.9 kg) and by the turn of the century to about 132 pounds (59.9 kg). Nevertheless, most butchers were small family businesses, sourcing their meat from nearby farmers whom they knew well and dealt with regularly, and salting and storing it in a cellar beneath the shop. Most small butchers bought animals at a local market and drove them to their own premises to kill them, for the butcher was a slaughterman as well as a retailer. When meat imports increased at the end of the century, local butchers often stuck to their trusted suppliers and proudly displayed a sign saying, 'No foreign meat'.

The small size of most High Street butchers meant that many usually slaughtered no more than one cow and a couple of sheep a day, or a few pigs per week if the business specialised in pork butchery. Most butchers survived on this

STOP HERE FOR
PEARCE'S
BEEF STEAK
PUDDINGS.
As Nice as Mother
Makes Them.
IF YOU DON'T BELIEVE IT
ASK ANY WORKING MAN.
6,760 Customers in a Day.

THE VICTORIAN BUTCHER

SAUSAGE-MAKING

Sausages and similar dishes such as haggis may have begun as a way of using meat such as offal that was perfectly edible but which some people found unappetising. But traditional pork sausages are commonly made with a mix of meat: many recipes suggest a roughly equal blend of lean shoulder and fat belly pork. Although some sausages were 100 per cent meat, some butchers added a proportion of cereal – breadcrumbs or rusk – to eke the meat out and add some texture. The other ingredient was seasoning, which varied widely from one region to another, from a simple mix of salt and pepper to a blend including spices (nutmeg, mace or ginger) or herbs (most commonly sage, but alternatively parsley or thyme). Sausage skins were the intestines of the animal, another example of the ways in which the traditional butcher put the whole of the pig to good use.

THE PROCESS

The butcher minced the meat, finely if he was using cheap meat and wanted to disguise it or more coarsely for a more interesting texture. Then the meat and other ingredients were mixed together and passed through a sausage machine. This had a hand-cranked handle and forced the meat through a nozzle, to which the sausage skins were attached. When a long length of skin was full, it was twisted or knotted to form the individual sausages. Butchers displayed these in the shop by hanging them in 'chains' and people liked sausages that had been kept for a day or two after making, so that the herbs and meat had a chance to blend.

LEFT *When you got used to feeding in the mixture and turning the handle steadily, sausage-making using the Victorian sausage machine was not difficult. The job was often done in full view of the customers.*

small-scale trade, which was given a boost at Christmas or when there was some special local celebration.

A good display of meat, often with carcases hung outside the shop, was a common way in which the Victorian butcher attracted trade. At time of festivities, such as Christmas, the butcher would put on a special display to water the mouths of customers. Sometimes this was advertised or reported in the local paper, as in this example from the *Montgomeryshire Express* in 1888:

CHRISTMAS SHOW. – *Mr. John Eaton's show of Christmas cheer consisted of two splendid maiden heifers, fed by the Ex-Mayor W. Jones, Esq., six Welsh wether sheep, fed by Mr. Owen, Jamesford, two by Mr. W. Rogers, Bacheldre Hall, and some nice porkers by Mr. Hamer, Montgomery. The premises were neatly decorated on Friday and presented a very attractive appearance.*

Notice how the report specifies which farms the livestock came from, so that potential customers were assured that the meat derived from reputable local sources. The whole account shows how shoppers were in much closer touch with the origins of their food than most of us are today. And in many places, people could be confident, when their food was so locally sourced, that they were getting good quality. However, there were exceptions, and one estimate from the

Below This is the kind of display of meat and poultry that would have made any Victorian butcher proud. Customers would have flocked to the shop to have a chance of a piece of the prize-winning meat.

1860s alleged that up to one fifth of all meat purchased at butchers' shops was from animals that were diseased. In most cases a butcher's meat was hung for longer than a lot of the meat that is sold today. People liked the taste of meat that had been well hung, and expectations about freshness were very different – the domestic refrigerator was, after all, a long way in the future.

WATCHING THEIR LANGUAGE

Butchers were famous for a form of language that enabled them to talk among themselves without customers understanding them. This was especially useful because in Victorian times prices were not usually fixed. Instead retailers often charged what they thought they could get away with, adjusting prices upwards for the better-off customers but charging less to the poor. The language butchers used for this purpose was called backslang, and was something they picked up from costermongers, although by the late 19th century the costermongers seem to have dropped it. Basically, backslang worked by reversing, or roughly reversing, the letters in each word, so 'bit' became 'tib' and 'boy' became 'yob', a word that has survived to become standard English. If a simple letter reversal produced something that was not easy to pronounce, a slightly different form was used, and sometimes a different form caught on anyway. So 'pork' was turned into 'kayrop', 'lamb' into 'bemal' and 'sausage' into 'swag'. All this of course allowed fast-talking butchers to adjust prices, give short weight and so on, without the customer having the least idea what they were talking about. But whether or not they used backslang, butchers built up close relationships with their customers, who came week after week to buy their meat. The bond between shopper and shopkeeper, such a vital part of Victorian shopping, was as strong here as in the other shops of the time.

Above The Victorian butcher did a lot of his work on a wooden block in the front of the shop, where his customers could see exactly what he was doing. Shoppers would watch every cut, and be quick to complain if the butcher did not give them exactly what they wanted.

THE PHOTOGRAPHER

For the Victorians photography was a fairly recent invention. The first practical photographic processes had been devised in the 1830s, and it took a number of years before photography was widely accessible. By the 1870s, photography was still the preserve of professionals, and a few amateurs with plenty of money, space and time. You needed not only a camera, then a costly hand-made item, but also a darkroom in which to process the photographs, as well as time to learn about the chemicals and processes involved. But there was enough interest for photographers to begin to appear on the High Street in the late-Victorian period.

Photography caught the imagination of the Victorians. Before photography, if you wanted a likeness of your loved ones, you had to have your portrait painted or drawn – and that really was for the rich. But now studios were springing up and travelling photographers were setting up in business, and for customers it was simply a matter of turning up, keeping perfectly still for a few minutes and paying the photographer's fee. It was portraiture for the masses, or at least for the middle classes, and it caught on.

EQUIPMENT

Below In the Victorian period, everyone who could afford it wanted their portrait taken. Both single portraits and group shots showing a whole family were popular.

At first, the combination of bulky equipment and complex chemical processes meant that photographers were confined to the studio and darkroom. If you wanted your photograph taken, you had to live in a big town where there was enough business for a photographer to set up on the High Street. It could be an awkward undertaking for photographer and sitter alike. Exposure times could last several seconds or even one or two minutes, and the sitter had to keep perfectly

still. One piece of equipment used by early portrait photographers was a head clamp, to limit the sitter's movement to an absolute minimum.

But by the mid-Victorian period photographers were on the move. Pioneering photographers such as Roger Fenton set up mobile darkrooms, often in horse-drawn vans. A cheaper option was a 'dark tent' mounted on a large wheelbarrow. In 1855 Fenton took his camera and horse-drawn darkroom to the Crimea and recorded the war. Others followed a safer route, travelling from one town to another to take the portraits of the inhabitants and to photograph local scenery for the production of postcards.

In the 1870s, photography was still novel enough to provoke excitement. Having your portrait taken still carried an air of glamour (people remembered how Queen Victoria and Prince Albert had had their photograph taken) but prices were by now within the reach of many. So when a travelling photographer arrived in town, there would be lots of interest, with enquiries ranging from families wanting portraits to local shopkeepers interested in having a photograph of their premises or in selling postcards produced by the photographer. Photographers soon realised that there was money to be made, and some became a fixture on the vibrant Victorian High Street.

Above This Victorian photographer's 'van' is in fact little more than a small cart, but the interior was lightproof and full of all the equipment and chemicals needed for processing film.

Overleaf
A selection of images show a variety of activities on the Victorian High Street.

Chapter Three

THE EDWARDIAN HIGH STREET

1901–1917

WHEN QUEEN VICTORIA DIED in 1901 her eldest son became King Edward VII. The new monarch was a worldly *bon viveur*, and his lavish lifestyle, aped by many in the upper classes, encouraged consumption and appreciation of the good things in life. This was good news for retailers, and the Edwardian period was in part a time of well-stocked shops and glittering window displays, of huge cakes and big steaks. But there was still a wide gap between rich and poor, a division that continued to be reflected on the High Street.

For the rich, there were still a huge number of high-class small shops offering everything from game to jewellery. But increasingly these were joined by large, prestigious department stores that offered a cornucopia of goods and encouraged the well-heeled to spend a great deal of their time shopping. Department stores were not an Edwardian invention, but they multiplied during this period, encouraging people to see shopping as less of a chore and more of a leisure activity.

The equivalent of the department store for the poor was the 'penny bazaar'. It also had a wide range of stock, but with cheap prices for those on a tight budget. Most were local businesses, often ones that had grown out of Victorian drapery or hardware stores. But there were also chains such as Woolworth's and Marks & Spencer Ltd, which grew quickly in this period. Like the department stores, they transformed the High Street, posing a threat to some of the smaller shops.

With both department stores and penny bazaars thriving, traditional shopkeepers had to find ways to keep up and attract business. While catering for

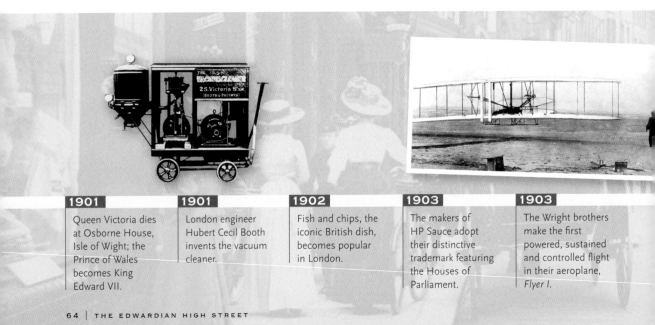

1901	1901	1902	1903	1903
Queen Victoria dies at Osborne House, Isle of Wight; the Prince of Wales becomes King Edward VII.	London engineer Hubert Cecil Booth invents the vacuum cleaner.	Fish and chips, the iconic British dish, becomes popular in London.	The makers of HP Sauce adopt their distinctive trademark featuring the Houses of Parliament.	The Wright brothers make the first powered, sustained and controlled flight in their aeroplane, *Flyer I*.

basic local needs, they also did their best to follow fashion. A baker, for example, might extend the range of loaves and cakes on offer, while a shop owner with the space could cater for the Edwardian love affair with the bicycle. Or they might upgrade their premises, building a new shop front to draw in customers.

At the end of the period, shoppers and shopkeepers alike had to face a stark new reality. The First World War brought terrible loss of life and hardship for those on the battlefront. It also led to shortages, hard work and austerity for many at home. Every shopkeeper had to adapt to survive.

New century, new styles

By around 1900, many architects and designers were leaving behind the old-fashioned revivalist styles of the Victorian era and following new fashions. Some stayed faithful to the ideals of the Arts and Crafts movement, which had begun a few decades earlier as a reaction against Victorian clutter and machine manufacturing. The hand-crafted aesthetic of Arts and Crafts still had a wide appeal.

Another design movement, Art Nouveau, also seemed to signal a new start. Instead of Victorian rectitude, Art Nouveau designers introduced sinuous curves and relief panels depicting alluring young women. Instead of the natural hues of Arts and Crafts they offered a jewel-like palette of exotic colours. This eye-catching style was well suited to shop fronts and arcades, brightening up the High Streets of many cities as well as enlivening interiors.

High society

British society was just as rigidly class-based in the Edwardian period as it had been during Victoria's reign, and in some ways it seemed even more so. Edward VII, famous for his love of horse racing, good food and beautiful women, presided over an upper class that went in for big meals, extravagance and house

1904
Shell introduces its famous scallop shell symbol, which eventually becomes one of the most widely known of all trademarks.

1905
Neon signs are made for the first time.

1905
During the campaign for votes for women, Annie Kenney and Christabel Pankhurst become the first suffragettes to be imprisoned.

1906
The Liberal Party wins the general election with a landslide victory. The new government introduces social reforms.

1906
The triode amplifying valve is patented in New York, making radio receivers more practical.

parties on an enormous scale. The Edwardian era was the last heyday of the country house, when the rich families of the land threw open their doors to their friends for days on end, laying on endless shooting expeditions and multi-course banquets as part of the entertainments.

LIFE FOR THE MASSES

The rest of society went about its business quite separately, working to maintain British supremacy in trade and industry, which was now under threat from competition as other countries, notably the USA and Germany, caught up with Britain's pioneering industrialisation. But there were signs of social change. Women were starting to campaign for the vote. The ideas of socialism were starting to take hold, although Parliament was still dominated by the Conservative and Liberal parties.

A number of campaigners saw through the glitter of Edwardian high life to the desperate plight of many at the bottom of society. Among the most prominent were William Booth, founder of the Salvation Army, whose book *In Darkest England* (1890) reminded people of the shocking conditions faced by many Londoners. The philanthropist Charles Booth took a longer and still more sober look at the London poor, surveying the entire city between 1886 and 1903. He created a series of maps that classified the capital's streets according to the class and wealth of those who lived there, from the rich upper classes to the 'Vicious, semi-criminal'. The work of these campaigners forced politicians to recognise that they should do more to help the poor and there were hopes that the lot of ordinary people would improve. Science was bringing improvements in medicine; the Old Age Pensions Act provided non-contributory pensions for people over 70 who had an income of less than £21 a year; and the National Insurance scheme was introduced to protect workers from the poverty resulting

1907	1907	1908	1910	1912
Robert Baden-Powell founds the Boy Scouts.	Marmite open a new factory at Camberwell Green, London, in response to high demand.	Kenneth Grahame publishes *The Wind in the Willows*.	Edward VII dies and his son becomes King George V.	Suffragettes smash shop windows during a protest in London. Emmeline Pankhurst is arrested and Christabel Pankhurst flees to Paris.

from unemployment. Such measures signalled the beginnings of the welfare state, and of a more financially secure life for working people.

So the shoppers on the Edwardian High Street were as mixed a bunch as they had been under Queen Victoria. At the wealthy end of the spectrum were the upper classes, who could afford the exclusive shops of fashionable haunts such as London's Burlington Arcade, who ran accounts at the best local grocer and employed the finest craftsmen to make bespoke furniture and other household items. Lower down were the middle classes, sustaining many High Street shops but also getting on the train to London to visit the expanding department stores such as Harrods. These huge emporia were largely unknown to the working and jobless poor, who shopped locally, bought cheaply and often had to rely on credit.

THE FIRST WORLD WAR

This picture was shattered by the First World War. The widespread conflict caused shortages of food and interrupted the global trade that had made Britain rich. It destroyed many country estates, whose owners lost male staff in the war and in many cases faced multiple death duties after it. It made people question values such as patriotism and ideas such as the power and influence of Britain that had previously seemed obvious and absolute. The war changed the lives of many women, who went to work for the first time and had a taste of independence. They also had to cope with food shortages and rationing.

Histories of the period used to say that the war destroyed the optimism and confidence of the Edwardian period. The era of house parties, flowing dresses and tea on the lawn was over. But such luxuries were only ever for the few. In reality, life in Edwardian times was as varied as in any other. And the High Street, with its butchers, bakers and bazaars, reflected this variety.

1914
The First World War begins after the assassination of Archduke Franz Ferdinand, heir to the Austro-Hungarian throne, in Sarajevo.

1915
The Battle of the Somme is a disaster for Britain, with some 57,000 casualties on the first day alone.

1916
The Easter Rising, by Irish republicans fighting British rule, takes place in Dublin.

1918
The Representation of the People Act gives the vote to women over 30.

1918
The First World War comes to an end when hostilities cease between Britain and Germany.

THE GOLDEN AGE OF SHOPPING

Many Edwardian shopkeepers were still the skilled craftsmen that their Victorian parents and grandparents were – bakers still baked bread and butchers made sausages and meat pies. But there was a huge pressure to adapt and in some areas of trade shopkeepers did this by buying a greater variety of stock. This tended to mean that they used more of their sales skills and fewer of their craft skills. The proprietor of a bazaar, for example, might buy in all kinds of trinkets, knick-knacks and imported goods. The wide range of stock drew people in, as did the keen prices. In the 19th century many shops had not operated a fixed-price scheme, instead charging what they thought the customer could pay. But these Edwardian bazaars adopted a more modern fixed-price approach, emulating the likes of Woolworth's, who promised 'everything for a sixpence'.

There were also new forms of display. More and more shops abandoned old-fashioned counters, which acted as a barrier between the customer and the goods. Instead they placed items in baskets or on table-top counters so that shoppers could examine and even handle them before buying. When this innovation was added to new kinds of shop decoration influenced by fashionable movements like Art Nouveau, it made shopping a very different experience. Shopkeepers found that, although it encouraged browsing that did not result in a purchase, it was also more likely to make people buy goods on impulse.

So some shops were changing in the early 20th century. But there was still a need for small local shops offering basic needs in the way they had done in

Opposite The Edwardian grocer stands at his counter with a variety of jams, pickles and sauces on display.

the century before. And shopping in these places was very similar to Victorian shopping, not least in that it was still overwhelmingly seen as 'women's work'. One shopper, reminiscing about life in around 1910 in North London, put it like this:

> *Women shopped locally when I was a child in the early 1900s, and I sometimes went with my mother to our local shops. (Never with my father, as it was unheard of for men to be seen doing women's work.) There were no supermarkets to sell everything in one visit. So we had to go to numerous different shops which made shopping a lengthy business. This was especially so because even being served took quite a time, as social chit-chat was expected and many of the goods had to be weighed out specially for each customer.*

On the Edwardian High Street there was still a place for small shops, the traditional skills and the personal approach.

SHOPS GET BIGGER

One thing that was changing retailing in the Edwardian period was the steady rise of the department store. Department stores in Britain were essentially a Victorian invention, beginning in London and spreading to major cities such as Birmingham, Newcastle and Edinburgh as the 19th century went on. They grew not only in number but also in size. In some cases a store would buy up neighbouring properties to increase its selling space, often with the ultimate aim of owning an entire city block, with entrances and windows on three or four streets.

In the Edwardian era department stores also spread widely across larger towns. A study of West Midlands towns, for example, shows that while Birmingham and Wolverhampton both had them in 1870, by around 1910 there were department stores in Coventry, Kidderminster, Leamington, Walsall and Worcester. The number increases further when other kinds of large store are added, such as multi-front shops and partial department stores, this second being shops that had originally specialised in one kind of retailing but had expanded by adding one or two other departments.

High-profile London stores were expanding too. Harrods, which had first

Below Fashionably dressed London shoppers crowd the streets on a summer's day in 1908. Many have paused to scrutinise the goods for sale – window shopping was becoming a popular pastime.

opened in the 1880s, completed its long Brompton Road façade in 1905, putting its glamorous Art Nouveau stamp on West London in a way that emphasised the fashionable, aspirational attitude of department-store shopping. This expansion coincided with another development – department stores extended the range of their goods and services. For example, an analysis of records of one large store, Cockaynes in Sheffield, reveals that by 1913 it was employing a small army of tailors, carpet-makers and fitters, cabinet-makers, milliners, removal men, painters and decorators and restaurant workers. Less than a quarter of the shop's staff were directly involved in sales.

If stores like Cockaynes carried a huge range of goods, the London stores were larger still. Many could claim, as London store owner William Whiteley did, to be 'universal providers', offering services as well as consumer goods, so that customers could reasonably expect to get anything they wanted from under a single roof. Major department stores like Harrods even acted as agents for prefabricated building manufacturers, who would send a flat-pack barn, house or even a church anywhere in the British empire.

The profile of department stores got even higher with the arrival, in 1909, of Selfridges in London's Oxford Street. This was a purpose-built store planned along the latest lines. It was designed to offer not just shopping, but leisure too, with its restaurants, roof-top tea garden, smoking rooms and art gallery. Such stores were effectively entire High Streets in their own right and the middle classes in London and other large cities patronised them with enthusiasm.

Above In 1913, Selfridge's large Oxford Street department store was four years old. Its palatial façade towered over the cars and open-topped buses in the street.

Small towns could not sustain monster stores like Harrods or Selfridges, but many market towns had a shop that over time grew to embrace several departments. This business might have begun as a draper's, for example, whose ambitious owner saw the chance to buy up adjacent properties and expand. While stores like this were a challenge to the smaller shops nearby, they were in one way a benefit. They kept shoppers on the local High Street and away from the temptations of the much bigger city stores, many of which were easy to reach by rail.

LIVING IN

Below Department stores with a large live-in staff, like this London one in *c.* 1900, provided meals in a dining room where workers sat at long tables. Here, as was typical for this period, the vast majority of the staff members are men.

Department stores were attractive to shoppers, but not always for those who worked there. Many stores required that a high percentage of their assistants live on the premises, usually in cramped, unpleasant accommodation and with very few basic rights. This practice had developed in the Victorian period, when shop assistants were often regarded in a similar way to domestic servants – as low-status beings with minimal employment rights who were at the constant beck and call of their employer. 'Living in' was still widespread in the first decade of the 20th century. It was the norm in many department stores in London and the South, but was less common in the North and Scotland. It did not always mean literally living above the shop, for many owners of larger stores bought up nearby buildings to serve as workers' hostels.

Having staff living in helped department-store owners keep a close eye on them, and it gave them more control, for employees were less likely to leave when they lost their home as well as their job. The owners also argued that the practice was beneficial to workers in that it gave young assistants, some of them just arrived in London from the provinces, the certainty of a square meal and a bed when these could otherwise be hard to find or expensive. Others saw it differently, especially as conditions in some staff accommodation were appalling. Philip Charles Hoffman, who began as a draper's apprentice in the 1890s before becoming a trade union organiser and eventually an MP, left a vivid account of living in the capital in his book *They Also Serve*. This passage describes his first night as an apprentice living on his employer's premises:

> *That night I found myself along with half a dozen other young shavers in a small dirty room with six beds packed very close together, covered with coarse red and black counterpanes. The ceiling was very low and could be reached easily by stretching our young arms. Both walls and ceilings were bare, grimy and splotched. The two windows, being curtained with dirt, needed no other obscuring. The naked gas jet had a wire cage over it. The boys undressed or dressed sitting or standing on their beds – there was so little room otherwise. But there was no bed for me; I had been overlooked. The steward with one eye, who was one of the porters, said I must sleep with one of the others. I refused. I had never done that before. He brought me from somewhere a blanket and a pillow. I lay down with them on the floor between two of those crowded beds. The gas was turned out at the main at 11.15. One of the boys lighted a piece of candle and they hunted for bugs on the wall, cracking them with slipper heels. When standing about and above me they lifted up their nightshirts and asked will this pass, will this pass, I thought my sensitive heart would break. I sobbed through that dismal night.*

Hoffman also records that staff living in had to obey a strict and bewildering series of rules, and the penalties for failing to do so were steep. At one store there were fines of twopence for taking too long for meals and sixpence for allowing a customer to leave the shop unserved. But at a high-class draper's in Knightsbridge there were much steeper penalties, including a fine of up to two shillings and sixpence for being absent longer than the permitted lunch break. Hoffman hated this system and soon became a leader of the trade union campaign to end it. The campaign began in 1901 and lasted several years, during which there were meetings, demonstrations and, from 1907, strikes. Eventually the publicity forced department-store owners to give in, and London stores such as Debenham & Freebody and DH Evans ended living in. Provincial stores followed suit and soon living in was optional for most staff. Even so, at the beginning of the First World War some stores still insisted that the most junior assistants and female staff live in, to protect their morals.

SERGISON'S

THE RISE OF THE MULTIPLES

Above Even if he ran quite a small shop, the Edwardian grocer needed several staff as well as family support to ensure that customers were served without having to wait.

A further development was the chain store with a network of branches. Enterprising department-store businesses such as London's Bobby and Company began to open branches in the provinces, especially in towns with a reputation as resorts or centres of fashion. Most of these stores were aimed squarely at female shoppers – for example, an advertisement of 1911 for Bobby's in Leamington described 'exclusive departments devoted to gowns, costumes, wraps, blouses, furs, dresses and fancy drapery etc.'.

But the rise of the multiples went far beyond department stores. The process had begun back in the 1870s and 1880s, when chain grocers began to spread and when new developments in shoe manufacture took hold, allowing machine-made footwear to be made and sold by multiple shoe retailers. Multiple tailors, selling ready-made men's and boys' clothes, also developed at the same time and expanded rapidly in Edwardian times. One of the most successful was the chain of menswear shops belonging to Joseph Hepworth, who had started in Leeds.

The 20th century saw growth for other kinds of multiple stores. Chains of butchers had begun in the 1870s, selling imported and frozen meat from South America and the British colonies. The River Plate Fresh Meat Company,

James Nelson & Sons, Eastman's and Dewhurst were all active in this market, spearheading the development that turned the food market into a global rather than a national concern.

There were also multiple chemists, a field in which Boots quickly became dominant. From its base in Nottingham, Boots expanded rapidly in the late 1890s, especially in the Midlands and northern England. By the end of the century it had 181 stores, and between 1900 and 1914 it grew still further, buying up existing chain chemists, including William Day. Day had 65 shops in southern England, giving Boots even greater geographical reach. By the outbreak of the First World War it had 560 shops selling medicines, toiletries, books, stationery, artists' materials and a variety of 'fancy goods'. These were almost department stores.

BAZAARS

Whereas Boots aimed at the middle-class market, a number of more downmarket shops, known as 'penny bazaars', offered a similar variety of stock to poorer customers. The uncrowned kings of this market were Michael Marks and Tom Spencer, who started in Yorkshire with market stalls in Leeds, Castleford and Wakefield, before opening shops with a similar style. They sold items such as cotton and buttons with the slogan, 'Don't ask the price, it's a penny.' When Marks died in 1907 the company had 34 shops and 15 stalls and the shops had a sign saying that Marks & Spencer Ltd were the 'originators of penny bazaars' to reassure people that their shops were more authentic than the many imitators

Above By 1913, when this advertisement was produced, Boots were offering a range of goods, including gifts designed to attract fashionable customers as well as the medicines available at their pharmacy counters.

that had sprung up. With some of the stock displayed on the pavement in front of the shop and more in baskets on counters, Marks & Spencer's shops encouraged people to come in and browse. The formula worked, the business did well and competitors started lookalike stores in towns that didn't have a Marks & Spencer.

But one visitor to Britain in 1890 was not impressed by Marks & Spencer. In his native USA Frank Winfield Woolworth had opened a chain of 'five-and-dime' stores, where goods were displayed on counters to attract browsers and were simply and cheaply priced. Woolworth criticised the small size of British shops and the way in which the shop windows were so full that passers-by could not see into the shop. He had grasped the essence of this kind of retailing – that you need to get the customers and stock as close together as possible, then people will buy. Would this approach work in Britain, he wondered. 'I think a good penny and sixpence store run by a live Yankee would create a sensation here, but perhaps not.'

By 1909 Woolworth had made up his mind and opened his first British store in Liverpool. He expanded rapidly and 27 further stores followed over the next two years. The popular formula consisted of simple pricing – everything was either threepence or sixpence – and a wide range of stock, from glassware to toys, haberdashery to stationery. It was a winning formula, and more and more branches of Woolworth's opened in towns and cities across the country.

Below In their early years, Marks & Spencer Ltd did well selling goods at a penny from stalls in covered markets. Customers were encouraged to look closely at the stock, and even handle it, before buying.

Stores for the poor

In towns where there was no Woolworth's or Marks & Spencer, there was an opening for an independent bazaar and some shopkeepers who had traded as drapers or ironmongers saw an opportunity to expand their business by following this fashion. The range of stock varied according to both the local market and the shopkeeper's preferences, but the mode of display was similar. Rather than keeping the stock behind the counter on shelves or concealed in drawers, shopkeepers displayed items on the counter. Customers were encouraged to pick the goods up and examine them, and this kind of shopping transformed retail design, making the shop more enticing and more welcoming to customers.

These new stock-intensive bazaars, big on display and happy to see browsers, proved very popular. They posed a major challenge to traditional ironmongers, drapers and other specialists, and their clear, cheap pricing made them especially attractive to the poor. More often than not, what the middle classes bought from their local department store or from a 'high-class' specialist, the lower classes bought from the bazaar – or from Woolworth's if there was a local branch.

Woolworth's was the eventual winner in this game of providing poorer people with choice. Its stores multiplied and were taken for granted on Britain's High Streets right up until the demise of the business in the recession of 2008–9.

Above The Edwardian bazaar, like many such enterprises, is run by a former ironmonger. Used to handling a huge variety of stock, he is well qualified to run this kind of business.

Traditional values still count

Although many shops in the Edwardian era were embracing new ideas, whether under the influence of bazaars, department stories or the Co-op, some retailers carried on as they had in Victorian times. Good, well-established businesses still had loyal customers, and a new business that supplied what people wanted at keen prices and provided good service was still likely to succeed. The arrival of a bazaar or Co-op did not mean that old-fashioned ironmongers, for example, were no longer needed.

In some towns people even started new businesses on the Victorian model. In her account of shops in the High Street in Hounslow, West London, Susan Higlett describes the shop of ironmongers Alfred and Louise Hooper. The Hoopers set up their ironmongery business in the early 20th century, by which time Arthur was already established as a wheelwright, cart painter and signwriter. The business went slowly at first – takings in the first week were a

THE CO-OPERATIVE MOVEMENT

Another way of providing better shops for the poor was offered by the co-operative movement. This emphasised ethical retailing that gave customers the chance to benefit directly from the shop's profits. It proved a successful formula, especially in the area of food retailing. The 'co-ops' were based on the ideas of Robert Owen (pictured right), a rich cotton trader who wanted to do well by his workers in the early 19th century. Owen believed that working people should be properly educated, fed and housed, and that the best way to lift workers out of poverty was to give them the chance to grow their own food, while living co-operatively in communities that would become self-governing. Owen's communities in Scotland and the USA did not last, but his ideas lived on and inspired others.

Among those fired by Owen's ideals were a group of 28 artisans in Rochdale, Lancashire, who pooled their capital and in 1844 started a co-operative shop, initially selling essentials such as flour, sugar and oatmeal. From these small beginnings a whole co-operative movement grew, with hundreds of shops offering an increasingly wide range of goods owned and run by the customers and redistributing the profits to the members of the group. Although some of the early co-operatives failed because of a combination of economic downturns and poor management, the co-operative movement had grown hugely by the beginning of the 20th century. It was bolstered by the Co-operative Wholesale Society (CWS), which centralised buying for the whole movement, so, although individual co-operatives remained small and local, they could benefit from the economies of purchasing on a large scale.

The co-ops were popular because they were reliable, sold good, unadulterated food, set reasonable prices and offered people the opportunity to save money as they spent it. They did not offer credit, but people accepted this because of the advantages. Many customers also liked the co-ops' support of education, which was one of the original principles of the movement laid down by the Rochdale pioneers. So for working people the co-op came to stand for good value, prudent saving, social responsibility and self-improvement.

FOR AND AGAINST

On the High Street, the Co-op became a popular name. While in 1875 Britain's Co-op shops had only about 2 per cent of the nation's retail trade, by 1910 their share had increased to some 7 to 8 per cent and it was probably greater still in the North, where the movement was especially strong. Their success hurt some private traders, and in some places there were noisy campaigns against the Co-op network. This was especially the case in northern England around 1902. In towns such as St Helens, Hull, Leeds and Newcastle, Traders' Defence Associations were set up to attempt to defeat the Co-op. Private shopkeepers refused to employ people who shopped at the Co-op, tried to persuade suppliers to take Co-op stores off their lists of customers and put up anti-Co-op candidates at council elections. But the campaign did not work. Leaders of the anti-Co-op faction found that, rather than forsaking the Co-op, customers were refusing to shop at their stores, and the campaign of opposition was giving the Co-op the oxygen of publicity. The anti-Co-op protests fizzled out, private traders realising that the best way to succeed was to try to emulate the Co-op's winning combination of reliability and value.

Many employees liked the Co-op too. The shops' opening hours tended to be shorter than those of the competition, and many societies offered benefits such as staff outings. The co-operatives' commitment to education also meant that there could be courses to interest the employee and offer a chance of career progression. Although many spent their working lives as assistants, some rose through the ranks from assistant to branch manager, which brought them an increase in responsibility and pay that would be unlikely for an assistant working in a small, owner-run business.

BELOW AND RIGHT *The Co-operative store in Lewisham in 1915 had a butchery department with an outside rail for hanging carcases (right). The interior of this kind of large Co-op (below) also included a substantial grocery section offering both tinned and fresh foods. In wartime, a few of the men on the staff had been replaced by women.*

mere two shillings and sixpence (12.5p) and the couple must have been glad of the income from Arthur's business. But eventually they thrived, displaying a wide range of stock:

> *Hooper's shop at 37 High Street was crammed with household articles, and the following list of goods were for sale: brushes, brooms, carpet beaters and feather dusters, matches, candles, gas mantles and glass shades, odd cups and saucers, small quantities of glass for mending windows, putty, nails, pumice stone, hearth stones for whitening front door steps, and also for the cement round the copper, carbolic and Sunlight soap, washing powder (Rinso), soda, paraffin, paint and paintbrushes, whitewash and distemper, in powder form.*

The distemper, which was used for painting interior walls in the way in which emulsion paint is used today, was available in various colours, and Mrs Hooper put samples of these in saucers to show the full range. The Hoopers' shop survived into the First World War, when the stock embraced items such as cap badges, lanyards and medal ribbons. Mrs Hooper, who like most people saw Britain's soldiers as heroes, kept some cigarettes behind the counter and if a member of the armed forces came into the shop he was always offered a few as a gift. During the First World War patriotism meant business.

THE IMPORTANCE OF SERVICE

Whatever the kind of shop, old-fashioned or modern, good service was still at the heart of good shopkeeping. There were no self-service stores and every customer had to be served quickly and with civility. To allow a customer to enter a shop and wait to be served was considered both rude and the worst business practice. If a large store was full and several of the staff were having their lunch in a back room, there was an instant solution. Speaking tubes linked the sales floors with the room where the staff took their meals. Each tube had a whistle at either end; the speaker would remove the whistle at his end and blow, producing a piercing noise at the other end. As Philip Charles Hoffman recalls, there would be a whistle from the tube and a voice would shout, 'Two wanted for the dresses.' The staff from the dress department would be expected to leave their half-eaten meal immediately and dash at top speed to the dress department before the customers left the shop without making a purchase.

Not that being courteous prevented dishonesty. Long before trades description legislation, shopkeepers and their salesmen often thought nothing of telling a lie to secure a sale. Hoffman relates how a female acquaintance of his came into the shop where he worked. The woman asked Hoffman if a particular fabric was pure silk, and he replied truthfully that it was not all silk but contained some jute. Another shop worker overheard him and butted in, grabbing the material, which he fondled appreciatively: 'He don't know nothing at all about it, ma'am; it is silk, all silk, bee-u-tiful silk.' The customer bought 13 yards.

But that was not the end of the story for Hoffman. Each shop worker had a 'premium card', on which his sales were entered. A bonus for each sale was given, and as assistants were on very low wages, these extra payments were important. When Hoffman went to get his card signed to show that the 'silk' had been sold, the worker who had lied about the fabric snatched the card from his hand. 'I think I've earned that premium, mister,' he said to Hoffman, tearing up the card so that he lost all the other premiums on it as well.

FREEDOM ON TWO WHEELS: CYCLING IN THE EDWARDIAN PERIOD

The bicycle had come of age in the late-Victorian period. Two inventions made this possible. The first was the 'safety bicycle', which had equal-sized wheels, a chain drive and a steerable front wheel. Pioneered in the late 1880s by John Kemp Starley, it replaced the penny farthing (which had been hard to get on and easy to fall off). Starley did not patent his safety bicycle, so many lookalikes appeared, and this form of bicycle became popular at the end of the 19th century. The second key invention, introduced at around the same time, was the pneumatic tyre. Inflatable tyres, developed by several inventors, including John Boyd Dunlop, made the ride more comfortable than with the solid tyres used until then.

By the Edwardian era, the bicycle was a cheap, comfortable, convenient machine. No longer did you need to own a horse to have personal transport, and moreover bicycles were inexpensive and low-maintenance. And with the demise of the precarious penny farthing, cycling was no longer seen as a rather dangerous sport for adventurous young men. Anyone could have a go: working men bought bicycles to travel to the workshop or factory, while women found a new freedom on two wheels.

It was probably women who benefited the most, for few had enjoyed the freedom of personal transport before the bicycle came along. And with cycling came more freedom and practicality of dress. Bustles and crinolines were impractical for cycling, and the craze for two-wheeled transport helped to make the elaborate dresses popular in the 19th century unfashionable. Simpler dresses and skirts became the norm, but the greatest innovation of all were cycling bloomers, invented by the American journalist and feminist Amelia Bloomer. The editor of the pioneering women's paper *The Lily*, Bloomer promoted her loose trousers in print as a way of achieving sartorial equality with men. She had introduced her bloomers in the USA in the 19th century, but it took cycling to make them popular with the Edwardians.

The personal approach

A draper might be able to get away with a deception about a piece of fabric. But in a food shop, where a customer was going to return at least once a week or even every day, the relationship between retailer and customer was different. Many people, especially members of the lower social classes, saw High Street traders as their friends. Successful shopkeepers cultivated these relationships, offering helpful advice about the stock. A good butcher, for example, then as now, would be expected to know how best to cook each cut of meat; a grocer would offer advice on the latest blends of coffee or tea.

All this meant that shops in small country towns were often seen as more than places to buy goods. They were more like social centres for the community, where people went for advice, help and a good gossip. Poorer people, of the working class or lower-middle class, had little money to spend at restaurant, club or even the pub, so sometimes they would meet up at a local shop for a chat.

One study of lower-middle-class life in Britain describes Charlie Clifton's shop in Bicester, Oxfordshire, which was part butcher, part general store and sold everything from fresh meat to paraffin, even delivering coal. Charlie's wife made an important contribution, making jams, ginger beer and pickles for sale in the shop. The pickles were especially popular late at night when people emerged from the nearby pub to buy a savoury treat. During the daytime people liked to come into the shop to pass the time of day. Charlie's daughter, Mrs Lovell, described her father's manner and his ease with the customers: 'he was a jocular man, he'd laugh with them all, he'd make a joke out of nothing with them – and that was their entertainment . . . he'd be telling them such tales . . .'

The customers didn't come only for entertainment – they also got advice and practical help, and this could go far beyond information about the goods they wanted to buy. For example, many customers around the turn of the century were illiterate, and they went to Charlie if they wanted help writing an official letter: 'if there was a bit of . . . an argument anywhere he could put a letter together for them – they always came to Charlie.' It must have been an invaluable service for people who would not have dreamed of consulting a solicitor, even if they had had the money to do so.

Above all, when customers ran short of cash, Charlie offered credit. Like thousands of other small shopkeepers, he would understand that credit could help a shopper whose purse was empty towards the end of the week. Nearly all his customers were regulars, and he knew that they would pay up when they got their next wage packet.

Charles Booth, who surveyed the life and labour of Londoners in the years on either side of 1900, described small shopkeepers as the bankers of the poor. He was referring not only to the practice of giving credit. Shops often acted as stores of wealth in kind. Most poor families could not afford to buy in bulk, simply because they did not have enough ready money to stock up a larder. So they had to buy small quantities, and a poor housewife, as Booth said, went to the shop 'as an ordinary housewife to her canisters'.

Opposite A selection of scenes in the Edwardian grocer's shop. Clockwise from top left: tinned and packaged goods kept in secure cupboards; Heinz soup, already a popular brand; the grocer keeps an eagle eye on his assistant; exotic nuts for the luxury market; the grocer and his staff get to grips with the latest gadget, a bacon slicer.

The personal approach also meant the ability of the small business to be flexible and to take advantage of local opportunities. An example of this was in the area of meat sales. In a country town there were often people ready with a gun who would supply rabbits and hares – and who would poach game too. If a shopkeeper was not too fussy about the origins of a pheasant or a partridge, the poacher would quietly empty his pockets in the back room of the shop and the birds would soon find eager buyers.

But a lot of people preferred more legitimate meat on their tables. For them, many butchers and general-store owners fattened their own meat. The shopkeeper would buy a few sheep or cattle at a time and keep them on some grazing land, having them slaughtered when they were ready. If he had a garden somewhere with a few sties, he could keep a handful of pigs in a similar way.

All these services turned the Cliftons' shop into a haven for locals. The personal approach kept customers loyal at a time when there were many temptations to go elsewhere. In Bicester there were no chain stores, but there were several other grocers and general stores eager for custom. Keeping the customers happy and building a personal relationship with them made a great deal of sense.

The specialist butcher worked on a larger scale, going to market once or twice a week and either sending livestock home by rail or driving it home through the streets. Cattle driving was often a job for the younger members of the family and did not always go smoothly. The son of a Kent butcher remembered how he once had to drive home several bullocks for his father, plus a single bullock for another trader:

> *At the top of the High Street, when I got opposite the telephone exchange which was a big house laid back in a garden, a dog ran straight across in front of these bullocks. They went for it and he ran into this telephone exchange! They went on in after him and one went right in the doorway and chased this dog downstairs into the basement. Pulled the banisters down. They had a hell of a job to get this bullock back out from the basement into the road again. They had to get some chaps to come and take the window out.*

Each butcher had his own slaughterhouse and killed his own stock. These were the days before humane killing, so butchers learned to be quick with the knife or poleaxe to dispatch the creatures rapidly. Then the meat was stored in cold rooms and, since there were no refrigerators, in ice boxes that had to be filled every two days with large quantities of ice.

Below Edwardian butchers, such as Frederick and Ada Hills of Brighton and Hove, were proud not only of the meat they sold but also of their delivery service. The cycles bore painted signs with the shop's name, so they acted as moving advertisements for the business.

As well as being a slaughterman, the butcher had to be able to dress the meat, creating the cuts that would sell in the shop, to arrange the meat to make an attractive display and talk knowledgeably to customers. He also had to be resourceful, offering new cuts such as cow's heel and sheep's head during the food shortages of the First World War. And of course he would oversee the staff throughout the working day.

Above A display of game fronts the butcher's shop. The window is open, allowing customers to see other meat hanging on the rail inside.

The butcher's day was long, beginning at about six in the morning when the joints were put on display in the shop and the salt beef was removed from storage tanks where it was kept in freezing brine. For many the day ended late – at 8 p.m. during the week and as late as midnight on Saturdays, when housewives left the pub and did their shopping for the weekend. Most butchers also offered deliveries, sending out a boy or roundsman, usually with a horse and cart.

A good butcher knew his customers and what they wanted. Often the business used an upmarket title such as 'purveyor of meat', to suggest that its meat was of the best quality. In such a shop marble slabs and stainless-steel rails for the carcases were the order of the day and the people who bought the best steak were the most valued customers. But good butchers also welcomed the poorer shoppers who bought odds and ends that were left over from the larger orders. A Kent butcher explained that people from different social classes or even different occupations preferred different kinds of meat. Local farmers and farm workers liked fat pork, while hop pickers and itinerant workers went for sausages.

So, once again, the personal approach of the shopkeeper meant that, when things went well, the right joints of meat were ready and waiting for the

Above A selection of images from the butcher's shop shows an assistant selecting game and the master butcher preparing and cutting up a boar's head and other meat.

customers when they arrived. But sometimes things went too well. In areas where there were fluctuations in trade, perhaps because of an influx of tourists in the summer, there could be a sudden demand. As the Kent butcher remembers:

> *Then in the summer time, if we had an extraordinarily good trade, such as holiday makers coming down, a lot more than expected, we'd probably sell out. One of the chaps, even two, would have to come in Sunday morning and kill half a score more sheep or lambs ready for Monday and Tuesday's trade. That often used to happen.*

As in any small shop, the butcher's work entailed keeping a constant eye on supply and demand, even if satisfying demand meant working on Sunday, the day that nearly everyone expected to spend at home with the family.

APPRENTICESHIPS IN DECLINE

One change in many retail businesses was that they were becoming less skilled. Whereas the Victorian grocer had to know how to blend tea and know the difference between the various kinds of flour and oatmeal, by the Edwardian era many products were available ready packaged. The grocer was less of an artisan and more of a salesman. This development changed the way people trained to go into the retail business. The traditional route was through an apprenticeship, when a parent paid to have their son trained, and the apprentice was bound for a set period to work in the business and learn the trade. There were fewer and fewer of these traditional apprenticeships in the 20th century. Boys or girls might join a shop as an 'apprentice' but there were not the same binding conditions or the same skills to be absorbed. If there was a binding agreement, the period of the apprenticeship was likely to be much shorter and the 'premium' paid by the parent much smaller. As a result there was a looser bond between shopkeeper and assistant, and staff changed jobs more often than they had done. Some went to a big city or even London to gain advancement. Others tried to save some of their wages in the hope that one day they would be able to start a business themselves.

It would be wrong to paint the Edwardian period as a time of great social mobility, though. The bosses still held most of the cards. A man arriving for a job interview with one of the large department stores might be asked to say what was the lowest wage he would accept. He would be shown the door if the figure he came up with was too high.

Overleaf At a livestock fair in Crawley in 1905, farmers have brought cattle to the market place to sell. Prosperous citizens pass through the square in a solitary car.

CASH VERSUS CREDIT

During the Edwardian period many people found it hard to make ends meet, but lavish shop displays and advertisements made them all too aware of the kinds of goods – luxurious and not-so-luxurious – that were available to those with the money. The upper classes still ran accounts at their favourite local stores, but not everyone could get credit, and many of the new multiples traded only in cash.

But there was another source of temptation – travelling hawkers who offered credit. Known as tallymen, these itinerant traders sold all kinds of goods. Some were drapers who brought round samples of cloth that people could order. Many an Edwardian housewife made her family's clothes with material bought this way, so that the credit system in the end offered a way of saving money. But there were also tallymen who offered all kinds of goods that were far from essential – pianos, gramophones and pottery ornaments were popular choices. The tallyman would call during the day, when the husband was at work, offering the woman of the household a tempting deal and sometimes buttering her up with flattery in the process. All too often the victim would give in, but the husband could do nothing about it when he returned home. The tallyman would call in once a week or fortnight to collect the instalments. One way to handle this problem was to take the offending item to the pawn shop, where it could be left in exchange for a loan.

A tallyman would be unlikely to accept payment in kind as a way of discharging a debt, but some shopkeepers occasionally did so. Whether or not this could happen depended on whether the debtor had something the creditor wanted and was prepared to accept. Traders sometimes accepted luxury items, but were more likely to favour supplies they needed anyway, farm produce, for example. E.W. Martin, in a study of life in a community in Devon, mentions smallholders who ran into debt paying off part of their account with produce such as fowls, ducks and potatoes. But for many this was not an option and it was not uncommon for shopkeepers to go out of business because of bad debts.

So, for many people, life was a matter of very careful money management. And because it was generally the woman of the house who did the shopping, she was also usually the one who managed the money. In her famous account of how poor families in London made ends meet, *Round About A Pound A Week*, Maud Pember Reeves eloquently described how the figures added up. Sidney Campion, brought up in a poor part of Leicester, offered this graphic account of how his mother budgeted: 'Every penny of her twenty shillings was placed on the table. With pencil and paper she reckoned where each halfpenny was going – and wondered how she could cater for us after having paid the fixed amounts like rent, insurance, clothing club and payment of debts.' Women had to be very careful with money, but there was a severe limit on what even a practised budgeter could do with one pound a week.

Shop workers were not highly unionised and had little power to improve their lot. Most of the workers' efforts were devoted to winning shorter hours. Since many shops stayed open late into the evening to catch customers leaving the pubs, 90 hours a week was not uncommon, and with no compulsory early-closing day there was little respite except on Sundays. Workers' campaigners and trade unions tried to get opening hours limited. The Shops Act of 1911 imposed a 60-hour week, but it was not until after the First World War that compulsory shop closing at 8 p.m. became law.

Shopping could continue late into the night on a Saturday. This extended opening not only allowed people to shop as they left the pub in the evening, but also enabled shopkeepers to sell off stock that would otherwise go off by Monday. W.F. Turner, writing about life on Walthamstow High Street, North London, in the 1900s, remembered this late-night shopping: 'the shops and stalls were out until ten o'clock, and meat was auctioned at rock bottom prices to save it going off in those days of no fridges.' At Christmas the shops were open even later, and their displays were ablaze with paraffin lamps.

Below The Popular Café in Piccadilly, London, was owned by Lyons and opened in 1904. The picture shows some of the 2,000 places set ready for the opening. The café also had a resident orchestra.

FROM BANQUETS TO CAFÉS

There was not much leisure for shop workers but in Edwardian times even the middle classes wanted a slice of the leisured life that the rich and the aristocracy so publicly enjoyed. If they could not afford a banquet, shoppers might at least

manage tea and cakes. In London and other big cities there were many cafés to supply this need, and the different social classes had their own preferred eateries, priced accordingly.

J. Lyons & Co. led the way, opening its first tea shops in the 1890s. There were soon many branches, kitted out in uniform style with distinctive opal-glass ceiling panels. They were pitched at the upper end of the market, whereas people of more modest means headed for the tea shops run by the Aerated Bread Company, familiarly known as ABCs. At a time when it was unacceptable for unaccompanied women to enter most pubs and restaurants, alcohol-free ABCs were known as safe places for women. When the International Congress for Women was held in London in 1899, ABCs were recommended as a safe place for delegates to eat. Virginia Woolf mentions ABCs more than once in her fiction. In *Jacob's Room* Florinda reads her love letters in an ABC and when, in *Night and Day*, Katherine Hilbery wants somewhere to put pen to paper, she goes into an ABC, orders a coffee and sits down to write her letter.

Above From china cups to floral wallpaper, bentwood chairs to potted plants, the Edwardian tea shop had an elegant décor designed to appeal to women shoppers.

More imposing than either ABCs or Lyons's tea shops were Lyons's major Edwardian venture, the Corner Houses. First opened in 1909, these were huge, multi-storey restaurants, laid out on a lavish scale, with orchestras entertaining the diners and a contingent of kitchen and waiting staff attending to the customers. With their modern layout and decoration the Corner Houses seemed the ultimate in eating out.

In provincial towns that lacked a Lyons or an ABC there was an opening for an enterprising baker to find room in his premises for a small tea shop or café. As they were already producing the bread and cakes they needed to do this, many bakers could create this extra business with quite a small outlay. Floor space, furniture, somewhere to prepare food and wash up and some waiting staff (often family members) were the main requirements.

Running a café or tea shop could be an attractive option for a small-town baker. As well as bringing in extra money, it offered a way of employing family members who might not be strong enough for the hard work of kneading the

CELEBRATION CAKES
AN EDWARDIAN PASSION

The Edwardians loved cakes, from rich fruit cakes to light sponges, Madeira cakes to Dundee cakes. They had a particular passion for iced cakes and today's multi-tier wedding cakes, decorated all over with white icing, became popular in the Edwardian era.

ROYAL ICING

The best celebration cakes were decorated all over with 'royal icing'. This is a form of icing that sets very hard and can be used to create very flat, white surfaces. It is also ideal for intricate patterns and designs created by piping. Royal icing is simply a mixture of fine icing sugar and egg whites. To make it, the baker sifted the sugar to make sure that it was as fine as possible and separated the whites from the yolks of the eggs. The whites were stirred slightly to break them up, but without introducing too many air bubbles. Then half the icing sugar was added to the eggs, mixed and beaten for up to ten

minutes. The mixture was left for half an hour or so, by which time the air bubbles had risen to the surface. Next the rest of the sugar was mixed in, until the icing had a stiff consistency. The traditional test was to stand the wooden spoon upright in it and watch it fall – if it fell gradually to one side you had the right blend. The mix was then left covered for a while in a cool place.

APPLYING THE ICING

Many people liked a perfectly flat surface, which was ideal for adding extra piped decoration. To flat-ice a cake, the top was done first, by spreading the icing evenly with a palette knife, working it carefully to expel any air bubbles. An icing ruler was drawn smoothly over the surface to make it flat. Next the sides were iced with the aid of a turntable, and again a ruler or baker's card was used to make the surface flat. After the join between the top and the sides had been tidied up, the cake was left for at least 24 hours to harden. Sometimes a second layer of icing, thinned slightly with water, was added later to make the surface even smoother. Only after the flat icing had hardened for several days was any piped decoration added, also using a royal icing mixture.

BELOW *Using square biscuit tins as improvised stands, workers ice wedding cakes at the Co-operative Wholesale Biscuit Factory in Crumpsall, Manchester.*

LEFT *Amid a confusion of scales, bowls, and storage jars, the ingredients for royal icing are mixed together in the bakery.*

ABOVE AND RIGHT *Decorative swags and flourishes are applied to the cake using a piping bag (above). When the icing has set the sections of the cake are assembled carefully (right).*

dough. The trade left its mark on the baker's body, as one trader remarked: 'A baker, you could always tell a baker! He always walked like this [feet splayed out] because he couldn't stand close enough to his bench without turning his feet out.' And though grocers did not normally sell bread or cake, making it essential for shoppers to visit the baker for these items, it was often hard to make a living from a bakery alone. There was competition from multiples and, in spite of machines such as dough mixers, baking remained a hot, laborious business. Customers expected a wide range of loaf types too, with tin-baked loaves like the sandwich, wholemeal loaves and speciality breads in demand alongside the standard kinds. Profits were slim on them all.

So, for the baker, running a tea shop provided more income, the chance to chat to customers, get feedback, improve customer relations and show off the latest cakes and biscuits. Not all bakers followed this route: some stuck to the old formula of baking mainly bread for sale in the shop and through a delivery round. But those who baked more cakes, opened tea or dining rooms, and perhaps branched out into confectionery too, had a better chance of prospering.

THE EDWARDIAN DRESSMAKER

A striking difference between the Edwardian High Street and today's shopping centres is the change in the number of shops selling clothes. Today towns are full of clothes shops, but in the Edwardian period there were very few. A certain amount of mass-produced clothing was available, ranging from men's suits from new chains such as Hepworth's to plain clothes for everyday wear by working people. Major department stores in big cities also offered a dressmaking service.

But many women preferred to vary their wardrobe by making their own clothes – sewing was a valued and valuable skill for Victorian and Edwardian women – or taking fabric to a local dressmaker and having a dress made. In the Edwardian era most towns had at least one or two 'little dressmakers', women who were skilled at cutting and using the now-popular Singer sewing machine, and who made clothes to order. They were respected, discreet women, and dressmaking was one of the few respectable occupations open to an independent or unmarried woman. It was also attractive to many women because setting up as a dressmaker did not require a large capital investment or the purchase of a lot of stock.

A woman could take an illustration from a fashion magazine to a dressmaker, who would copy or adapt it for her customer. Having a dress made to order was costly, but clothes were not the ephemeral fashion items they often are today, and most people expected them to last a very long time. Besides, a good, specially made dress was one of the few major indulgences available to Edwardian women. For those on a tight budget, an alternative to making a dress from scratch was to buy a partly made garment and complete it to produce a perfect fit. Partly made garments could be completed by the purchaser or taken

THE EDWARDIAN DRESSMAKER

DRESSMAKING

Working from a comfortable, quiet room, typically above a shop and perhaps adjoining her living accommodation, the Edwardian dressmaker was a well-known but discreet presence on the High Street. She was likely to be a single woman who valued her independence, and combined flair with colours and fabrics, a knowledge of the latest fashions, and skill with both traditional needle and sewing machine. She also had to be good with people, getting to know her clients and their likes and dislikes.

The dresses and skirts she made usually had narrow waists with a line that was smooth over the hips but flared out near the ground. Lace was much favoured as a decoration, both on blouses and at the corsage of evening dresses. For everyday wear, women often chose a plain skirt and a blouse, which could be quite elaborately decorated with much tucking and trimmings of muslin or lace.

The dressmaker would make more practical, tailored clothes for working women such as governesses or those working in shops. In addition, dressmaking involved repairs and alterations such as letting out or taking in a dress, often one made by the dressmaker herself some time ago, that had been passed on to another member of a family.

So the dressmaker had to know not just about basic needlework, but also about materials such as lace – and cheaper substitutes such as Irish crochet for those who could not afford real lace. She also had to understand corsetry, as in a small town there was usually no specialist corsetiere. The corset, which held in the waist and tended to throw the bust forward and the hips backward, was at the heart of the Edwardian look, and the dressmaker had to understand both its whalebone construction and how to trim it with lace in the most pleasing way.

ABOVE AND RIGHT *Although she uses a sewing machine, the dressmaker still has to be a skilled needlewoman. She adds a decorative flourish to a corset, a key feature of Edwardian fashion.*

GILL COCKWELL
Dressmaker

Before I started this project I had this romantic idea about days gone by being nicer, people being kinder to each other and taking more pride in their work. So far, I've been proven right. I went to the grocer's this morning to buy tea and biscuits for my customers and the service was amazing – I walked in and somebody took my coat and gave me a seat and found everything I wanted and then said: 'We'll bring them over to you.' It was just lovely.

At home I get really bad backache and I thought my backache would get worse when I was working as an Edwardian dressmaker because of having to lean forward to see things. But actually I haven't had a single twinge. I've had a hard-backed chair, which I think is really good, and the first time I've had any hint of back trouble was as soon as the sewing machine arrived, so it's ironic. But now I'm happy again, doing my hand sewing. And I've got some great projects to do tomorrow with or without the machine. I'm also going to have a little bit of help from the young girls. That will be really fun because I'll be able to teach them something and they're such enthusiastic girls that they'll really enjoy it.

to a dressmaker. Another compromise was to buy a ready-made skirt together with matching material for a bodice. The dressmaker could style the bodice individually to the wearer's preference, and the result would still be unique.

All this meant that Edwardian women valued their dressmakers highly. But dressmakers were not a major presence on the High Street. They usually either worked from home or took a room above a shop. Because they were making goods to order they did not have stock to display in the window, and a quiet room was the ideal place where customer and needlewoman could discuss the next dress in privacy.

THE END OF AN ERA

The comfortable life of tea shop and dressmaker was brought to an end with the coming of war. One shop worker who wrote a description of her life, Winifred Griffiths from Hampshire, was in domestic service when the war began but soon left this for a new job in the grocery department of the Co-op in Basingstoke. She recalls that she was one of three new women staff members, the others having travelled all the way from Somerset and Yorkshire to take up their posts. Even if grocery was not the skilled business it once was, there was still much to learn:

> *I had to take payment of bills and the method of receipting had not been explained to me. When trying to serve customers I did not know where things were kept, nor yet had I memorized the prices. I had not acquired the knack of making tidy packets for goods like dried fruit, rice and tapioca, and numerous others which were kept loose in drawers and had to be weighed as needed. To crown all, most customers expected their goods to be done up in a large paper parcel.*

Although many Edwardians had experienced a little luxury in their lives, and had seen their High Streets become more modern with the arrival of Woolworth's and similar stores, much basic food retailing was carried out in ways that the Victorians would have recognised. As the war went on, and many food supplies were diverted to soldiers on the front, life became still more austere. When the longed-for end of the war finally came in 1918, things would never be quite the same again.

Below In 1917, a family pause to look at a window display. The man is in uniform and the end of the war is still a year away.

Overleaf A selection of images of activities on the Edwardian High Street. Clockwise from top left: preparing sandwiches in the tea shop, tying a parcel at the butcher's; the dressmaker at work; the owner of the bazaar keeping accounts; cottons and lace; tea shop scene; the finishing touch to a celebration cake; a perfectly decorated table.

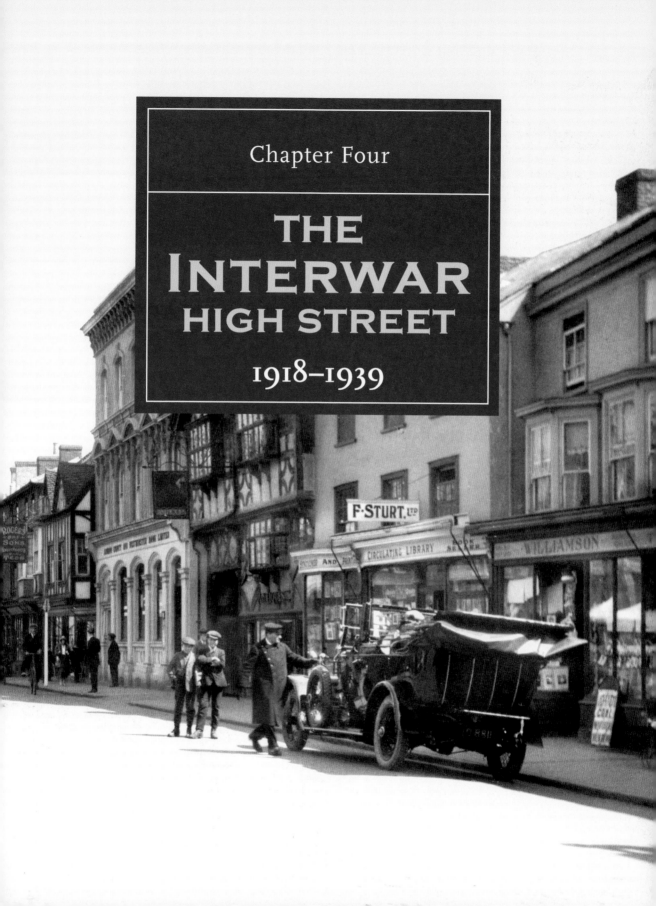

Chapter Four

THE
INTERWAR
HIGH STREET

1918–1939

THE 1920s AND 1930s were a time of change on the High Street. Optimism after the end of the First World War gave way to high unemployment and economic crisis. Shoppers were looking for good value and shopkeepers were seeking ways to innovate and attract customers. For some shopkeepers this involved taking on new kinds of goods; for others it meant buying a van, getting on the road and making deliveries. For all, it was an interesting but challenging time.

The interwar period was a chapter of economic accidents. Britain emerged from the First World War into a slump and although there was some recovery in the early 1920s, there was a further setback because the exchange rate in the second half of the decade made exports more expensive. Many employers tried to reduce their costs by cutting wages and this provoked the General Strike of 1926, a nationwide stoppage in support of the coal miners, who were in dispute with their employers. The strike brought industries such as iron and steel, construction, printing and transport to an almost total standstill. The government recruited middle-class volunteers to run some services and troops took to the streets to maintain order. After nine days the General Strike collapsed, without winning any benefits for the miners, who stayed on strike for several months.

In 1929 an even worse disaster struck. The New York Stock Market crash led to a worldwide depression. The market for British exports disintegrated and unemployment, already high at 1 million, increased to 2.5 million (one fifth of the workforce) by late 1930. Every town and village, almost every family, was affected in some way by the crisis.

1918	**1919**	**1921**	**1922**	**1923**
The First World War comes to an end with the signing of the Armistice.	Wartime rationing comes to an end, but there are still shortages of many foods and other goods.	The Gramophone Company (HMV) opens a new shop in Oxford Street, London.	The small, mass-produced Austin Seven brings down the cost of motoring for many families.	Burton's, by now well established as a menswear retailer, begins to build purpose-built stores, many with the company's trademark billiard halls in the rooms above.

FROM DEPRESSION TO RECOVERY

The crash damaged the industrial areas of northern England and Scotland and the mining towns of South Wales particularly badly. British heavy industry found it hard to compete with foreign rivals and there was mass unemployment in mining, metalworking and shipbuilding. Southern England was hit less badly, partly because there was still a market for products such as electrical goods produced in the modern factories in London and the South-East. There was also a housing boom around London, where many of the suburbs were built in the 1930s, and low interest rates helped to sustain the capital's expansion. Some Midlands cities also did well thanks to a growing car industry, in which Austin, Morris and Ford were key players. But even in the South, if people kept their jobs it was often with a cut in pay.

A change in economic policy – devaluing the pound and withdrawal from the gold standard – made British exports more competitive and from 1934 onwards there was a slow recovery. The government further stimulated the economy with schemes such as road-building programmes and loans to shipyards. After Hitler's rise to power in Germany, it also ordered a massive rearmament, which created many new jobs from 1936 onwards. As a result some families became prosperous. While the middle classes hoped to buy a new Morris or Austin car, or set up house in an attractive suburb, the less well-off began to eye household gadgets such as radios and vacuum cleaners. By the end of the 1930s three-quarters of British families had a gas cooker and a quarter had a refrigerator. And in 1936 holiday pay for the employed was enshrined in law. But many families still struggled to make ends meet. The government estimated that a quarter of the population was managing on or around subsistence level and malnutrition was common.

1925
Contributory state pension scheme is introduced for workers over 65.

1926
The General Strike interrupts major industries and transportation, but ends after nine days.

1927
The BBC gets its royal charter, establishing it as a broadcasting monopoly and the world's first public service broadcasting organisation.

1929
The Wall Street Crash begins an economic slump that affects all industrialised countries in the West.

1930
Bird's first uses the 'Three birds' logo for its popular custard powder, which is advertised widely in this period.

FROM JAZZ TO THE MOVIES

Cultural historians often see the 1920s as the jazz age, a period dominated by cocktail parties attended by bright young things listening to gramophone records of the latest sounds from Harlem and New Orleans. Although many people in Britain had neither the money nor the social connections to go anywhere near a cocktail party, they did have the chance to distract themselves from the harsh realities of life in the depression in new and interesting ways.

The interwar period was a golden age of the cinema. Although there had been cinemas before the war, many of them had closed for the duration and in the 1920s a new generation of cinemas, larger and more elaborate than before, began to open. Some were combined with a ballroom and restaurant, and by the end of the decade they were showing movies with synchronised sound. The cinemas of the 1920s, and even more so the 1930s, were like fantasy palaces. Some were even called 'Palace' or 'Dreamland'. Cinema owners like Otto Deutsch of the Odeon chain commissioned architects who pulled out all the stops to design breathtaking interiors in the sleekest modern or Art Deco style or using ancient Egyptian, Medieval or baroque decoration. The aim was to take the movie-goer into another world – and given the depressing outlook for many in the 1930s, most people were all too eager to be seduced.

As in retailing, chains developed. The three most prominent were the Gaumont, Associated British Cinemas and Odeon companies, all of which were established by 1930. They colonised the larger towns and the growing suburbs; smaller, local independent cinemas were also built in places without a chain cinema or where the market was big enough to support several picture houses. The movies were popular, but some people also liked home entertainment, buying gramophones or radios. Gadgets like these provided retail opportunities, and electrical shops started to appear on the High Street.

1931
Labour Prime Minister Ramsay MacDonald forms a National Government consisting of members from all three main parties.

1932
George V begins the tradition of regular Christmas broadcasts on BBC radio.

1933
Unemployment reaches almost 3 million.

1933
John Boot, backed by a group of bankers, buys back his family firm of chemists from Louis Liggett of the United Drug Company, who had lost a fortune in the Wall Street Crash of 1929.

FOOD FASHIONS

Many women enjoyed the freedom that had come with the First World War. They had earned good money and new friends working in factories and shops and did not want to return to domestic service, the main employment for women before the war began. This left many middle-class women without domestic servants and coping with cooking and housework for themselves for the first time.

When rationing ended in 1919, the emphasis at the grocer's moved towards more pre-packaged and processed foods, in part to satisfy the demand of the new breed of home cooks – both the middle-class women without domestic help and single women living alone. So a host of new brands appeared, and older ones enjoyed a revival. Grocers stocked Paxo stuffing, Chivers jams and Edwards' Desiccated Soups. Sliced bread began to appear. Ready-shredded suet became widely available. And old flavouring standbys such as Bovril became still more popular. Dishes that were simple to cook, such as casseroles, gained a new vogue. A good stew was nutritious, could be left simmering while the cook did other things and involved minimal washing up after the meal. Those with the money for a fridge used it to store meals that had been prepared in advance. And those without such conveniences dreamed of the new modern hygienic kitchens that were appearing in magazines and at the Ideal Home exhibitions.

People, conscious of the USA through the movies, also looked across the Atlantic for food and fashions. Hot dogs and hamburgers made an appearance on British tables, and housewives cooked Chicken Maryland and Baked Alaska. The culinary world was slowly starting to shrink. Tinned foods, seen as the latest technology, were on the increase too. People embraced convenience foods enthusiastically. What was occasional convenience for the well-to-do could be the one source of variety for the poor – if they were lucky. For the interwar period was always one of mixed fortunes and varied tastes.

1934
Robert Lutyens, consultant architect to Marks & Spencer plc, develops a grid system to plan shop fronts for the company, giving all its stores a similar uniform design.

1935
Nylon fibre is first produced in the laboratory, heralding a new era of artificial textiles.

1936
During the Abdication Crisis, Edward VIII quits the throne and his brother becomes King George VI.

1938
To avoid war, Prime Minister Neville Chamberlain makes a compromise agreement with Hitler for 'Peace in our time'.

PEACE AND PROSPERITY

Susan Higlett, in an account of traders in Hounslow High Street, gives a short summary of a group of shops along one stretch of the street. Although not a full list (the bakers, butchers and grocers were clearly in another part of the town centre), it conjures up a vivid picture of the period. Together with the Hoopers' ironmongers, a clothes shop and a restaurant called The Dining Rooms were the following traders and businesses: 'Rainbow – fried fish; Loves – tools, keys and ironmongery; Nicholes – sweets and tobacco; Rowles – chimney sweep; Lamb – watch repairs, sweets and tobacco; Underdown – greengrocery; Reed and Hann – corn and seed merchants; Poultons – toys; Kemp – fishmonger; Turner – yeast merchant; and Lawson – chemist.' It is a traditional-looking list, containing many trades that might have been there in Victorian times. But the 1920s and 1930s were also a period of change. The first radio shops were opening, for example, along with electrical retailers selling other kinds of household gadgets. More restaurants were opening, continuing an Edwardian trend that had been interrupted by the war. And as people started to buy cars and commercial vehicles, garages, sometimes extensions of ironmongers' or bicycle dealers' shops, began to open to service them.

With the war over it was a time of optimism for many, but retailing still posed challenges. One of these was bad debts. Credit was still common on the High Street and unpaid bills brought some businesses to their knees. Peggy Hancock remembers working in a music shop and piano dealer's in Devizes, Wiltshire, in the late 1920s. Although the business did well selling and tuning

Opposite The butcher offers a joint for inspection by the customer.

pianos – many houses had a piano in those days – there was still a problem collecting the debts: 'We used to send out bills for tuning, five shillings [25p] a time or a pound for five times a year. The number of bad debts you got at that rate was terrific!. . . I knew when I sent some of [the bills] out that it was going to be a dead loss and that I might as well have torn them up straight away.'

As the period went on and Britain began to face the economic hardships of the 1930s, this problem increased and some shops closed. Increasingly, too, shop assistants found themselves working harder than ever for lower wages.

THE WORKING DAY

During the 1920s and 1930s working conditions in shops were hard and harsh for many. The working days were long, there were few breaks and assistants were reprimanded if they ignored a customer, talked among themselves or even, in some shops, sat down. Most shops had little heating and some shopkeepers insisted on keeping the door open permanently, to lure customers in. After the First World War many of the economic privations continued. Nor did the food shortages go away, with rationing for meat lasting until late 1919, while butter and sugar were rationed until 1920.

Another wartime restriction on trading was continued too. During the war the government had brought in compulsory restrictions on shop hours to conserve fuel. On four days every week shops had to close at 8 p.m. and on Saturdays they were allowed to open until 9 p.m., but on the remaining weekday early closing at 1 p.m. was enforced. Workers liked the rules, but shop owners were doubtful at first. However, their customers got used to shopping earlier in the day, and shopkeepers came to appreciate the shorter hours too, and even closed earlier than the law required.

When the war ended many shop workers feared that their hours would go back to pre-war levels. But the restrictions on hours continued and were made permanent in 1928. There were exceptions – extensions of trading hours were allowed for sweets, table waters and fruit, for example – but on the whole shop workers did not have to work such punishing hours as they had in the Edwardian era.

HARD TIMES

One result of the Armistice was that many men returned from the front to take up their old jobs. Their arrival meant that a lot of the women who had found work on the High Street during the war were now sent home. If a woman worker received a couple of weeks' notice to quit because men were returning from the army or navy, there was nothing she could do about it – it was accepted that the men had priority. But the picture was not a simple one. In spite of the returning servicemen, the total number of women working in retailing in the 1920s was still higher than it had been in the Edwardian period and by 1930 around half of shop workers were women. There were many women especially in shops selling clothing, shoes and fabrics. Businesses such as butchery and grocery, on the other hand, were still dominated by men. And these figures confirmed that there was a huge prejudice against women in these trades. For example, one grocer argued that young women should receive no more than half the suggested minimum pay because 'you have to teach them the business and lose by their errors, breakages, clumsiness and mistakes in charging, weighing, etc.'. As there was no law imposing equal pay, or regulating assistants' wages generally, shopkeepers could get away with paying women much less than their male colleagues.

The situation did not improve during the slump of the early 1930s. Shops came under pressure in many ways. Good public transport meant that many small local shops had to compete with town shops that offered lower prices or a better choice of goods. Small shopkeepers often had to compete with multiple stores, which were on the increase. The shopkeeper could cut prices to match the multiples – food prices in the 1930s, for example, were around half what they were after the end of the war – but this slashed profits. And lower wages for customers meant a lower spend too, reducing the shopkeeper's income still further. For many shop workers this meant either dismissal or a cut in wages. Many had their earnings reduced by a third or even more, yet those who had to cope with this thought themselves fortunate compared with men and women who were dismissed. With all shops feeling the pinch there was little chance of another job, and shop workers faced long-term unemployment. According to one study, as many as one in five male assistants in the grocery, butchery and footwear trades was out of work by 1931. Jobs in retailing were rarely secure, and

Above The work of the small-town grocer and his wife diversified during the interwar period. Those behind the grocery counter found themselves cutting cheese and selling family provisions one minute and handing out the latest sweets to children the next.

many older, experienced employees were dismissed and replaced by younger, cheaper workers.

Those who managed to keep a job did not always do badly. Although many suffered wage cuts, prices had fallen still faster. So the employed still had some disposable income, and manufacturers were busy introducing radios, gramophones and vacuum cleaners for them to spend their money on.

DELIVERING THE GOODS

In Dorothy L. Sayers's 1937 detective novel *Busman's Honeymoon*, Lord Peter Wimsey and his new wife Harriet move into their country home and find themselves investigating a murder instead of enjoying a few weeks of married bliss. Their house is in chaos because of the death of its previous owner, and, as policemen, chimney sweeps, vicars and a host of typical interwar characters come and go, the couple and their servant have to buy food and other supplies in an isolated village with no shop. This being the 1930s, the shopkeepers come to them. Drink is sent around from the pub and they are soon visited by a local grocer and baker, and are being told by a neighbour that the Home and Colonial, the chain grocer in the nearby town, is cheaper but calls on a different day of the week. In the interwar period, deliveries – which save, or at any rate provide, Lord Peter's bacon – were becoming a way of life.

The men and boys from the High Street whose job it was to deliver the goods used various kinds of transport. The milkman might come with a horse and cart, while the baker's boy could arrive on a bicycle with a huge

Below In Conisbrough, Yorkshire, confectioners Drabble and Co. had a small fleet of delivery vehicles. Here, the drivers stand proudly by their trucks, which advertise some of the goods they carried, including toffee made by Mackintosh's, itself a Yorkshire brand.

basket overloaded with loaves. As the 1920s and 1930s went on, quite a few traders drove vans, which were ideal for grocers with their wide range of goods, and for hardware stores with their clanking dustbins and sloshing cans of paraffin.

Bakers were among the most widespread traders who delivered. People liked their bread fresh and a daily delivery, or a call every other day, was just right. In town it was often the job of the 'boy', the youngest member of the staff, who whizzed around the streets on a bicycle. Jack Pritchard, one of the contributors to an oral history of the Forest of Dean in Gloucestershire, remembers his first job, delivering bread. In this period

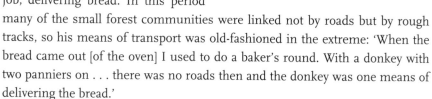

many of the small forest communities were linked not by roads but by rough tracks, so his means of transport was old-fashioned in the extreme: 'When the bread came out [of the oven] I used to do a baker's round. With a donkey with two panniers on . . . there was no roads then and the donkey was one means of delivering the bread.'

Above The baker loads his shining green van with trays of bread and cakes. With motorised transport, shopkeepers were able to cover a wider geographical area than in earlier periods.

Where the roads were better, bakers increasingly abandoned horse-drawn transport and invested in a motor van, which was faster and could carry more stock and cover more miles in a day. A van, painted with the owner's name and address, was also a moving advertisement, one that stood out boldly in the days when there were very few vehicles on the road. But vans had their downsides too. They cost a lot of money. They needed maintaining and filling with fuel, and there were few petrol stations, so you had to be organised and keep the tank full.

Butchers often delivered too. One butcher in Devizes remembers his father's assistant in the 1920s going out with a horse and cart to collect carcases from the slaughterhouse and then using the same vehicle to deliver meat to customers. Later the business bought a Ford Type T van, which the family used for leisure trips at the weekend. It was vital to keep the tank filled up: 'It had three gears; high, low and reverse and gravity feed petrol. If you were going up a steep hill and the petrol was a bit low it would stop. When we went out at weekends we filled up when we saw a garage because they were few and far between.'

Retailers came to value their vans, and many shop owners, like the family from Devizes, discovered the freedom of motoring by using a commercial vehicle at weekends. Soon garages were more common, and there were more delivery vans – and private cars – on the road.

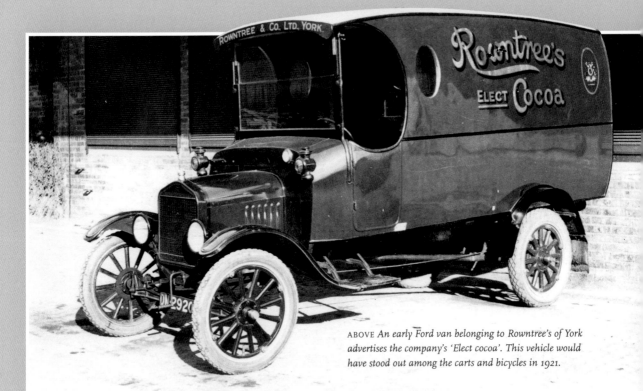

ABOVE *An early Ford van belonging to Rowntree's of York advertises the company's 'Elect cocoa'. This vehicle would have stood out among the carts and bicycles in 1921.*

INTERWAR TRANSPORT

DELIVERIES AND VANS

Bakers were among the first trades to take up motor vehicles in a big way in the interwar period. For many it was a plunge into unknown waters. In the early years there was no compulsory driving test – this was introduced in 1935 – and bakers and their staff learned to drive these early delivery vehicles by trial and error. Although there were relatively few vehicles on the road, there were still accidents, which sometimes happened in the most unexpected ways. A resident of the Forest of Dean, then a coal-mining area, remembers how a baker's delivery man, stepping down from his van on to a tram rail, had his leg amputated by a runaway truck used for transporting coke.

Most drivers, though, soon learned to be road-aware, and the baker's van became a familiar sight to customers and a commercial asset to the owner. It was not just that families wanted their 'daily bread' to be delivered to the door. A baker with a van could deliver his whole stock – cakes,

crumpets, tarts and the rest – and a good salesman could sell more by turning up on customers' doorsteps with a tempting basket of goods.

The range of vehicles was smaller than it is today but surprisingly diverse. At the larger end were vehicles like the 1920s Morris One Ton, with its roomy, box-like body, straight windscreen and cart-like spoked wheels. Slightly more compact, and seen all over the world, was the equally antique-looking Ford van based on the Model T car. The body types included some with open cabs and overhanging roof, and the wheels were usually spoked and similar to those on the Morris. These Fords were among the earliest mass-produced vehicles to sell in large numbers. Smaller models included the popular seven-horsepower Austin, equally boxy but much more compact – altogether a more practical proposition for short-haul deliveries in both town and country.

LEFT *Boots the chemists mostly delivered smaller items and this compact delivery tricycle was an eye-catching sight on the streets of South London in the 1920s.*

BELOW *By the late 1930s, more modern-looking vehicles like this one from Crawley were on the road. More streamlined design and a fully enclosed cab attracted owners who wanted better comfort and an up-to-date image.*

BREAD AND BASICS

The baker might have had the latest in transport, but what he was baking was often very much the same kind of bread as his father before him. Although big, city-based bakers had factory-type facilities with large industrial ovens and huge, motorised dough mixers, many small bakers in country towns still used old-fashioned brick ovens, and more than one remembers the bits of soot and charcoal that stuck to loaves as a result of using wood as fuel. Most customers came to accept these black marks on the crust, as long as the bread tasted good and kept well.

By the 1930s, with poverty on the increase and war becoming increasingly likely, life was hard for many people. Bread, cheap and filling, was a key staple for poorer families, and for some, bread and butter was almost a meal in itself. In some northern towns children snacked on a 'penny chunk' – a quarter of a loaf spread with butter. The baker would cut a loaf into quarters and place these in the oven to toast. When they were ready, he would take them out, spread them with a good dollop of butter and sell them for a penny. Some children liked a chunk of buttered bread as much as a bag of sweets. And their mothers were no doubt grateful that they were eating a filling snack.

In some places there was a major change in the way bread was sold – the introduction of sliced bread. This began in America in the early 1930s with a brand called Wonder Bread. The sliced bread was soon available in Britain and in the 1930s some enterprising bakers even bought slicing machines to slice their own loaves. Sliced bread was popular with people who made a lot of sandwiches, but most customers bought their bread unsliced until after the Second World War. More common than bread slicers were mechanical dough mixers, which began to be popular among smaller bakers just before the First World War and became more widespread still after the war. These gadgets took a lot of the hard physical work out of baking, and gave the baker more time to spend on making other goods, such as cakes. But not every baker could afford an expensive machine like a dough mixer. Some were content to carry on with muscle power, just as the previous generation had done.

Many bakers reacted against the trend for sliced bread and factory-made products. One indication of a move back towards craft-based bakery was the bread-baking competitions of the 1930s. In an atmosphere rather like a flower show, master bakers and their

Below Hovis, by the interwar period a familiar household name, was always advertised as a brand that promoted health. This advertisement also reminds the customer that the bread was baked locally.

The Gateway of Health

HOVIS is fine food for young or old. It builds strength and stamina; nourishes brain and body; brings radiant health.

YOUR BAKER BAKES IT

Previous page As well as bread, the interwar baker was producing a range of cakes including rock cakes, fruit cakes, and the marzipan-covered Battenberg.

apprentices would submit loaves to the discerning palates of a panel of judges. These connoisseurs would prod and poke each loaf, smell it, examine its crumb and measure its crust, before tasting it and pronouncing one the winner. To be the baker of a 'prize-winning loaf' helped bring in more customers, and especially those who were prepared to pay for quality.

LOCAL LUXURIES

Many bakers also made cakes, and as soon as the First World War ended, customers rejoiced that, with food restrictions lifted, they could once again buy more varied cakes, ranging from sponges to traditional recipes such as Eccles cakes and simnel cakes, as well as items like cheesecake. Some of these cake recipes were not just attractive to the consumer but a boon to the baker. For example, many cakes do not keep long and bakers often had stale sponge cakes left over. A way of making money out of these 'stales' was attractive and some cake recipes actually included bread or sponge crumbs in the mix. This was the reason why bakers sold some kinds of cheesecake, treacle tart and other lines. Traditional, local varieties of cakes and buns were still very strong, and had loyal followings. Banbury cakes, Bath buns, Coventry puffs, Eccles cakes and the greasy Cotswold lardy cake or 'dripper' are a few examples, but there were many more.

A lot of bakers sold these cakes in a café adjoining the bakery, just as they had done in the Edwardian period. They still found this a useful source of extra

Below Bakers made full use of window displays, lining up both large iced cakes and smaller lines such as pastries and buns. The displays were entrancing to passing children, most of whom could only dream about expensive iced cakes like these.

income, but these cafés varied widely in the amount of money they brought in. In a prosperous town such as Bath or Cheltenham there were quite upmarket cafés serving a clientele of well-heeled women shoppers. But in many towns the cafés were pitched much more downmarket, with tea rooms or 'refreshment rooms' offering, if you were lucky, quick, courteous service and a cheap cup of tea.

THE BUTCHER'S BOY AND BIKE

Like bakers, butchers were usually expected to deliver to customers, and by the 1920s most butchers had at least one delivery bicycle, operated by the 'boy', often the proprietor's son who was learning the trade. Many larger butchers had a small fleet of these bicycles, and the butcher's boy, flying along the street under pedal power, became a frequent sight.

Above One popular type of delivery bicycle featured a small front wheel. This kind of bike gave plenty of space for a deep basket, enabling the delivery boy to go out on longer trips – provided they could keep the bike steady with a full load.

The typical delivery bicycle had a large frame at the front to take a rectangular willow basket. At the start of the round this was piled high, and more than one delivery boy remembers sitting on the saddle during loading, to act as a counterweight and prevent the whole lot from toppling over. Making the first few deliveries, while the basket was still full, must have been a perilous business. Across the middle of the bicycle, beneath the crossbar, there was usually a sign with the name of the shop. Like the delivery van, the bicycle was a form of moving advertisement, although it was often ridden at such speed that few could read what the sign said. Even in the 21st century, some butchers still have a bike or two, because of their convenience for short-distance deliveries and the chance they give to show the company name around town.

In the interwar years the fast and furious pedalling often continued over the lunch hour, because delivery bikes were considered a fringe benefit of the job and many butchers allowed their apprentices to use them for personal journeys during their lunch break.

The personal use of delivery bicycles became a legal issue in 1932 when in London a member of the public was injured in an accident involving a butcher's delivery bicycle. The bike was being used by the rider in his lunch hour, with the butcher's permission, and the injured passer-by claimed damages from the business. The butcher had to pay £300. He appealed and finally the Law Lords ruled that an employer was not liable for injuries caused by a bicycle used by an employee for his or her own purposes, even if it was used with permission. So butchers' boys continued to zip around town during working hours and to benefit from this useful perk at lunchtime.

Above In the 1930s, Colchester carnival featured a 'derby race' for delivery boys on their bicycles. This photograph shows them practising for the big occasion in 1934.

LEARNING THE TRADE

If the butcher's boy was learning the trade, he would expect to do a lot more than delivery duties. A key aspect of the business was buying the best meat at the keenest price, and this involved regular trips to market. A history of butchers' shops in the North London borough of Camden contains a reminiscence by Phillip Cramer, a member of a family of butchers in the area. Phillip was learning the business from his father in the period between the two world wars.

The Cramers being London butchers, they made the journey to the large Smithfield meat market by Underground, in the early hours of the morning, a trip that soon became second nature to butchers all over the capital. The vast market, criss-crossed by hundreds of men and full of the apparently random shouts of the buyers and sellers, seemed a place of chaos to the newcomer. But the young butcher soon mastered the maths needed in dealing, and picked up the knowledge of meat that would help him buy the carcases he needed. It was tough, rapid, on-the-job training, as Phillip Cramer explains: 'There was much to be learned in being a buyer in Smithfield that could not be learned by reading a book.' For much of the period there were no weighing machines in markets, so a butcher had to get used to judging a beast by eye. This was a matter of experience, but after years of going to market with a master butcher, an apprentice knew what to look out for. Eventually he would be able to tell not only which animals would yield the best meat, but also an animal's weight to within a few pounds.

Once the meat was bought, the butcher arranged for a specialist meat carrier to deliver it to the shop on his lorry, and then there was time for a breakfast at one of the nearby pubs with an early-opening licence before going back to the shop to open up for the long day behind the counter. For butchers all over the country, the working week followed a similar pattern, although in a country town the early-morning journey would be to the local market rather than the vast, echoing hall of Smithfield.

FRESH BUT CHILLED

If things went well, those pre-dawn trips to market yielded good, fresh meat, although the butcher had to have a clear idea of what his customers were looking for. But in the 1920s and 1930s more and more butchers had a secret weapon that was available to few before the First World War – the refrigerator. Although refrigerators were invented in the 19th century, they were not taken up widely until much later. This was partly because of the cost, partly because few people or businesses had access to the electricity or gas needed to power them. The situation changed in the 1920s and 1930s because more businesses were hooked up to the electricity supply. In addition, safer coolant chemicals came in during the 1930s, making fridges still more popular.

The fridge or cold room made life easier for the butcher. He did not have to buy quite so often, and there was not the rush to sell off meat before the end of the week. For some it also meant that more variety of stock could be held, because the butcher could afford to hang on to cuts of meat that were less popular than the mainstream items. Used with care, therefore, refrigeration could turn into the chance to make more sales.

In some rural areas, however, electricity arrived late and refrigerators were not installed until well into the 1930s. In many places, such as the Forest of Dean, that meant that there was a pressing need to sell off meat at the end of the week, and so regular meat auctions were held. These took place on Saturday evenings, starting at around 7 p.m., and by nine they were in full swing. Most butchers had opening shop windows and a crowd of bargain hunters would gather round on the pavement outside to examine the stock and make their bids. In poor areas customers liked the meat auctions because of the chance of a good deal – and also because the butchers' patter was good free amusement. One Forest of Dean resident remembers the humour of some of the sales talk, a mixture of talking down the meat available at competing butchers and wittily talking up what was about to be sold: 'Look at these lovely legs [of mutton] like London barmaids with blue garters on.' As so often was the case, shopping also involved entertainment.

The layout of the interwar butcher's shop had been familiar to shoppers since the Victorian era. In the window – either a single window or twin openings on either side of a central door – were marble slabs on which the meat was displayed. The wooden floor was dusted with sawdust twice daily. Inside the shop were two butcher's blocks, a large one for cutting up carcases and a small one where the meat was cut into small joints for the customer. There was a shiny metal rail suspended from the ceiling and carcases hung from this rail. Somewhere at the back was the cash office where bills were drawn up and people paid.

At the beginning of the day the first job was to cut up the meat for customers who had placed orders. These joints were then loaded on to cycles or vans ready for the delivery round to begin. This work was done early in the

CELLOPHANE

When in 1900 Swiss chemist Jacques E. Brandenberger watched spilled wine seeping into a restaurant tablecloth he decided to do something to stop this kind of damage. He experimented with producing clear, waterproof coverings for fabric and one trial coating, made of viscose, tended to peel off the cloth. Brandenberger realised that he had something else – a clear plastic film that had potential for packaging. He improved it by making it softer and more flexible, and designed a machine to produce it. He patented his product in 1912 and called it Cellophane. By the 1920s, further modified to make it truly moisture-proof, the new material was changing the world of retailing. In Britain the material became especially popular in the 1930s, when it was produced on a larger scale by the company British Cellophane at their large factory in Bridgwater, Somerset.

Confectioners and other food retailers loved Cellophane. It helped preserve the food that was wrapped in it, but was perfectly transparent, so customers could see exactly what was inside the wrapping. Because the see-through material was shiny, it even gave an attractive sheen to the packaging, making the items inside look just as tempting as fresh, unpacked foods on a shop counter. Cellophane made pre-packing goods much more practical than before. Instead of weighing everything out for each customer, a shopkeeper could make up packages in advance, and present them straight to the customer. This speeded up the sales process because there was less waiting around for things to be weighed and wrapped. And it made things more convenient for the shop owner, because packing of goods could be done by an assistant, behind the scenes. Cellophane packaging also meant that goods could even be pre-packed elsewhere and brought to the High Street ready for sale, eventually accelerating the main change in retailing in the mid-20th century, from the sale of fresh goods individually weighed for the customer to standardised pre-packed items.

morning, before breakfast. After the breakfast break the items for delivery went out, and in the case of a butcher in a market town deliveries would be made both in the town itself and in the surrounding villages.

Back in the shop some of the carcases were cut into large pieces and displayed in the window, and the premises were ready for business. When customers came into the shop they usually knew exactly which cut of meat they wanted and would ask for particular joints – meat from near the horn of the animal for stewing, for example, or from towards the rump for roasting. The butcher would reach for the appropriate piece in the window display and cut the joint from it for that customer. This was important, because shoppers expected to see the meat before it was cut and have it cut to their personal requirements. If the customer didn't like the look of what was in the window, the butcher would turn to the whole carcases hanging on the rail and offer to cut a joint from one of those.

Service was personal, but the orders were often very small and made by women who came in every morning. A butcher hoped for a good mix of customers, with poorer people going for cheap cuts such as brisket of beef and better-off customers buying best steak. Mrs West, the daughter of a butcher in Market Harborough, Leicestershire, remembers customers buying very small quantities of steak, including some who would come in regularly for 'is worth of steak for my husband's dinner'. In the days before pre-packaging, everyone's requirements, from the poor single person buying a few pence worth of meat to a rich family investing in a whole sirloin, were met by the local butcher.

Above The lavish display of meat, all hung for long enough to bring out its flavour, was still the preserve of the master butcher. Full use was made of outside hanging rails and the butcher's traditional open shop frontage.

Many people in villages relied on deliveries from the butcher in the nearest town, but some villages had a butcher of their own, although these were usually very small businesses. Often the village butcher could barely make a living from butchery alone, so many also had a few acres of land, working as farmers and raising meat for slaughter and sale in the shop. The other difference between town and village butchers was to do with specialisation and range of stock. In towns there were still specialist pork butchers, who made pork pies, haslet, potted meat and faggots, as their Victorian parents and grandparents had done; there were also general butchers who stocked all kinds of meat but made few products apart from sausages. In most villages, by contrast, if there was a butcher at all, he had to keep a general stock, including pork, beef, lamb and sometimes poultry, in order to make a living.

Above Unwrapped boiled sweets go sticky when exposed to the air, so they were kept in glass jars with tightly fitting lids. Their colours looked tempting through the glass, and the jars were easy for an assistant to open and scoop out the contents.

FROM GROCER TO SWEET SHOP

For the grocer, times were changing in the years between the wars. A number of convenience foods were starting to appear, products such as Bird's custard, which speeded up preparation times and became instant hits with the housewife. Stocking items like these meant the grocer was more than ever a reseller – the days of the Victorian 'high-class' grocer blending tea and drying fruit were virtually gone. But there were also small 'general stores' that supplied pre-packaged goods, often at competitive prices. And, in a period when many were feeling the pinch, the Co-op was still strong. Many High Streets, even in quite small towns, had a Co-op where foods of good quality were offered at realistic prices, with the addition of a dividend for members. Some estimates give the Co-op around 20 per cent of the total grocery market in this period.

By the 1930s the multiples had a similar slice of the business to the Co-op. They bought in bulk, sold cheaply and encouraged their managers to cope with a small staff to keep prices down. The manager of a multiple grocery also had support from headquarters. Many produced magazines for their staff that gave hints and tips that would help them achieve higher sales. Managers were given instructions in the art of window display and in the best way to deal with a difficult customer. This all added up to stiff competition for the small local grocer.

What could a small grocer do to compete with the Co-op and the multiples? Some responded by working harder, even to the point of breaking the law and opening for longer hours or trading on a Sunday. They risked prosecution, but frequently magistrates, who were local people and well aware of the difficulties faced by small traders, imposed the lowest possible fines.

THE SWEET SHOP

A better answer was to expand into another area of sales. Some grocers tapped into the British love of sweet things and opened a confectionery counter. This offered the shopkeeper the chance to open on a Sunday, because sweets were exempt from Sunday trading restrictions. In the interwar period the sweets on offer were a mix of traditional items – boiled sweets, toffee, fudge and the like, which had to be weighed individually and were the confectionery equivalent of pre-packaged goods – and others ranging from chocolate bars to sherbet fountains.

The interwar period was the time when pre-packaged bars and packs started to take off in sweet shops. Chocolate bars had been around for some time – Cadbury's Dairy Milk was an Edwardian creation – but now all kinds of ingredients were added to make enticing new bars. Everyone liked them – manufacturers found them easy to distribute, retailers valued their keeping qualities and the way in which you could just hand a bar straight to the customer without any weighing or wrapping. Customers soon came to like the new variety on offer. The Mars Bar was one example that lasted. This toffee, nougat, and chocolate bar was first produced by Forrest Mars (son of Frank C. Mars, who had launched another successful bar, the Milky Way, in the USA). His factory in Slough started with just 12 staff, but was soon producing hundreds of the bars. Crunchie (1929), Kit Kat (1935) and Aero (1935) were other successful bars that appeared at around this time.

Mars Bars and Aero were impulse buys, sweets that you could buy cheaply for a quick snack. At the same time manufacturers saw a more upmarket opportunity in pre-packaged chocolates. Boxed chocolates had been sold before, but Black Magic, Dairy Box, Cadbury's Roses and Terry's All Gold, all of which appeared in the 1930s, made them more widely available.

Below 1930s confectionery brands were distinctively packaged. Many, such as Mars, Rolo and Kit Kat, still use variations on the original interwar typography on their packaging.

SAY IT WITH SUGAR

A few grocers who had the space and the willingness to learn the necessary skills began to make sweets on the premises. 'Home-made' sweets sounded appetising and reassuring, and for someone with dedication there was money to be made from them. Making boiled sweets entailed following instructions carefully, boiling sugar-based mixtures to punishing temperatures and passing the resulting mix through a hand-cranked machine with interchangeable rollers to produce the various shapes of popular sweets –

ovals for barley sugars, pear-shapes for pear drops and the special twisted form for humbugs.

There was also a huge range of traditional hand-made confectionery, from coconut ice and tablet, to toffee, butterscotch, and rock, the latter especially popular at the seaside. Then there were chocolate products, to which a newcomer was added in the 1930s: white chocolate. This is a mixture of cocoa butter, milk, and powdered sugar, which are stirred together to produce a viscous paste. The mixture is then subjected to a process called tempering. This involves heating it, so that excess fat comes to the surface and can be removed. When cool, the resulting chocolate paste can then be put into moulds. Confectioners also found that its taste and colour made a pleasant contrast with that of dark chocolate, and the two could be used in layers in luxury chocolates and other products. In the 1930s, innovations like white chocolate brought the traditional confectionery counter bang up to date.

Coconut Cream
Bon-bons
Tablets
Butter Scotch
Rock
Vanilla Creams
Fondants
Turkish Delight
Russian Toffee
Coconut Kisses
Date Balls
Walnut Toffee

SWEETS : SOME WHOLESOME AND DELICIOUS SWEETMEATS WHICH CAN BE MADE AT HOME

LEFT *A selection of traditional confectionery. Most of these sweets are made by boiling sugar to a specific temperature that influences the consistency (from soft and yielding to hard and brittle) of the finished product. A range of flavourings from butter to vanilla adds to the variety.*

ABOVE *Chopping pieces of white chocolate ready for heating and tempering.*

RIGHT *The tempered chocolate forms an ivory-coloured viscous paste that is pushed carefully into the mould to eliminate air gaps.*

ABOVE *When the mould is full, the excess mixture is scraped off to create a perfectly smooth surface.*

Traditional boiled sweets, sold by weight, were still popular too. Packed into glass jars with metal screw-caps to stop the contents going sticky, the colourful sweets were an eye-catching draw for customers. Often bought by the quarter-pound (0.1 kg), wrapped in conical paper bags or twists of paper, they were a favourite treat of many children.

For the more sophisticated customer there were delights such as fudges and the traditional butter-flavoured confection often known as tablet and popular in Scotland. Butterscotch, other kinds of toffee and coconut ice were also favourites. When well made, confections like these could bring customers back to the shop repeatedly, and if the shop was in a tourist area they often appealed to visitors. None of these sweets, even luxury lines like coconut ice, generated individual sales of much value. But they were attractive and, for some, almost addictive, and customers soon added a few sweet treats to their order when they went to the grocer's or general-store sweet counter. Added to small orders from children, the proceeds from the sweet counter could make a difference to the balance sheet of the small-town shopkeeper.

SAFFRON
Grocer's daughter

I think the 1930s are great. The main reason is that we have every type of chocolate that we can think of. We walked in and as we started to see all the sweets and chocolate I fell in love with it. We have thousands of jars for sweets – the bad thing is that the sweets to fill these haven't arrived yet, so I'm really looking forward to that.

There's a lot more stock that you could recognise in 2010 than there was in the Edwardian times. The rooms are pretty similar but with different wallpapers and furniture – like a wardrobe – and also the chairs and couches are really comfy.

When the kids first came into the sweet shop it was manic because everyone tried to push into the front of the line – they were knocking over sweets and I was trying to pick them up. But after that it was more orderly. It's a bonus having the sweets because they're amazing to eat – we have so much overstock that I can just eat all I want and there will still be loads left for the customers! It's also good because everyone keeps coming round for them so we're making money as well.

THE POST OFFICE

There was another vital service for a small town or village in the early 20th century: the Post Office. In the 1920s and 1930s few people had a telephone. The only easy way to keep in touch with people was by letter or postcard, so the Post Office, the only place where stamps were sold, letters posted and parcels processed, was the communications hub of any community. To take on a Post Office was a big commitment for even an experienced shopkeeper. You had to open for fixed hours, be scrupulously reliable and willing to offer the range of additional services provided by the Post Office counter – postal orders, for example, which offered an efficient way of transferring money when many had no bank account and so could not send a cheque. On the other hand, to be the shop where the Post Office was located put your business at the centre of town or village affairs. Everyone came through your door, you would talk to them all and they would often buy goods in the retail part of your premises too. Your business was the hub of the High Street. So, even though it meant a lot of hard work, running a Post Office was very worthwhile.

Many grocers in the interwar period added a Post Office, sweet shop, newsagents or tobacco counter – or all of these – to their business. They had discovered that the whole is more than the parts. People who came into the shop for one thing remembered that they needed something else, and so takings increased. It was one way for a small shop to prosper, and to benefit from some of the advantages that were enjoyed on a larger scale by multiples and department stores.

Above Diversification was the way forward for many retailers in the interwar period. This Northamptonshire business combined the traditional trades of butcher and grocer with running the local Post Office, becoming a one-stop shop for the local community in the process.

Overleaf A selection of 1930s brands includes many that are still household names today.

WOMEN'S CLOTHES

During the interwar years women had quite a wide choice when it came to where to buy their clothes. Although many women owned a sewing machine and learned needlework from their mother or at school, fewer made their own clothes than was the case in the Edwardian period. This was because mechanisation was bringing down the price of ready-made clothes. The interwar linen draper's shop stocked not only a selection of fabrics, but also many ready-made garments for purchase.

Plenty of market traders sold clothes, and at prices cheaper than the draper's. Chains such as Woolworth's and Marks & Spencer plc stocked clothes for women on a budget. And for those with even less money there were still dealers selling secondhand clothes, although these were less common than in earlier decades. So there was plenty of choice.

In addition many towns had one or two small clothes shops selling a more exclusive selection at higher prices. These shops liked to project an image of sophistication and high fashion and, Paris being the headquarters of European fashion, frequently tried to imply a French connection in their name. They were often known as 'Madame shops'. Even a small town could have several. A history of retailing in a small Leicestershire town, for example, recalls: 'Market Harborough had several of these small costumiers. The shops had names like

Below The interwar dressmaker shows off some favourite designs.

"Maison Eve", "Violette" and "Madame Gertrude's", which was opposite Boots. The latter sold "very high-class stuff".' In a Madame shop the customer expected attentive personal service, clothes that she would not find elsewhere and a feeling that the goods were a cut above what could be bought at one of the multiples. The air of luxury that filled some of these shops added to their attraction for customers.

THE CUSTOMER IS ALWAYS RIGHT

But for the staff it was a different story. In *The Other Side of the Counter*, Marjorie Gardiner wrote a memorable account of working in a hat shop in the interwar years and during the Second World War. The working conditions she describes in this Brighton milliner's were probably little different from those in dress shops up and down the country. The first surprise to a modern reader is how cold it was in the shop:

Above A commission to design a new evening dress is the best kind of work for the dressmaker – a task that calls for creativity and flair, and also one that brings in more income than the usual round of simple jobs and alterations.

> *By nine o'clock the door was open and even in winter remained open throughout the day, no matter how bitter the weather. The girls suffered acutely from the cold and most of them had chilblains for which mittens did little or nothing. Occasionally they tried to sneak a moment in which to warm their frozen fingers on the one tiny radiator which was all that the shop possessed in the way of heating. Incredibly, this was not allowed!*

There were no tea or coffee breaks, but the young female assistants dashed to the kitchen to make a quick cup of tea to warm themselves up, although they were often called back to serve someone before they had finished. At lunchtime they heated food in a gas oven in the kitchen, and also stuck their feet inside to warm them a little.

The staff had to put up with these conditions for a long day, typically from 9 a.m. until 7 p.m., and longer on Friday and Saturday. And if there were still customers in the shop at closing time, the assistants had to work on. There was never any question of asking a customer to leave because the shop was about to shut, in spite of the law restricting opening hours.

When a customer came into the shop, she was invited to sit down in front of a mirror and the assistant brought her a succession of hats. If they were really busy, an assistant might have to serve two or three customers at once, but the rule was that however busy they were, a customer had to be greeted and seated as soon as she entered the shop. As the customer tried on the various hats, the manageress prowled around, checking the assistant's sales technique and ensuring that the most expensive hats were offered. It was in the assistant's interest to do this too, as she was paid commission on sales. Whatever the

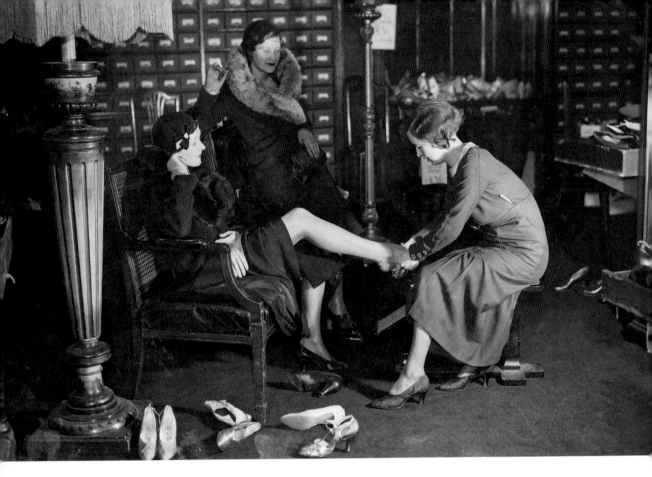

customer's reaction or behaviour, the assistant had to be deferential. As in every branch of retailing, the motto of the business was, 'The customer is always right,' and even the customers who came in with no intention of buying anything, or who were critical of the assistant or the goods she was offering, had to be treated with the same deference.

Each assistant had a book in which every sale was recorded. The manageress collected these at the end of the day's trading, and if there were few or no sales, the assistant was reprimanded, even if she had spent most of the day serving the customers who were notorious for never buying anything. Staff members could benefit from the system if they did well on commission, but those who made few sales faced a telling-off – or, if sales did not pick up, dismissal. Jobs in retailing were notoriously insecure, and for most of the interwar period unemployment was high. So, whether in a dress shop or a grocer's, shop assistants tended to toe the line, work hard and do what they could to keep their employer's favour.

WORKING WITH WINDOWS

The 1920s and 1930s saw modernist architecture catch on in Britain, and this had an impact on shop design. Modernism used a mixture of plain white walls, big plate-glass windows and austere lines. Shop designers picked up on these ideas to provide more generous but simpler shop windows in which the goods inside could be seen clearly, without all the the distracting carving or gilding of Edwardian shop fronts.

The proprietors of dress shops and shoe shops were especially keen on these new window designs. They were in the business of supplying goods that were not everyday purchases, so success relied on tempting customers into the shop, and a more modern approach to window design was effective for this. And because their business was all about fashion, they were also more receptive to new trends in design, especially ideas imported from the most famous designers in Europe, than many more traditional retailers.

The fashion for Art Deco, the more decorative, jazzy style of design seen most famously in Odeon cinemas and on ocean liners, also influenced the way shops looked. Art Deco encouraged bold styles of lettering, the use of neon lights and elegant contrasts of shiny black tiles and dazzling chrome metal to attract the eye.

Below The big plate-glass windows and strong lighting used in Art Deco shop fronts were intended to catch the eye of the passer-by. The simple, elegantly spaced letterforms of the sign were also typical of the style.

Whether the designer used Art Deco or was a follower of modernism, the new kind of shop design worked in two main ways. First, the shop front was kept simple. The emphasis was on clean lines, narrow glazing bars and big expanses of glass. Some designers used discreet bands of ornament and mouldings, but these were kept simple. The customer's eye was directed towards the goods in the windows. Secondly, shop designers went in for deep lobbies, lined with more windows. You could look at the goods here under cover but without actually entering the shop, and sometimes the lobby was very deep, like a miniature shopping arcade. An additional touch was that the floors of these entrances were often paved

with a form of mosaic. This distinguished them from the pavement outside and enabled the architect to incorporate the shop's name or logo in the design of the floor, a clever piece of subliminal branding.

Deep lobbies and 'arcade entrances' were an effective way of putting a lot of items on display, and of slowly drawing the customer nearer and nearer the door until they were no longer able to resist going inside and perhaps buying something. In addition the lobby sometimes also contained 'island units', full-height display cabinets that acted as further extensions of the shop window.

With good modern electric lighting, windows like these displayed items such as dresses or shoes very effectively, so this kind of shop layout was very popular among shopkeepers who could afford a refit. Arcade entrances worked

THE TOY SHOP

If dress shops helped broaden the amount of choice on offer to women, toy shops did something similar for children. There were more toy shops on the High Street in the 1920s and 1930s than before, and this was partly the result of a changing view of childhood. As children went to school for longer and started work at an older age than they had in earlier decades, they had more time to play. Toy manufacturers took advantage of this growing market. Before the First World War many toys, from teddy bears to tinplate models, had been imported from Germany. But

the anti-German feelings that welled up during the 1914–18 war put an end to the imports, and British toy manufacturers stepped into the breach. Some of these were very successful, and filled the shops with a new variety of toys. The construction toy Meccano, for example, was devised by Frank Hornby in 1901 and was selling well by the First World War. In 1914 the company built a large new factory in Liverpool, which was to supply toy shops for more than half a century. Frank Hornby began to produce clockwork O-gauge trains in 1920, and Hornby trains became a popular boys' toy in the

ABOVE *The construction toy Meccano and games such as Ludo were popular with children. Toy shops and department stores would stock up on these at Christmas time.*

interwar period, joining those from other successful train-set manufacturers such as the Leeds Model Company.

Toys like train sets and Meccano construction kits were costly, but retailers made sure that they stocked a wide range of items, including many that could be bought with pocket money. As a result toy shops were crammed with coloured pencils and catapults, model soldiers and miniature boats, soft toys and dolls, mostly produced by British companies. Made of both traditional materials, such as wood and metal, and newer substances such as celluloid, these exciting, multicoloured playthings turned the toy shop into a place of fun and enchantment for children lucky enough to have one in their town.

RIGHT *Glove puppets, like these traditional Punch and Judy characters, were old favourites and make a colourful splash in a window display of toys.*

LEFT *This group of mothers and children in the early 1930s are admiring the latest window display in their local toy shop. A regularly changing display attracted admiring glances.*

well for the retailers who tried them, but towards the end of the 1930s some people objected that, while the lobbies were brightly lit and inviting during the day, at night they tended to be haunted by 'courting couples'. So, by the time of the Second World War, the fashion for this kind of shop entrance was in decline.

WIRELESS COMES TO THE HIGH STREET

Another side of 1920s and 1930s modernity was that radio became a mass medium. The British Broadcasting Company began radio services in 1922, and because the government saw it as having a similar message-carrying function, the company was originally put under the auspices of the Post Office. At the end of 1926 it became the British Broadcasting Corporation and was given its first charter and control of the airwaves. Under its first director, John Reith, it embraced the ideals of public-service broadcasting, aiming to inform and educate, as well as to entertain.

What the BBC had to offer proved popular, and many people invested in a radio receiver. Most of these were large devices, using glowing valves for amplification, although there were also the smaller crystal radio sets, often made by amateur enthusiasts. Listening to a crystal set was generally a solitary business, involving the use of headphones and the careful tuning of the device. But the new valve radios were different. They were more like pieces of furniture, and families gathered round them to listen to the news, music or drama.

Below Interwar radio receivers often had Bakelite cases moulded in a streamlined design. The large tuning dial, with the names of radio stations across Europe, would light up when the set was switched on.

As radios became more affordable, the broadcasts proved hugely popular, and radio entertainment was to some extent a welcome distraction from the troubled times of the 1930s. Especially popular was *Band Wagon*, a light entertainment offering on Wednesday evenings, which led to drops in cinema and theatre attendances on that evening, and classic serials on a Sunday, which made clergymen complain that many members of their congregations were cutting evensong. However, radio also brought people closer to world events. News broadcasts kept people up to date with the latest happenings both at home and abroad. If radio meant that people got used to hearing the voice of the king for the first time when he made his popular Christmas broadcasts, it also allowed them to hear the chilling speeches of Adolf Hitler and made them concerned about the likelihood of war.

As the 1930s went on, almost everyone who could afford a receiver wanted to have radio in their home and radio ownership increased dramatically. But the

whole business of receivers, valves, aerials and radio stations was a closed book to most people. Customers needed help using the receiver and maintaining it, so whether selling new sets, supplying replacement valves or offering advice about aerials, the radio dealer became a valued presence on the changing High Street of the interwar years.

The 1920s and 1930s were often difficult times in Britain. People were faced with economic depression, unemployment, wage cuts and strikes. The High Street responded to these tough times well. Shopkeepers still upheld the old values of retailing such as personal service and good value. But they also took up new ideas and technologies enthusiastically. This was the age when delivery vans, radios, cinemas and more and more pre-packed convenience foods took the High Street by storm. Increasingly, the shops that sold these goods were often repackaged too, in shining Art Deco architecture, with expanses of plate glass and bright, shining signs. This combination of traditional service and new ideas helped many shops survive the difficult times. They prospered because their approach gave customers what they wanted and made them feel good. From the temptations offered by sweet shops and traditional bakers to the kind of attentive service provided by everyone from the butcher to the 'Madame shop', successful interwar shopkeepers remembered the golden rule and always put the customer first.

Above In the 1930s, many people did not own a radio, so people gathered around any available receiver to listen. This group are listening to a broadcast of the Grand National.

Overleaf A selection of images of the interwar dressmaker, grocer, baker and butcher.

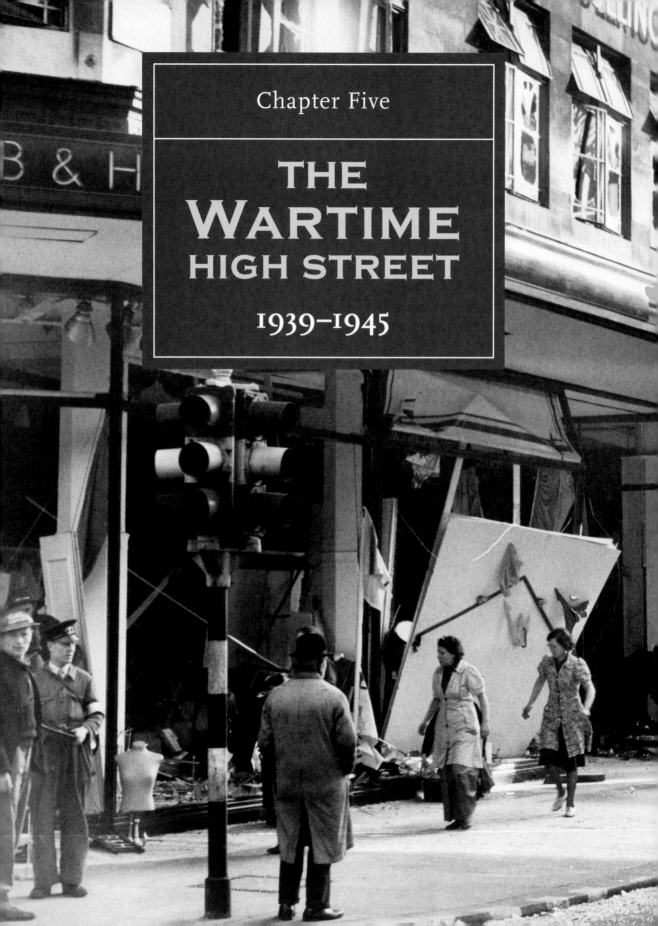

Chapter Five

THE
WARTIME
HIGH STREET

1939–1945

LITTLE MORE THAN 20 YEARS after the end of the First World War the world stood once more on the brink of global conflict. This new war was very different from that of 1914–18, involving the civilian population more completely than before and creating a 'total mobilisation' that affected the way people all over Britain lived and worked. On the Home Front, shortages and rationing transformed the High Street and the population found ways of surviving, and even thriving, on the basic necessities alone.

In the Second World War the conflict was brought right into people's homes. Although there were fewer military casualties than in the 1914–18 war, the widespread bombing caused tens of thousands of civilian deaths and major disruption of life in the main target zones such as big cities, ports and industrial areas. In cities and towns especially, people became used to the idea that their homes or businesses might be destroyed or their loved ones killed.

There was also a huge impact on supplies, and this affected everyone. Before the war, Britain had been dependent on imported food, timber and other essentials. Now, with shipping under attack, imports virtually dried up. Only essentials, and that meant mostly vital military supplies, were shipped. The country's limited resources had to be channelled, and military needs had priority. So the civilian population found itself striving on the Home Front to make the best use of resources – coping with limited food supplies, mending clothes rather than buying new ones, making do with very little consumer choice and saving fuel by staying at home unless a journey was absolutely necessary.

1939
APRIL Britain's farmers, helped by government grants, begin a huge ploughing campaign to increase the production of wheat.

1939
MAY Conscription is introduced, in anticipation of the coming war.

1939
3 SEPTEMBER Britain declares war on Germany.

1940
8 JANUARY Rationing begins in Britain.

1940
MAY The Nazis invade France, Belgium and the Netherlands; Allied troops are evacuated from Dunkirk.

Every minute of every day, from the lack of a breakfast egg in the morning to the blackout at night, the British were reminded that there was a war on.

Most people made the best of these privations, and the government encouraged them in this, providing information leaflets on how to make the best of your rations and grow your own vegetables, and commissioning helpful radio broadcasts on similar topics. The hardships of the home front were a genuine and essential part of the war effort, which would result in the defeat of Hitler and, it was hoped, a better world. And there was satisfaction too in growing your own food, mending things and making a little go a long way. These little pleasures, and the hope that things would soon be much better, carried Britain through.

PREPARING FOR THE WORST

Twenty minutes after Prime Minister Neville Chamberlain announced that the country was at war with Germany, the air-raid sirens sounded in London. It proved a false alarm – Britain was not to face aerial bombardment for several months. The false alarm began a jittery period known as the 'phoney war', a relatively inactive stage in the conflict that lasted from September 1939 to April 1940 and during which both sides planned their first moves. The phoney war enabled the Allies to continue their preparations for fighting, including pressing on with the rearmament measures that had begun earlier in the 1930s, and introducing the legal framework for National Identity Cards, conscription and a substantial increase in taxes.

Food rationing began in January 1940, confirming everyone's fears about the regime of austerity that would be necessary in wartime, but also ensuring that there were fair shares for all of what food and resources there were. By this time many children, and in some cases their mothers too, had been evacuated from major cities to the countryside. As the phoney war dragged on, however,

1940
MAY The Home Guard is formed to protect Britain from invasion.

1940
10 JULY The Battle of Britain begins.

1940
7 SEPTEMBER The Blitz, with its sustained aerial bombardments of British cities, begins.

1940
14–15 NOVEMBER The Germans bomb Coventry.

1941
11 MARCH President Roosevelt signs the Lend-Lease Act.

many of them returned home. Then German invasions of Norway in April and of France and the Low Countries in May saw the fighting start in earnest. In July the Germans began their aerial bombardment of Britain.

LOCAL DEFENCE

As the fighting raged in Europe and bombs were dropped on cities and factories, preparations were made both to equip people to withstand air raids and to defend Britain from a potential invasion. In addition to military precautions – anti-aircraft posts, pillboxes and the paraphernalia of coastal defence – there was a host of domestic measures involving the whole population. Windows were blacked out at night to mask lights that might guide bombers. Signposts were removed in case of invasion. Air-raid shelters were erected in back gardens.

Many civilians joined the Home Guard, the amateur fighting force of men not yet called up or too old to join the regular forces, which was intended to be the last line of defence in case of invasion. Others became air-raid wardens or fire watchers. As the bombing continued, minds were sharply focused and practically the whole country got behind the war effort.

A WOMAN'S PLACE

Women were mobilised too. Every woman who cooked and kept house was in effect fighting on the Home Front to conserve resources, help in the drive towards food self-sufficiency and keep the population fed and clothed. But many went further than this. Thousands joined the Women's Land Army, doing vital farm work as men went off to fight. These 'land girls' made a key contribution to the big push that was needed in agriculture with the cutting off of food imports. A further group of women took over other kinds of jobs vacated by men who had joined the forces. As well as munitions factories and the essential office work that

1941
JUNE The Utility scheme for retail goods is introduced by the Board of Trade.

1941
7 DECEMBER Japanese aircraft bomb the American base at Pearl Harbor, bringing the USA into the war.

1942
JANUARY American forces begin to arrive in Britain.

1942
JUNE Dried egg is introduced.

1943
JANUARY Unemployment falls to zero.

was needed to keep the country running (administering the rationing system, for example), many women worked in shops. Although some were welcomed only grudgingly, retailing had already become less male-dominated, so women shop workers were generally more widely accepted.

ON THE MOVE

What was happening to women was one example of the beginnings of increased social mobility during the war. Changes in work, the new perspectives opened up when American airmen or Italian prisoners of war arrived in the country, the sense that there might be different roles for women in the post-war world – all these things signalled that the conflict could lead to social changes for the better. One symbol of this was that many people learned to drive for the first time. Whether they were getting used to controlling a tractor on a farm, or learning how to drive a lorry, as Princess Elizabeth did, many Britons had a tempting taste of the freedom that driving could open up. During wartime they could not always exercise this freedom, because petrol was scarce and cars were expensive. But learning to drive was a skill that opened doors into new areas of work and leisure when the war ended. There was a sense too that some benefit had to come from the terrible casualties and sacrifices of the war, and people hoped that the war would usher in a better life for more people.

So it was that at the first post-war general election – hardly post-war, as it took place in July 1945, before victory in Japan in the following month – a Labour government was elected with a landslide at the polls. Labour's transformative list of social reforms in health, social security and other areas defined the welfare state of the second half of the 20th century. There was real optimism that life was indeed going to be better for all.

1943
6 JUNE D Day:
Allied landings
on the beaches
of Normandy.

1944
13 JUNE The first
flying bomb hits
London.

1945
8 MAY Victory in
Europe (VE) Day.

1945
26 JULY Clement
Attlee succeeds
Winston Churchill
as Prime Minister.

1945
14 AUGUST
Japan surrenders,
bringing the
Second World War
to a complete end.

MAKE DO
AND MEND

By 1940 it was clear that Britain was facing shortages across a range of major foodstuffs and that the country's shops were heading for a crisis at least as deep as in the First World War. Action was needed, but that very action sometimes caused as many problems as it solved. For example, a move in many places from dairy farming to growing cereal and other crops led to the slaughter of dairy herds and a reduction in the milk supply. The answer was to ration essential goods. This was a huge operation, employing a dedicated government department – the Ministry of Food – and a whole structure of ration books (issued to every individual), coupons and record-keeping. It required a huge publicity and information machine, with countless posters and leaflets telling people how the rationing system worked and giving them helpful hints about how to get by on meagre supplies. For the duration of the war, and a few years afterwards, it transformed the High Street and altered the way in which the public and shop staff interacted.

A wide range of items was rationed, and the list of rationed goods changed with availability. But broadly, food rationing affected meat, fats (butter, margarine and lard), dairy produce (cheese, milk and eggs), tea, jam, sugar and sweets, so grocers and butchers were affected in a major way. Bread was not rationed, but any baker who made cakes was affected by the rationing of sugar and eggs. Other rationed goods included clothes and fuel. The amounts of these goods allowed varied too. The amount of cheese per person, for example, varied between 8 ounces (227 g) and just 1 ounce (28 g) per week; the allowance of bacon and

---

Opposite Mending and alterations become a major part of the wartime dressmaker's work.

Above The butcher's shop has been prepared for the worst, with sandbags piled up and sticky tape on the windows to minimise the effects of a bomb blast.

ham ranged from 8 ounces to 4 ounces (113 g); that for fats from 8 ounces to 1 ounce.

People were allowed between half a pint (0.3 l) and two pints (1.1 l) of milk per week, but here the government had a secret weapon to supplement the allowance: National Dried Milk. People could buy a tin of this every four weeks, giving the equivalent of an extra four pints (2.3 l) of milk. There was a similar dried substitute for eggs, and a packet of dried egg yielded the equivalent of 12 eggs every eight weeks. Neither of these dried substitutes was as good as the real thing, and the government tacitly admitted this by issuing helpful leaflets suggesting ways of disguising the flavour.

WARTIME AND THE SHOPKEEPER

From extra taxes to the need to allow staff time to train in civil-defence duties, shopkeepers faced many problems and challenges during the war. Many of the difficulties endured by retailers and their staff were similar to those faced by the rest of the population. In big cities especially, there was the real chance of having your premises bombed. If you did not receive a direct hit, there was the prospect of injury and damage from shattered bits of shop window if a bomb dropped nearby. While it was possible to patch up a broken window, bombed-out premises were often simply abandoned because there were severe limits on building and building materials until well after the end of the war. And there was more than one way to lose premises – some shops, again mostly in cities, were requisitioned for government use.

Then there were staff shortages. Many male shop workers joined the armed services. Retailing (with the exception of some of those engaged in the food business) was not a reserved occupation, so when men were called up they had to go; and in any case, many volunteered. Single women joined the forces or the Women's Land Army, or did essential war work in other areas. This left many retailers short of staff. One solution was to employ men who were too old for the services, and experienced men, recently retired, found themselves asked to take on management jobs. Another was to hire married women, who were exempt from war service. This meant a period of training, but many women took well to shop work and more were able to remain in retailing when the war ended than had been the case at the end of the First World War. This was because the returning men often wanted to take up more interesting or better-paid jobs outside the retail sector.

WORKING WITH RATIONING

Rationing was a challenge to the shopkeeper just as much as it was to the shopper. Small shopkeepers complained that they were losing out because of the registration system. The way this worked was that a customer had to register with a specific retailer for their meat, groceries and later other goods such as clothes and petrol. Many registered with a larger shop because the bigger the business the wider the range of goods on offer. So the smaller retailers claimed that they were being cheated of business. This problem was made worse for small businesses in 1941, when the Ministry of Food stipulated that to remain in the business of selling rationed goods a shop must have at least 25 registered customers. Some retailers expanded to attract more customers, others went to the wall. A study of shops selling sugar showed that the number of retailers in this area dropped from 170,000 to 133,000 between 1940 and 1941.

Once the shopkeeper had hit the registration target and got used to the limit on how much you could sell, there was the challenge of the bureaucracy involved. Here there was also a continuous process of change and adaptation, in that the amounts of different commodities that were allowed kept altering to keep pace with availability. Because the amounts could go either down or up, this sometimes meant that shoppers went over their allowance in the month in which the change was made, and as a result they had to forgo some of their ration in the following month.

Below A number of wartime processed foods, like this dried milk, came from the USA, in packaging that clearly reminded the housewife of the assistance that was coming from across the Atlantic.

RATION BOOKS AND COUPONS

Rationing worked like this. Every member of the population was issued with a ration book. This contained a certain number of coupons for the rationed items and when you went to the shop, as well as handing over money you had to hand over coupons too. The ration books were issued by the local Food Office, which also collected the coupons from the shopkeepers.

Special concessions were made to pregnant women and nursing mothers, who were issued with a special green ration book containing extra coupons for certain foods. There were also special arrangements for young children. Other beneficiaries of extras were heavy manual workers, including farm workers, who were allowed additional cheese, for example. But for one and all it was a case of living on what by modern, and indeed pre-war, standards was a meagre diet.

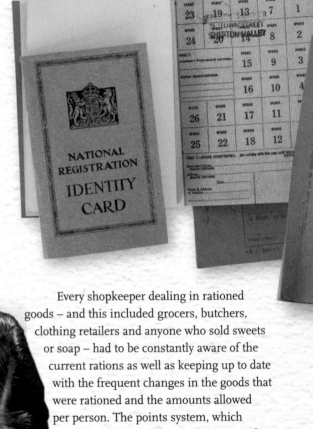

BELOW *Working out the household budget was no longer simply a matter of money – the housewife had to count the coupons too.*

Every shopkeeper dealing in rationed goods – and this included grocers, butchers, clothing retailers and anyone who sold sweets or soap – had to be constantly aware of the current rations as well as keeping up to date with the frequent changes in the goods that were rationed and the amounts allowed per person. The points system, which introduced additional 'points' coupons for certain goods, created further problems. Grocers complained that demanding points coupons for some items, such as particular tinned goods, put people off buying them altogether. Pamela Horn, in her book *Behind the Counter*, quotes the president of the local Grocers' Association in Tynemouth objecting to the points imposed on tinned salmon – would buyers 'waste' their cherished points on what was basically low-grade fish?

RIGHT *The grocer's wife got used to explaining how to cook with the new wartime products.*

BELOW *Most adults had buff-coloured ration books; those for children were blue.*

Then there were the accounting procedures. These meant a huge extra job for the shop workers who had to count the ration coupons they had received. Shop staff, often busy all day, frequently took coupons home to count, and there were often thousands to get through in one evening. Inevitably, the worker's family were often roped in so that they could get through the task.

If coupon counting sometimes forced people to work longer hours at home, one advantage of wartime conditions was that they brought shorter hours for many. A combination of the blackout and the drive to save energy meant that earlier closing in effect helped the war effort. So earlier closing times for most shops were brought in for the winter months, with exceptions for newsagents, tobacconists and sweet shops. Not every shop owner liked this change, complaining that it took away potential business, but it remained in force for the duration of the war.

ABOVE *Used coupons were either removed from the ration book or cancelled by the retailer, who got used to a huge amount of extra paperwork.*

To their surprise, most people were well nourished by the wartime diet. The British population had been used to eating meals rich in meat, but under rationing a switch to a low-fat diet was imposed before such a thing was fashionable, and the protein intake was also severely limited. The Ministry of Food knew about this, and in designing the rationing system they were aware of the problems of food shortages and the bad effects these had had on people's health during the First World War. The main danger was the lack of vitamins, and this was not so much because of rationing as because the supplies of imported fruit dried up almost completely. People spoke of never seeing a banana for the duration of the war. Even fruit grown in Britain, such as apples and pears, though not rationed, was snapped up quickly. Many wartime shoppers remember queuing for an hour to buy a pound (0.5 kg) of apples. The government responded with a campaign to get people to consume supplements such as rose-hip syrup.

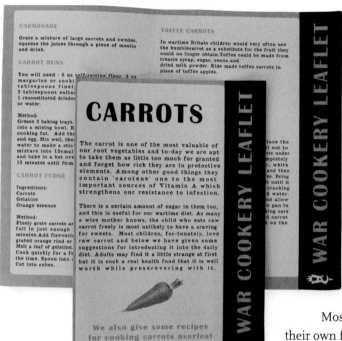

Above This government cookery leaflet about carrots contains information on the nutritional value of the vegetables as well as recipes using ingredients that were available during wartime.

Most of all, people were encouraged to grow their own food in a campaign that became one of the most famous of the war – Dig for Victory. Vegetables were in short supply at the beginning of the war because farmers were concentrating on growing essential cereal crops and fodder for cattle. But with the restrictions on the supply of meat, vegetables were needed more than ever before. So a huge advertising campaign was launched to persuade people to turn over their gardens to vegetable production. Millions of leaflets on vegetable growing were distributed, posters went up and everywhere there were slogans such as 'Lend a hand on the land' and 'Turn over a new leaf'. A couple of cartoon characters, Potato Pete and Doctor Carrot, extolled the health advantages of eating vegetables, suggested recipes and doled out advice.

Some of the posters and leaflets offered specific advice on what to grow and how to grow it. The aim was to get people as close as possible to self-sufficiency in vegetables, and one wall chart laid out a list of vegetable crops, with planting times and suggested sizes of plot, that was designed to produce vegetables all year round. The chart was divided into 'Miscellaneous Crops' (peas, dwarf beans, onions, shallots, broad beans and runner beans), root crops (potatoes, carrots and parsnips) and 'Winter & Spring Green Crops' (cabbages, savoys, sprouts, broccoli, kale, swedes and beet). You needed a good-sized patch of land to grow all these vegetables in quantity (the government suggested an area measuring about 90 by 30 feet). But for those in the country, or with one of the new suburban gardens or an allotment, the challenge was inspiring.

The Ministry of Food encouraged people to try wild food too. Increasingly, people kept their eyes open in the country, picking both familiar delicacies such as blackberries and unusual items such as nettles (for soup) and wild rose hips (to make rose-hip syrup and jam, both rich in vitamin C). People even banished their fears of being poisoned and tried a range of wild mushrooms.

The Dig for Victory campaign was a success. A 1943 survey showed that half of all manual workers were growing vegetables either in their garden or on an allotment. And it was not just in the country, where people were used to growing things, that this happened. Encouraged by such high-profile projects as the conversion of the moat at the Tower of London to allotments, town people cultivated what space they had and urban gardens across the country were given over to food growing. Vegetable consumption increased steadily between 1941 and 1945.

The economies that wartime imposed, the big push to grow vegetables, save eggs and eke everything out, were seen as patriotic duties, a point that was pressed home in a host of government leaflets about food, economy and rationing. Growing your own food, and enjoying it fresh from the garden, was a huge morale booster too. Digging for victory made people feel much more in control of their lives than if they relied solely on the sometimes meagre selection of foods available for purchase in the shops. And in wartime, good morale is essential. By contrast, wasting food, or squandering anything else, was seen as diverting key resources away from our troops. In other words, squandering food was actually helping Hitler, and housewives in their kitchens were fighting on a domestic or home front that was almost as important as the battle front itself. The Home Front was vital, the housewife could be a war hero, and the Ministry of Food made sure that everyone knew it.

Overleaf A selection of wartime posters and advertisements from the 'Dig for Victory' campaign.

Below Even shopkeepers, who often lived in the centre of town where there was little available land, tried to find the space to grow vegetables and the time to look after them.

DOCTOR CARROT
the Children's best friend

VIT-A

DIG for... PLENTY

GROW FOOD
IN YOUR GARDEN
OR GET AN ALLOTMENT

POTATOES
feed without fattening and give
you *ENERGY*

NEW KINDS OF SHOPPING

Rationing, digging for victory and making do all meant that in wartime shopping on the High Street was a very different business from what it had been just a few months before the war. For rationed goods, people registered with a specific shopkeeper. But for non-rationed goods, people kept their ears open and shopped around. A whisper would go around that a certain shop had just received a supply of apples, say, or tinned peaches, or offal (which was not rationed) and a long queue would form instantly.

There was also a less public and more sinister development – a flourishing black market. It was inevitable, because sooner or later there would be a surplus of rationed goods – more meat, for example, than there were coupons – and the retailer would be unable to sell it legitimately. Under-the-counter deals were the result, and slices of steak were exchanged for unofficial cash payments or 'gifts' in kind.

In this climate the archetypal spiv, dressed in a sharp suit and doing clandestine deals, could flourish. In a small community people knew who to go to in order to find either unofficial rationed goods or mysterious supplies of imported items that were hard to come by on the legitimate market. Deals like this were illegal, but customers were often desperate, and often succumbed. The spiv and his activities were looked on in two different ways. On the one hand, the spiv and the black market were unpatriotic. They stood in opposition to the good citizens of the Home Front, who were waging their battle against Hitler by economising and sticking to their rations. A person who stood against this effort could be viewed as a traitor. But on the other hand, spivs also stood for a kind of independence. Many found the ever-present wartime bureaucracy suffocating and this made some admire black-marketeers and what they did.

Sometimes the dealing was directly with the supplier, cutting out both spiv and shopkeeper,

ABOVE *Cash changes hands as two men do a black-market deal in September 1942.*

and a farmer would swap 'unofficial' meat for other goods or services, on the quiet and quite illegally. This activity was condoned both because of the temptation of acquiring illicit goods and because doing so was a blow against the ubiquitous rules and regulations. Barter, exchanging one item for another, was quite common. People who kept chickens in their back garden found they had a valuable currency on their hands – eggs could be swapped for anything. You could keep up to 20 hens, but if you had more you were obliged to register like a farmer and go through the bureaucracy of rationing. So, many people kept to the maximum number and offered some of their eggs to neighbours in exchange for other items the neighbours had and they did not.

THE MEAT MARKET

For most people the effects of war were not felt straight away. In the run-up to Christmas 1939, shops advertised a full range of seasonal fare. North London's largest butcher and provision store, Page's of Camden High Street, announced, 'Tons of Turkeys. Tons of dairy fed pork. Tons of Scotch beef,' and insisted that its shop was 'one of the Freshest and Cheeriest Places to Visit at Christmas Time'. Other traders, from grocers to toy shops, advertised with the same defiance. But by spring 1940 the Ministry of Food had a new head, the recently ennobled Lord Woolton, who had a background in shopkeeping, having been the manager of a department store in Liverpool. 'I suppose I am going to run the greatest shop the world has ever known,' he said.

It was a highly regulated market. The traditional wholesale meat markets in London, for example, were closed, and the meat trade was controlled by a number of regional Wholesale Meat Supply Associations. Dealers in meat had to be licensed, and slaughterhouses were taken over too. By October 1941 the entire industry was effectively controlled by the government. Retail butchers were each allocated a certain amount of meat per week, this amount being decided according to the shop's takings immediately before the war. Later this allowance of meat was adjusted to suit the number of registered customers the butcher actually served.

Below The Small Pig Keepers' Council produced appealing posters to encourage people to keep a porker. The publicity reminded people that pigs eat waste foods, turning it into more appetising and valuable food.

So, as the war dragged on, butchers, like other food retailers, faced shortages of stock and all the form-filling and bureaucracy of rationing. In addition, as in the First World War, many also faced staff changes as men went off to fight. Many of the new assistants were women, who took well to their new roles but were often resented. Sainsbury's admitted women to their meat counters, but had a rule that they should not be referred to as butchers. This was probably well-intentioned tact, but as butchery was also a respected skill it also implied that women were not being fully accepted into the privileged ranks of the craft.

MANAGING THE SHORTAGES

There were often shortages of meat because farmers were encouraged to concentrate on cereal crops. One meat in short supply was bacon, which people liked to eat for breakfast. In fact so important was bacon to the British diet that it was felt worth bringing back an old substitute based on cured mutton and known as macon. It was not popular and was discontinued in 1940. One solution to the bacon shortage was small-scale pig-keeping. The keeping of a pig had long been a perk for farm workers. Slaughtered and dressed as often as not by a travelling butcher, the cottager's pig provided a variety of meat that could last long and serve the owner well. The Second World War saw the extension

KEEP A PIG

SAVE Waste and make FOOD

FOR ADVICE AND INFORMATION ABOUT PIG CLUBS APPLY TO –
SMALL PIG KEEPERS' COUNCIL, VICTORIA HOUSE, SOUTHAMPTON ROW, W.C.I.

of cottage pig-keeping. People formed 'pig clubs', pooling their resources to keep and feed a porker. There were soon suburban pigs as well as country ones, and the animals hoovered up such scraps and leftovers as there were.

Home-grown pork was an attractive alternative to chicken for Christmas dinner, and many pig-raisers were enthusiastic and resourceful – there are records of pigs being kept in back yards, garages and fire stations in numerous towns. As with any wartime food production, though, there were rules and regulations to be observed. The creatures could not be killed until they reached a weight of exactly 100 pounds (45.4 kg), and strict inspection regimes were introduced to ensure that this was rule was observed. But it was worth the trouble for the rashers of bacon at breakfast, not to mention pork, ham and all the other kinds of pig meat.

TRYING SOMETHING NEW

When meat rationing was announced in March 1940, the government was clear about the necessity for limiting supplies. It was not simply that there was not enough to consume at pre-war levels. A lot of the available meat went to the armed services, and shoppers were encouraged to buy home-raised meat. As the government announcement put it, 'When you cannot get Imported Beef, bear in mind that our Fighting Forces, whose needs must come first, consume a large proportion of our supplies. Remember that the eating of Home-killed instead of Imported meat saves shipping space and foreign exchange.'

Below Pig clubs were intended for people, like these firemen in South-West London, whose regular work was outside agriculture and who had little or no land. The Small Pig Keepers' Council provided information to help each club run smoothly.

WYSE PIG CLUB

THE WARTIME COOK

FOOD FROM THE FIELDS

To protect essential crops from predators, people in the country were told to get out into the fields and shoot creatures such as rabbits, crows and pigeons that fed on what the farmer was growing. Many of these creatures were edible, and people in the country got used to rabbit pie, roast pigeon and other delicacies. There were suggestions from the Ministry of Food that people try rook pie – a prospect off-putting to all but the most adventurous.

The war was also a good time for poachers. Game was not rationed, and many a countryman, out to shoot pigeons, would bring down an occasional pheasant or duck for the family pot. A game stew or soup was a welcome treat for a family used to surviving on less than 1 pound (0.5 kg) of meat per person each week. Butchers also sold game, but it was usually an expensive luxury.

Even in the countryside, however, not everyone had access to this kind of free meat. For most, it was a question of making the best of what could be got from the butcher. And this was a blow to the British diet, which was based firmly on the 'meat and two veg' formula. Meat was seen as the heart of the typical British meal, and to be limited to maybe a couple of ounces (57 g) per person per day was hard for many to cope with. Families with several children did rather better than most. Children of five and older were entitled to a standard ration, the same size as an adult. So the children could be given slightly smaller portions and the meat went further. Women also sacrificed their appetites, giving more meat to their menfolk, many of whom had tough physical jobs and needed more calories.

RABBIT PIE

Ingredients
- 225 g (8 oz) shortcrust pastry
- The meat of two rabbits
- 2 peeled potatoes
- 1 onion
- 1 bay leaf
- Salt and pepper
- Stock or water

Method
—Preheat the oven to 200°C.
—Roll and cut out the pastry.
—Joint the rabbit and wash.
—Slice the potatoes and onion.
—Fill a dish with alternate layers of meat and vegetables, seasoning each layer.
—Half fill the dish with the stock or water.
—Cover with the pastry, making a hole in the middle to allow steam to escape.
—Bake for about 15 minutes until the pastry has set.
—Reduce the oven temperature to 170°C and bake for a further 1 hour 15 minutes.

Often, though, there was very little beef at all at the butcher's. What could the butcher offer customers to see them through the wartime low-meat week? Shoppers were reminded by the Ministry's information leaflets that liver, kidney, ox-tail and tripe were not rationed. As Marie Verrall, who worked in her father's butcher's shop in Epping, remembers: 'Offal was "off ration" and sausages called ARPs were made from anything and everything. We sold boiled sheep's heads with tongue, brains and everything left in.' Cookery writers and broadcasters offered recipes to make these kinds of meat more acceptable, as they were unattractive to many people raised on steak or shin of beef.

As Marie Verrall suggests, the sausage became a shadow of its former self. To reduce the amount of meat in sausages, various fillers were introduced. The Ministry of Food laid down guidelines, specifying the proportions of meat and other ingredients: 37 per cent meat, 7 per cent soya and 55 per cent filler and water, plus seasoning. It is no surprise that many shoppers, used to sausages with a very high proportion of beef or pork, were suspicious of these watered-down bangers and suspected them of containing horse flesh.

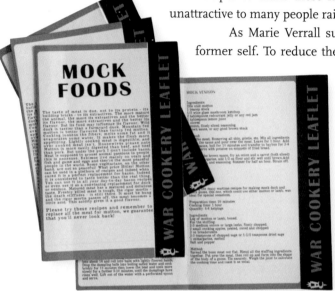

With meat shortages rife, it was a question of being as inventive as possible. The more unusual cuts of meat – bits that had previously been given to the cat's meat dealer, boiled for stock or shoe-horned into sausages – were offered as delicacies. Pig's feet in jelly and calf's head suddenly seemed worth trying. Offal was given new disguises as calf's liver mould or poor man's goose. Pig's cheek required repeated washing, boiling for more than two hours, and then baking for another half-hour, but in desperate times desperate remedies were occasionally needed. Some people even threw their British inhibitions aside and turned to horsemeat, which was sometimes sold illegally as mutton or venison.

Above 'Mock foods' were dishes that used cheap, available ingredients to imitate foods that were in short supply. Intended to keep people's spirits up, dishes like 'mock goose' made with offal were often the butt of jokes.

Opposite Comedy duo Gracie Allen and George Burns used American humour to promote the most American of all imports – Spam.

CORNED BEEF AND SPAM

Another way of eking out the meat ration was offered by corned beef and Spam, which were sometimes available from the butcher in larger quantities than fresh meat. Corned beef hash mixed the meat with potatoes to make it go further and corned beef could also be made into rissoles. The product widely known as Spam (officially written in capitals and used as an adjective, as in the phrase 'SPAM Luncheon Meat') came to Britain from the USA. It was a form of canned meat produced by the Hormel Corporation, which rebranded it as 'Spam' in 1937. The name is said to derive from 'Spiced Ham', 'Shoulder of Pork and Ham' or 'Supply Pressed American Meat'. Spam caught on during the war, when it was shipped to

Europe as part of the USA's lend-lease agreement, under which it supplied weapons and other supplies to the Allies. Spam was eaten cold or cooked, for example, by being fried in batter to create fritters, and was ubiquitous. As American journalist Edward Murrow reported from London in 1942, 'Although the Christmas table will not be lavish, there will be SPAM luncheon meat for everyone.'

During the war and for some time afterwards, chicken was a luxury, and many looked forward to it at Christmas to replace the turkey or goose that they had enjoyed in better times. And those who kept chickens for their eggs could not afford to be sentimental when a hen stopped laying.

Butchers did what they could to advise people on how to cook their meagre rations. Fritters – pieces of meat (or Spam) fried in batter – were a popular way of making the ration go further. Housewives would be encouraged to add oatmeal to their mince, or to add chopped potato and carrot and make a filling for pasties. Stews, bulked out with dumpling and given extra flavour with Marmite (meaty to taste but containing no meat), were also popular. Raynes Minns, in her study of the domestic front, *Bombers and Mash*, quotes a letter from a listener to the radio programme *Kitchen Front*. The listener describes how she ekes out 1 pound (0.5 kg) of steak to feed a family of four over three days:

WED – *Pasty, using one-third of steak supply, with turnip and sliced potato.*
THURS – *Beef olive (stuffing of brown crumbs, parsley, herbs, etc) with carrots and suet dumplings.*
FRI – *Steak and leek pudding. Remainder of steak with alternate layer of leek and sliced potatoes.*
Sprouts also served on those 3 days. Family: 4 adults.

With potatoes, breadcrumbs and a liberal helping of vegetables, a little meat could go a long way.

Through these shortages, rations and desperate remedies, the High Street butcher must have found himself sometimes the target of resentment, and sometimes, when offering 'delicacies' such as pig's cheek, of sheer disbelief. But, in the spirit of co-operation and effort brought on by the war, most customers accepted that butchers were doing their best

to help. Then as now, they accepted the advice of the butcher about which cuts to choose and how best to cook them.

So people trusted their butcher, and this extended to many areas – home deliveries, selection of meat, and so on. A butcher from Saffron Walden, Essex, remembers doing local deliveries. Often, the occupants were out: 'The housewife would leave the key for you and you would undo the door and if they hadn't got a fridge you knew just where to put the meat. People trusted you. They would leave a note on the table telling you what they wanted for the weekend. It was the way we lived.' But it would be wrong to look back with too much nostalgia to this time of open doors and unblinking trust. The trusting relationship between shopkeeper, customer and community was forged in an atmosphere of real austerity in which the greatest fear was of the enemy across the Channel. But it is an indication that there was often a close bond between customer and shopkeeper, and that the routine of regular deliveries meant that the householder would know exactly who had been in the house and when they would have been there.

FENCES, PENS AND COOPS

With thousands of people turning to chicken-keeping, one opportunity for the wartime ironmonger was in providing chicken coops. These structures were usually made of wood, and gave shelter for the chickens, while also giving them adequate ventilation. In the austere conditions of wartime, chicken coops were usually basic and well ventilated, unlike the climate-controlled coops, with warming electric lighting, favoured by some chicken-keepers today.

A coop needed to be sturdily constructed, predator-proof and easily cleaned. Inside there would be nest boxes in which the hens laid their eggs. The coop was usually set in an enclosed area fenced with wire sunk into the ground to keep out foxes. Making a coop involved simple carpentry – not the kind of intricate joint making used in furniture-making, but basic joinery with screws and nails. It wasn't difficult, and many ironmongers and hardware-sellers were practical enough to manage it. In addition they sold the other equipment needed for chicken-keeping, especially chicken wire to make pens. The ironmonger or hardware merchant would also stock all the components of the chicken coop – timber, nails, chicken wire, staples for fencing – plus the necessary tools.

LEFT *Chicken-keeping required a simple wooden house in which the hens could roost and lay, plus a small amount of protected land.*

THE WARTIME GROCER

By the Second World War the role of the grocer was much closer to that of today's general store or supermarket. Although there were still some 'high-class' specialists, weighing out tea and dried fruit like their Victorian grandparents, their business was hard during the war. Their supplies of imported goods were irregular, and few customers had the money to shop from upmarket food stores. So increasingly most grocers sold much more pre-packaged goods and carried a very wide range of stock. This change had already begun before the war and was partly thanks to the increasing influence of the big chain grocers such as the Home and Colonial and International Stores. These were trusted businesses that carried many different kinds of stock and offered home deliveries. As one Lancaster resident remembers, 'the Home and Colonial on Penny Street . . . sold bacon, cooked meats, tea, sugar, butter, everything. You could get all your week's rations there.'

The Home and Colonial had begun in late-Victorian times as a tea dealer, and was originally called the Home and Colonial Tea Association. It had thrived and grown through the first half of the 20th century, merging with Lipton's in the interwar period to form one of Britain's largest grocery chains. Its success as a general grocer was a sign of how the grocery business was changing and would continue to change after the war, and later rationing, came to an end.

Another way in which grocers were leaving behind tradition was in coping with new wartime products. One example was dried egg powder, which was introduced to cope with the shortage of fresh eggs. It was not much liked. Raynes Minns sums up people's memories of it as 'rubbery, leathery, biscuity and dull'.

Above Shop fronts often evolved over the years and few were redesigned during wartime – unless they needed to be rebuilt because of bomb damage. The grocer's shop still has Victorian details and an interwar Art Deco sign.

But dried egg was better than nothing, and supplies were fairly reliable. What more appropriate firm to produce and supply it than Bird's, a trusted and familiar brand because of their popular custard powder. Bird's had existed as a company since the 1840s, but became especially well recognised when its 'three birds' logo was introduced in 1929. During wartime Bird's advertisements showed the three birds singing, 'Save eggs! Save eggs! Save eggs!' and exhorting people to try their 'Substitute Egg Powder'. In urban areas, where few had the space to keep their own hens, it was hard to avoid it, and people were making everything from cakes to Yorkshire puddings with the stuff.

BAKING WITHOUT FRESH EGGS

Since long before the war, the British had loved their cakes, whether bought from the baker, enjoyed in a café or tea room or baked at home. But the wartime lack of eggs was a big challenge for most people, especially those living in towns who had little or no garden, because keeping chickens was out of the question. Apart from simply going without, both professional and home bakers were faced with two solutions: use the dreaded dried eggs or find recipes that excluded eggs altogether.

Dried egg powder was promoted by the Ministry of Food but many cooks disliked it because it could go lumpy and after a while started to smell 'off'. To get the best out of it people were advised to keep it in an airtight container after opening a packet, and to store it in a dry, cool place. Quantities also caused confusion – around two tablespoons of dried egg made up the equivalent of one fresh egg. However, people got used to recipes with dried egg, and both housewives and professional bakers tried recipes for Christmas pudding and for various cakes using dried eggs.

Many people tried making cakes without eggs at all. There were recipes for cakes such as the 'Eggless, fatless walnut cake', which was simply a mixture of flour, milk, sugar, baking powder and chopped walnuts, with a pinch of salt. A wartime Christmas cake recipe included butter (or margarine), milk and ground rice, as well as the usual sugar and dried fruit, but no eggs. Some people tried icing their Christmas cake with 'mock marzipan', a rather unappealing blend of sugar, fat, ground rice, almond essence – and haricot beans. Such were the deprivations of wartime.

IN THE WINDOW AND UNDER THE COUNTER

In wartime, supplies were often so low that it was difficult to make an enticing window display. Even so, some 'high-class' grocers made the effort, as one woman from Bishop Auckland, Durham, recalls about a grocer in the town: 'I remember their autumn display. One window had a stuffed pheasant, heather, and heather honey combs. The other window had special biscuits.' This kind of ingenuity, making a window display out of a few props and a couple of products that happened to be plentiful, was a way of standing out in a town with several grocers.

In wartime, however, rumour could provide advertising that was more powerful than a window containing a stuffed pheasant. The same Bishop Auckland resident remembers a cut-price shop that was especially popular, both because of its keen prices and because the proprietor seemed to be able to get hold of bananas. These were famously scarce so this was something worth queuing for: 'There was a cut-price shop and on Thursdays during the war there was a queue, when the word went round that they had bananas. You took your ration book and if you bought something else you got some from under the counter.' Putting the bananas under the counter was almost a more powerful way of selling these mythical fruit than displaying them openly.

DEBBIE SERGISON
Grocer's wife

Things are definitely going to get worse as the war goes on, but we just have to take one day at a time, because I'm sure that's what people did, and try and meet problems head on. We can't produce things we haven't got, so it's just a matter of apologising and giving service with a smile - that's the way it's going to be. As a working community we are definitely going to stick together - we're looking after everyone and everyone's looking after us. In the wider local community, though, you're going to see a lot of complaining going on - 'She got carrots and I didn't' - that's going to happen.

......

We spent the afternoon in the garden. We dug for victory. Not only did we plant some beans and other things, we also picked loads of veg, which will be on sale in the shop tomorrow. The colour of all the vegetables in the shop looks really nice, so hopefully people in Shepton Mallet will be eating lots of vegetables tomorrow.

......

Surprise, surprise, within an hour of opening the shop I had all the blackberry jam sold, which was 21 jars, and of the 26 jars of cherry plum, there are only 2 left for tomorrow.

FRUITS OF THE HEDGEROW

With sugar rationed, one traditional English product was in short supply. Jam, the staple of high tea, and even of cheap packed lunches for some people on low incomes, was not always easy to come by. One way around this was for people to make their own using fruit picked in the hedgerows. Although many country people were used to going out and foraging in the more relaxed years of peacetime, not everyone did this, so the Ministry of Food encouraged them with helpful leaflets listing 'Food for the Picking' and 'Hedgerow Harvests'. Many families got used to replacing their traditional strawberry and raspberry jams with preserves from the hedgerow. Blackberry and apple was one Ministry of Food suggestion, and many saved some of their ration of sugar (the only ingredient apart from the fruit and water) to make it. It might have reminded some veterans of the First World War of the notorious plum and apple jam supplied to the troops, but for most it went down well.

It was not only jam that the Ministry wanted people to make from foods they could gather for free. Other 'Food for the Picking' included: elderberries (good in jam or stewed with apples); sloes (for use in preserves); crab apples (valued because they provided a substitute for lemon juice); rose hips and the haws of the hawthorn (to make jams and jellies rich in vitamin C); and nuts of all kinds. There was a real feast waiting for people in rural areas, and those within reach of the country or the hedgerows on the fringes of towns.

One free food suggestion that went down less well was mushrooms. The Ministry of Food leaflet gave little indication about which mushrooms were safe to eat, and no doubt many were put off by the prospect of poisoning. For those in the know, however, mushrooms made a tasty supplement to the diet, not just to give extra flavour to stews with a low meat content, but also on their own. So farm workers came in from the fields with armfuls of puffballs, and people who could tell one species from another filled their baskets with ceps and chanterelles long before these mushrooms became the delight of middle-class devotees of French and Italian cuisine.

NATIONAL MILK

Many times during the war people in Britain found themselves looking at their allies across the Atlantic with envy. Americans seemed to live a charmed life: their cities did not get bombed, they had more money and their food was better and far more plentiful. When the USA joined the war, and American troops and airmen were based in Britain, they were famously seen as overpaid and apt to seduce British women with presents of stockings and other desirable gifts seldom seen in British shops.

Back at the start of the war, America was the envy of Britain for its diet. When the Ministry of Food looked at milk consumption, for example, it found that the average American drank a pint (0.6 l) of milk every day. In Britain the average was nearer half a pint (0.3 l), and in many poor families it was much lower, and as likely to be in the form of tinned condensed milk as fresh.

The authorities wanted to improve these figures, especially for those with special dietary needs, so a scheme was introduced that guaranteed pregnant women and nursing mothers a pint a day, a pint for children under five and half a pint for those between five and sixteen. This milk was free for those on low incomes.

As well as fresh milk, dried milk was available as a key weapon in the fight against shortages. It came in two forms: Dried Household Milk, a skimmed milk meant for general use, and National Dried Milk, a full-cream version with added vitamin D meant principally for feeding young children. People without children could only buy tins of the enriched National Dried Milk, normally sold by chemists, if it was beyond its use-by date.

Below The swastikas on the Squander Bug sent out a clear message: wasting money means helping the enemy.

MAKING DO

People learned to make do with products like dried milk, and the government made a whole campaign out of the idea of making the best of what people had. They called it 'Make Do And Mend' and it embraced in particular the skills of the housewife, who was encouraged to mend clothes, patch bed linen and not waste a scrap of material. Waste was one of the greatest enemies on the Home Front, so government publicity pushed the message home at every opportunity. In one publicity campaign – actually designed to encourage investment in National Savings – a pair of characters called the Squander Bugs boasted about how they'd encouraged people to spend money rather than put it into Savings Certificates, which could be bought in instalments of as little as sixpence (2.5p) and brought a return of around 33 per cent over ten years.

One High Street trader who benefited most from the new ethic of saving money and making do was the ironmonger. The stocks of timber and nails, chicken wire and fence posts, spades and forks, and all the other paraphernalia of what we now call 'DIY', was what every family needed in order to take full advantage of all the savings recommended by the government campaigns. From pig-keeping to vegetable-growing, the ironmonger offered the tools and the wherewithal. Perhaps ironmongers did not exactly prosper during the war. There was little market for fancy goods such as elaborate brass fire irons or ornate lamps. But the more practical side of the range did better than ever before.

Overleaf Children joined in the hunt for wild foods. As this image of children from Frensham, Surrey, shows, it was an activity that could be productive, messy, and fun.

WARTIME CLOTHING

The government's campaign to get people to repair what they had rather than buy something new was aimed especially at the housewife. 'Make Do And Mend' leaflets told women how to darn, unpick old woollen garments to knit new ones and give new life to old clothes by adding 'decorative patches'. This kind of mending was vital for most. Rationing meant that it wasn't always possible to buy new clothes – and anyway there were the shortages, both of the clothes themselves and, for many, of ready money. Some people – especially those who had never before had to worry about buying new when something wore out – found the advice offered by the government useful. But many poorer women had had to make do and mend before the war had even started. They had no money to buy new stuff on a whim. Darning and patching was a way of life for them. Some of them found it insulting that the government presumed to tell them what they already knew from hard experience.

Clothing was one area in which shortages were badly felt soon after the beginning of the war. Many people tackled the problem head-on, embracing all the inventiveness of the 'make do and mend' movement. They knitted jumpers and gloves, fashioned coats out of blankets, cobbled together shirts out of sheets and made wedding dresses out of nightgowns. Worn-out socks were darned, threadbare jackets patched and people made the best of it.

For those who wanted or needed to buy new clothes, choice was minimal. Keeping as close a control as possible of the import and distribution of fabrics and

Below Wartime fashions made a virtue of economy: tailored designs made the best use of the available fabric and could be elegant too.

other raw materials, the government took charge of the clothing business. A new range of designs was produced, with the aim of saving fabric and cutting down waste. Men's trousers, for example, no longer had turn-ups; collars were narrow; excess decoration or embroidery was axed; designers kept pockets and other fabric-intensive details to a minimum.

The government standardised these new clothing designs, and the garments were produced in large numbers. They were referred to by a standard name, Civilian Clothing 1941, and labelled with a 'CC41' logo, which became instantly recognisable. At first people resented buying clothes that were made to such standard designs, rather like military uniforms. But the CC41 garments were made using good fabrics and proved durable. They seemed right for the time and shoppers accepted them. Soon they became part of the patriotic effort to save resources, whereas people wearing highly decorated clothes, or garments with an excessive number of buttons, were looked upon with suspicion.

Above Posters like this one encouraging women to make the best use of their sewing time were backed up by leaflets and evening classes on sewing and mending clothes.

THE NATIONAL LOAF

Bread was not rationed during the war, so it might be thought that Britain's bakers survived the period much more easily than their High Street colleagues, the grocers and butchers. But with the coming of war the bakers faced a crisis of their own. Britain was dependent on imported wheat, but ships bringing in the precious grain were threatened by German U-boats, and many were sunk in 1942–3. In response to this problem the government encouraged farmers to begin a huge switchover to wheat-growing, and the deficit was partly filled by imports from across the Atlantic. But there was still a shortage. The government's answer was to take control of the flour mills and order them to mill the wheat at higher extraction levels – in other words, produce more flour per ton (0.9 tonnes) of wheat, which entailed leaving more of the wheat in the flour to produce a brown flour that had the extra advantage of being more nutritious.

The bread produced with this flour was called the National Loaf. In addition to the effect of the more wholesome flour, the nutritional quality of the bread was improved by restricting the use of bleaching agents and alkaline baking powders, and by adding calcium to make up some of the loss of this important element to the diet that was a consequence of butter and cheese shortages. The National Loaf represented a turn-around from the most popular pre-war loaves, because much of the population had acquired a liking for white bread. So people had to be persuaded to buy the National Loaf by means of the same kind of propaganda as was used for other wartime food measures. Publicity for the loaf sang its praises from every conceivable angle. Advertising messages included the point that the National Loaf was better – both tastier and more nutritious – than white bread; that although superior, it was no dearer; that eating it saved on flour, some of

Above At the National Loaf Exhibition in November 1942, judges inspect hundreds of entries from bakers. Baking a prize-winning loaf was always good for business.

which was imported; and that eating this patriotic loaf was in effect a way of helping to defeat Hitler.

Some startling statistics were brought to bear to persuade people to make the best use of their bread, too. People were encouraged not to waste a crumb, and the Ministry of Food worked out that even a wastage of half an ounce (14 g) a day, if added up across the whole country, meant throwing away some 250,000 tons (227,000 tonnes) of wheat a year, representing the cargoes of 30 wheat ships. Since every ship was in danger of attack from German U-boats, reducing dependence on them was also potentially a way of saving lives in the merchant fleet.

The National Loaf was not always quite what it seemed, though. Sometimes other grains – barley and oats – were added to the mix. Potato flour was also suggested by the government as an additive to eke out the wheat content, but it was not widely used. And there was a controversy over the loaf's nutritional value, leading to an exchange of letters between doctors in the *British Medical Journal*. This culminated in various pronouncements from a Dr Harris of Liverpool, who disparaged the loaf at public meetings, in the press and in a letter to the journal, and claimed that the bread was adulterated with chalk. A vigorous reply, defending the nutritional necessity of the loaf and its calcium content, came from a doctor in North Wales on 29 August 1941:

Dr. Harris's letter is full of half truths which are unlikely to deceive the medical reader, but I tremble to think of their effect on the layman. He says the loaf is to be fortified by calcium alone – he must know that the national wholemeal loaf has five times as much iron, twice as much fat, many times as much vitamins, and the unknown remainder present in natural whole grain but absent in the 73% extractions. He calls the calcium 'chalk.' Is it not a fact that calcium is added in the form of phosphate? He wants us to have our necessary calcium in milk. Is he unaware that the pre-war consumption of milk was one-fifth of a pint [0.1 l] per day per head, and that even then two and half million more milking cows were necessary to provide the optimum daily pint [0.6 l] per head?

. . . Again he says there is not a scintilla of evidence that there is a calcium deficiency. Has calcium nothing to do with teeth? Can he produce twelve adults in working-class Liverpool with sound teeth? They have not come to North Wales as evacuees, and if white bread is not responsible for their languid pallor then it is up to Dr. Harris and his colleagues with the advantage of local knowledge to tell us what is.

The controversy involved the politicians and civil servants too. But for ordinary shoppers the argument was academic: when the standard national flour was all that was available, people had to be content with the brown loaf. And, whether they knew it or not, their health benefited. The National Loaf was one of the foods that helped Britons remain well nourished during the war years, in spite of the shortages of many foods and the unappetising quality of much of the national diet.

The years of the Second World War were some of the toughest ever for Britain and its retailers. Shortages, the regulated market and slogans such as 'Make Do And Mend', could have been enough to drive retailers off the High Street altogether. But, like the rest of the population, Britain's shopkeepers did their bit to keep the country running. In doing so they displayed amazing resourcefulness – selling new lines, eking out supplies, offering advice, recipes and – some of the time at least – cheerfulness.

Britain's armed forces could not have won the war without the support of the Home Front, and the Home Front could not function without the commitment of the retailers. Whether it was selling National Milk or Utility clothing, offering recipes for rook pie or nails to make chicken coops, the retail sector did its bit, and more. As a result most Britons were better nourished than they were before the war. The resourcefulness of both shopkeepers and customers had triumphed. Their adaptability and resilience was remarkable, and an example to other businesses both then and now.

Overleaf A selection of photographs from the wartime High Street shows a range of activities from chicken-keeping to cutting a ration of butter, from sewing to rabbiting.

Below Food retailers' shelves were sadly bare during wartime, but it was the grocer's job to make sure people got their rations, explain new products – and serve his customers with a smile.

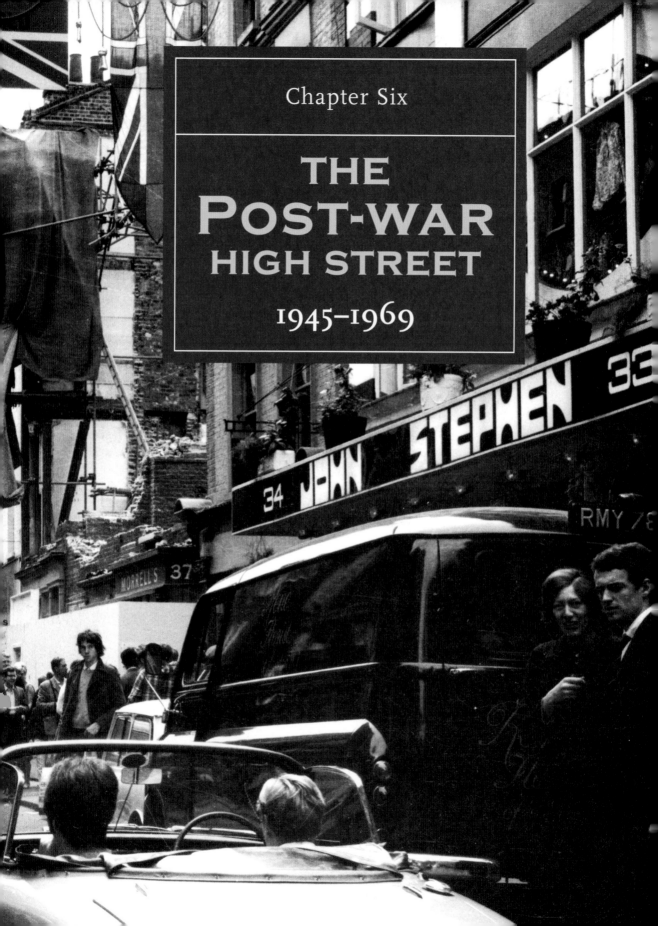

Chapter Six

THE POST-WAR
HIGH STREET

1945–1969

IN THE 1950s Britain began to emerge at last from the difficult times of the Second World War and its aftermath. Although rationing and shortages continued for several years, there were signs of new hope and, for some, prosperity. In a variety of ways, from the new kinds of design seen in architecture and household goods to the fact that there was a new, young queen on the throne, Britain seemed on the brink of an era of change. In every area of life, from the school to the workplace, from the living room to the High Street, the 1960s fulfilled that promise.

The 1945 Labour government laid the foundations of the welfare state, set up the National Health Service, began building programmes that replaced bombed town centres and provided much-needed new housing. But by the beginning of the 1950s many people were still to see the comfort and prosperity they had hoped for. So in 1951 the British people elected a Conservative government and welcomed back the wartime leader Winston Churchill as Prime Minister. Churchill's return was just one sign of change in the early 1950s. The year 1952 also saw the death of King George VI and in the following year his daughter Elizabeth was crowned queen. People hopefully compared the 'new Elizabethan age' to the 16th-century reign of the first Queen Elizabeth, a time when Britain had been a major sea power and when its writers and artists, above all Shakespeare, had given the country cultural supremacy.

Britain did not reclaim its 16th-century power under the new Elizabeth. On the contrary, the British empire was being dismantled and British power

1946
A group of new towns, including Harlow and Stevenage, is planned around London.

1948
The first large group of Jamaican immigrants arrives in Britain aboard the SS *Empire Windrush*.

1949
Britain's first tower block of flats is built in Holborn, central London.

1950
The Korean War begins.

1951
The Festival of Britain: British achievements are celebrated in events across the country.

seemed to be on the wane. And yet this very decline in power brought formative changes. Waves of immigrants from former colonies in the Caribbean and South Asia delivered vibrant new cultures and tastes, in food and music for example. And as Britain's power declined, the influence of America increased, fuelling all aspects of life from politics to youth culture.

This change had a huge impact on the High Street. Coffee bars, jukeboxes, beehive hair-dos, self-service shops – all these trends of the 1950s and 1960s were at least partly due to foreign influence. But this foreign influence was added to a rich British culture, with its innovativeness in design, to make a unique mix. The 1960s High Street could accommodate Italian cafés and home-grown milk bars, cut-throat supermarkets and thriving corner shops. It could seem both ultra-modern and very traditional at the same time.

THE NEW AGE

The Coronation heralded a new age – and not just because Britain had a new young monarch. The Coronation was also important because it was the first national event watched widely on live television. Before 1953, relatively few people in Britain owned a television. But prices of receivers were falling. Thousands of people bought a TV in 1953 so that they could watch the Coronation and those who did not have one crowded around their neighbour's screen. The estimated audience for this historic television broadcast was 20 million, and the entertainment habits of the whole country were transformed at a stroke.

Television became powerful, but not in the way it is today. TV ownership increased rapidly, but in 1953 still fewer than 25 per cent of households owned a set. There was just one channel, run by the BBC, and transmission times were severely limited – three hours in the evening and a couple of hours earlier in the day. But the very fact that broadcasts were so limited and concentrated into

1951
The Conservatives win the general election, and Winston Churchill returns as Prime Minister.

1952
Elizabeth II becomes queen after the death of her father, George VI.

1953
Elizabeth II is crowned and many buy their first television set to watch the ceremony live.

1954
Roger Bannister becomes the first person to run a mile in under four minutes.

1955
Britain's first pedestrianised shopping precinct opens in Coventry.

one part of the day gave the medium its power. Because there were relatively few programmes, millions of people made a point of watching them, devoting a large stretch of their evening to viewing. So television was becoming influential, and bringing entertainment, news, and information into people's living rooms as never before. In the 1960s TV ownership increased still more and television became a true mass medium.

Television was not the only electrical gadget that people rushed out to buy in the 1950s and 1960s. This was the era when plug-in appliances came of age, from labour-saving devices such as vacuum cleaners and electric irons to entertainment appliances like transistor radios, record players and vast wood-encased radiograms, the ancestors of today's hi-fi. For many these were major purchases and had to be bought on credit with a hire-purchase agreement.

NEVER HAD IT SO GOOD?

With access to all these consumer goods, better wages and a safer, more secure existence than people had known in wartime, many Britons enjoyed a good life in the late 1950s and 1960s. When Harold Macmillan, the Conservative Prime Minister between 1957 and 1963, famously told the population that they had 'never had it so good', many could put the Cold War, nuclear weapons and other disturbing issues out of their minds and agree.

But Britain in the 1950s was still very different from Britain today. More people rented than owned their homes, although the number of mortgages was growing. Most houses were heated with a mixture of coal or gas fires and plug-in electric heaters – central heating for most was a thing of the future. All but the rich and the adventurous holidayed in Britain, and holiday camps on the British coast were especially popular, particularly for families with children. Car ownership was far lower than today.

1956	1957	1958	1958	1959
The Suez Crisis: a military attack on Egypt by Britain, France and Israel follows Egypt's decision to nationalise the Suez Canal.	Harold Macmillan makes a speech alleging that most British people have 'never had it so good'.	The Campaign for Nuclear Disarmament is launched in London; the first Aldermaston March takes place.	The Preston Bypass (M6), Britain's first stretch of motorway, is opened.	The Mini enters production.

Slowly and surely, however, Britain in the 1960s was beginning to look more like modern Britain. Post-war rebuilding led to ever-expanding housing estates, each usually provided with a parade of shops. Town centres were reconstructed, leading to not only the replacement of bomb-damaged shops, but also the demolition of historic buildings to make way for more up-to-date structures. The shopping centre, a covered development with a variety of shops, became common and self-service stores began to appear.

The idea of self-service shopping was pioneered by several companies that still dominate food retailing today (Tesco and Sainsbury's, for example) but also a number (such as Pricerite and Fine Fare) that have long since disappeared from the streets. But in addition to these big names, there were small self-service grocers who brought the new kind of shopping to the small towns, suburbs and villages – places that were too small to sustain a supermarket. These pioneers got us used to self-service, but did much more too. They sold on price and value more than ever before. They stocked everything, enabling people to do the week's food shopping in one shop, and moved aggressively into non-food lines as well. And they encouraged an attitude of instant gratification – if you can pick an item from the shelves, you can buy it – which was completely different from the slower, more thoughtful approach of traditional retailing.

Today arguments rage about whether the benefits of supermarkets outweigh the drawbacks. But in the 1950s and 1960s issues such as 'food miles' and the grip supermarkets are able to keep on the whole food-production process had not arisen. Most people gladly embraced the supermarkets with their value-for-money ethos. Like so much else in the post-war era, from the foundation of the Health Service to the rise of television, this new kind of shopping seemed a good thing. And in this area of daily life, as in many others, it was a time of hope and looking forward.

1963
The Beeching report leads to the dismantling of a large part of the British railway network.

1964
The Bull Ring, Britain's largest shopping centre, opens in Birmingham.

1965
Comprehensive schools, already in existence in some areas, begin to be introduced more widely.

1967
Colour television broadcasts begin in Britain.

1969
The voting age in Britain is reduced to 18.

HELP
YOURSELF

Although the horror of war was over in 1945, life for shopkeepers kept much of its wartime austerity for years to come. Clothing and footwear, for example, were rationed until March 1949, bread was brought into the rationing system between mid-1946 and mid-1948, and rationing did not end fully until 1954. In addition, Utility furniture was still being sold several years after the war ended.

When servicemen returned to civilian life, some demanded their pre-war retailing jobs back, but large numbers applied for work in industry, where they could find better-paid and more interesting jobs. So, while some of the women who had taken to shop work in wartime were asked to leave, many stayed on and retailing increasingly became seen as women's work or work for the young – by 1951 more than 20 per cent of those working in food shops were under 20 years old. By the mid-1950s, though, things were looking up. Ranges of goods were extended, especially in the area of pre-packaged foods, enabling people at last to bring more variety to the dining table. The choice of shops was greater too. The number of department stores increased and London companies such as Harrods began to open provincial branches. It was shops like this that brought the newest fashions to the cities. Kendal Milne, the large department store in central Manchester, for example, introduced a range of clothes designed by Mary Quant in 1963.

With petrol more readily available distribution improved too, carrying this new variety of goods around the country. Although the rail network was disastrously pruned in the 1960s, companies took quickly to distribution by lorry, and even the most remote rural shop could extend its stock. Wages were rising

Opposite The hair salon was a social centre of the 1960s High Street.

too, and people began to afford luxuries again and to believe Harold Macmillan when he said that Britain had never had it so good.

The post-war period was a time of change in other ways, too. Self-service came of age, with the number of self-service stores in Britain rising from ten in 1947 to 6,000 in 1960 and more than 20,000 by 1966. This was a revolution in shopping, transforming life for both workers and customers and making a sector that had prided itself on service and old-fashioned courtesy into one that prized value and efficiency above all. This change transformed the High Street and remains something that influences the way we shop today.

NEW SHOPS FOR A NEW ERA

After the Second World War Britain faced the coming years in the knowledge that a huge effort would be needed to rebuild war-damaged Britain. The Labour government voted in at the 1945 election made huge strides socially with its numerous welfare reforms. But economically the country still faced shortages and rationing, while many shops, and sometimes whole streets, remained bombed out. With supplies of building materials restricted and money short, most new shop fronts in the late 1940s were plain and often temporary. But by the middle of the 1950s an increasing number of shop fronts designed in a modernist style appeared, especially in cities that had been bombed or in new towns like Harlow in Essex and Stevenage in Hertfordshire.

These new shops and renovated frontages exemplified the modernist architecture that designers and planners were convinced was the style of the future – plain walls, clean lines and lots of glass. The typical design was very simple and dominated by lots of plate glass extending from close to the pavement up to ceiling height. Above, a sign with large, bold lettering announced the name of the business. A popular design ploy was to recess the centre part of the window to make a covered lobby, drawing window shoppers nearer to the door and tempting them inside. This kind of design also provided a greater window area, meaning that lots of stock could be displayed. In this way customers of, say, a shoe shop would often have decided what they wanted before even entering the door.

Big areas of glass put the merchandise centre-stage, which was just what retailers wanted. But a shop front that was nearly all glass could also be rather bland, so designers often spiced it up with a splash or two of colour. A favourite material was mosaic tile, which could be used vertically up a narrow section of wall. The shop sign was all-important. Big 'Egyptian-style' letters were popular, as were letters in more than one colour. But in the 1960s there was a fresh development, the internally lit plastic sign, which brought light and brightness to the street and enabled customers to make out the shop name from a distance, and at night provided advertising. The second half of the 1960s brought the psychedelic shop front, the kind of boutique that was decorated in swirls of mixed vibrant colours. London's Kings Road and Carnaby Street had many such shops, but they were unusual outside London. Even larger towns usually had just one, a shop that catered to a young clientele and often occupied a small frontage in a side street. The High Street, on the other hand, stuck to its illuminated signs and clean, modernist lines.

MAJOR REBUILDINGS

During the 1950s architects and planners set about the serious business of rebuilding town centres that had suffered major bomb damage. Cities such as Coventry and Bristol had had their hearts knocked out of them, and there was a determined effort to turn this disaster into an opportunity to rebuild. Planners hoped to create new city centres for a new era, and this meant a complete rethink from the ground up. Car ownership was on the increase and many town-centre streets were narrow and unsuited to heavy traffic. Pedestrians, on the other hand,

Below The fashion menswear shop Lord John was opened in London's Carnaby Street in 1964 by Warren and David Gold. There were soon Lord John branches across the UK and in Europe and the USA.

Above Crawley was one of the new towns designated in the 1940s. The Broadwalk, a new 'pedestrian way', was opened in 1954 and was at the heart of the town's new shopping area.

needed space to walk and shop without for ever dodging cars and lorries. So the pedestrian precinct was born as a way of separating pedestrians and traffic – and with it, a host of other planning decisions involving everything from blocks of flats accessed from elevated walkways to bypasses and arterial roads.

Pedestrianisation was the change that most affected the High Street. Shops were separated by broad pavements; areas were set aside for seating, trees were dotted about and there were openings leading to green spaces. Car parks were tucked away behind the shops in the service areas, or turned into multi-storey towers. City centres with these features seemed to symbolise a new way of life and hope for the future, a future built largely of reinforced concrete and plate glass. Major redevelopment radically changed cities such as Coventry, Plymouth, Bristol and Nottingham. Modern consumer items, slowly becoming more plentiful as rationing ended, looked good in the big, bright windows. And new designs in furniture, improved televisions and radios, and a wider range of foods – not to mention steadily increasing wages for many – all attracted shoppers in greater numbers than before.

The strong lines, broad decks and thrusting towers of new shopping developments such as Portsmouth's Tricorn Centre and Plymouth's Mayflower Centre excited architects, but shoppers merely tolerated them, many disliking the windswept walkways and the concrete walls, which were pale and clean-looking when new but soon turned a depressing grey. A lot of 1960s city architecture was inspired by the work of modernist luminaries such as Le Corbusier in the south of France. These buildings needed the southern sun to look good and were less effective under Britain's overcast skies. If a large unit in a shopping centre failed to attract a tenant, the place could look dirty and unkempt very quickly, putting off shoppers. And the new buildings tended to swamp any old ones that remained. As *Images of Change*, a recent English Heritage study of post-war landscape and building, says of the ancient Quakers Friars site in Bristol, 'The building was . . . left stranded among industrial bins, worker smoking breaks and car parks . . .' Old and new found it hard to coexist.

So the concrete shopping developments of the 1960s have had a mixed impact on city centres. In the period just after the war they brought new life to bombed-out towns. But by the late 1960s they had passed their heyday, and many people were longing for the old-fashioned randomly developed towns of earlier years – and the traditional shops their High Streets had contained.

THE GENERAL STORE: KEEPING UP AND TAKING STOCK

Jack of all trades and master of none: the old phrase sums up as well as any other the role of the general-store owner on the High Street. In a small town with a limited number of specialist shops – or in a city where many other shops had been wiped out in bombing – the general store was a linchpin of the neighbourhood, the place where everyone went for basic foods and for those things that you couldn't get anywhere else. That could mean everything from string to firewood, candles for birthday cakes to Christmas tree decorations. For the store proprietor it was a nightmare, involving keeping contact with dozens of different wholesalers and other suppliers, and keeping tabs on a diverse stock without any help from computers.

The shopkeeper also had to keep an eye on the latest trends. People wanted their bread white and sliced, they were on the lookout for the latest varieties of tinned meats or fruit and more and more convenience foods, such as instant-mix desserts, filled the shelves. Cake mixes were popular with both working women and housewives in a hurry. Then there was the influence of America to contend with – everything from hamburgers to Coca-Cola was in fashion. The owner of the general store somehow had to cram all this into a small shop, and also remember where everything was, and how much of it was in stock. Although the store owner probably lamented the fact that shopkeeping was no longer the skilled craft it once was for the Victorian grocer or pre-war butcher, there was a new set of managerial and stock-keeping skills to learn and keep everyone on their toes. So the general store may look old-fashioned to modern eyes, with its seemingly chaotic shelves. But in reality it was a hive of activity and a valued asset for the High Street.

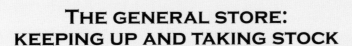

TRADITIONAL FOOD SHOPPING

Although there were huge changes in food shops and shopping during the post-war era, some old-style food shops survived. They preserved few of the skills of the traditional grocer, but their owners still prided themselves on personal service. Their staff were polite and deferential, engaging their customers in conversation and talking knowledgeably about the choice of goods on offer. They knew both their customers and their customers' preferences. But the traditional grocers of the post-war period were retailers rather than skilled weighers, blenders and packers. As one Market Harborough grocer put it, 'After the war you didn't need your skills. You only needed your skills after the war for bacon and cheese. Other stuff used to be all done for you . . .' In other words, all the other goods in the shop were pre-packaged by the manufacturer, and all the assistant needed to do was to hand them over and collect the payment. Some shopkeepers looked back fondly to the traditional shops. As one respondent to a survey on shopping in the 1950s recalls the old-fashioned grocer's approach, 'it was all cupboards and drawers and a bit like the chemist in a way . . . so you knew you had this expertise that you don't use now'.

In reality the relationship between shop staff and customers varied. In an upmarket grocer's, deference was the keynote. The people on either side of the counter would not get too familiar, service came first and customers valued additional services such as home delivery. In the small local food store, on the other hand, proprietor and customers knew each other closely. They might live in the same street, call one another by their first names and share a joke or some gossip. Shops like this were mostly in working-class districts and signalled the fact that there were still strong class divisions in British society, which were reflected in where people shopped and how they interacted.

Traditional shopkeepers seemed to offer a sense of continuity with the old values of the past – a continuity strengthened by the fact that there was a long-serving staff consisting either of family members or assistants who stayed in the job for years. Assistants stood behind an old-fashioned counter and there was often a chair for the customer to sit on. The shopkeeper wore a white apron. Inside one of these shops, the Victorian era did not seem so long ago, and even in the 1950s a few shops still had furniture and fittings that dated from before the First World War. For many people, traditional local

Below and opposite
In the new self-service stores, food was arranged on hygienic white shelves, all within easy reach of the customers, who were encouraged by helpful signs to select their own produce.

shops were the convenience stores of the time, places to pop into for everyday basics. Because customers and shopkeepers knew one another and customers were always calling at the shop there was strong loyalty. Small shops bolstered this by taking on extra lines and functions, just as they had done in earlier eras, so a corner food shop might also be a local Post Office or newsagent, or have a large sweet counter.

MEAT VALUES

In the post-war era most people still liked to buy their meat from a specialist butcher, and many customers stayed loyal to a specific butcher – usually the one from whom they had bought their meat rations during the war. Butchers were especially popular if they stocked local delicacies that might be overlooked by supermarkets and

chains. A Lancaster resident remembers a local pork butcher selling cuts of meat that harked back to earlier times: 'Their pies were nice. They sold tripe as well. You don't hear of it now but a lot of people used to eat tripe, and pig's trotters and pig's head . . . And you used to be able to get a wrap-up at the butcher's. You'd maybe get a little bit of everything in it: steak, chops, liver, sausage.' A 'wrap-up' was a butcher's way of selling a little of everything to a customer on a budget – a different kind of convenience package from the sort of thing on offer at the supermarket, but widely popular. In the 1950s, in other words, butchers and other specialist food retailers still had contact with local produce and local preferences. This was an area in which they could still beat the supermarkets, and they did so without any of the self-conscious 'traditional-food' revivalism of modern retailers and farmers' markets. They were just selling local people food supplied by local farmers.

SELF-SERVICE

But increasingly, butchers and grocers alike faced stiff competition from larger stores. The old multiple grocers such as the International Stores led the way and the Co-op chain was also still popular. Even though dividends had fallen during wartime and the austerity years after the war, the Co-op was still a trusted brand with its own loyal following. And some of the multiples made their business

more secure by trying a new way to speed up the purchasing process, cut costs, reduce prices and make shopping more businesslike: self-service. Self-service was an American concept. It had originated in the first decades of the 20th century with the Piggly Wiggly group of stores in Memphis, Tennessee, a chain owned by Clarence Saunders that sold pre-packaged foods. Big Bear, the most famous early American supermarket, opened in New Jersey in 1932. Based in a converted car factory, selling many other items as well as food and offering free parking, it gave a surprising glimpse of the future, but Britain did not get such vast out-of-town stores until towards the end of the century.

A few British shops had tried self-service before the Second World War, and some Co-ops tried a partial self-service system as a way of coping with staff shortages during the war. But these shops were not full-scale self-service stores and did not catch on widely. For this to happen the shops first of all needed the full paraphernalia of the supermarket – a row of checkouts, wire baskets (trolleys came later), dedicated shelving units and refrigerated cabinets for perishables. This kind of 'retooling' was not possible during the war, and self-service did not reach Britain in a big way until several years afterwards. In addition, during wartime many items still had to be packed by the shopkeeper, and self-service only really works if the vast bulk of the goods are pre-packaged. In the post-war period there were far more pre-packaged goods and customers were ready for something new.

Robert Opie, an expert on the history of packaging and brands, has pointed out how packaging changed in the 1950s to reflect this development. Packaging in the post-war years was simpler and bolder in design. Packets emphasised the brand as never before by using strong colours and clean lines. This kind of packaging worked well when shoppers no longer had advice from the shopkeeper on the virtues of different brands and had to make their own choices as they walked around the shop with their basket. Clearer, bolder packaging design meant easier brand recognition, helping both the shopper looking for a specific brand and the manufacturers trying to promote their product.

Multiples like the International Stores and Sainsbury's, along with more recent arrivals such as Tesco, pioneered self-service supermarkets. What they created was not always the well-planned shopping experience of a modern supermarket, partly because retailers often had to convert existing stores that did not necessarily have the space for shelves, generous aisles for circulation and checkouts. One shopper, Marion Dutch from Trowbridge, Wiltshire, remembers the beginnings of self-service in her town: 'The busiest shop was always the International Stores, which was on the corner opposite the Town Hall. That was always packed, because it was the only self-service store in the town. It was very tiny and you sort of shuffled round with your basket, filling it up and getting to the other end.'

Below Because self-service was a new concept for most customers, firms such as Sainsbury's produced guides explaining how to use the wire baskets and what to do at the checkout.

Sometimes a chain like the Co-op had several neighbouring shops – a grocer, butcher and baker, for example – and these could be knocked together to create one large self-service store. But a modern shopper would find even this kind of shop cramped by today's standards. There was still very much the feeling that you were on the High Street and these early self-service stores were a far cry from the vast, purpose-built supermarkets of the 21st century. But purpose-built supermarkets were also arriving: the Co-op began building them in 1949 and other chains followed.

Architects and retailers soon settled on a standard design for the town-centre supermarket. The frontages were very simple, with a long window looking in on to the checkouts; this window was often effectively a noticeboard for 'special offer' posters – no goods were displayed there. At one end there was usually a canopy sheltering the main entrance. Mothers often parked their prams here, and baskets and trolleys were left here too. Inside the products were on low shelves and in refrigerators. A standard arrangement also developed, with goods that turned over rapidly at the back, close to the stock rooms, and impulse buys such as sweets near the checkouts.

At Sainsbury's Self-service shopping is EASY and QUICK

1—As you go in you are given a special wire basket for your purchases.

2—The prices and weight of all goods are clearly marked. You just take what you want.

3—Are you a fast shopper or a slow? You can be either when you shop at Sainsbury's!

4—Dairy produce, cooked meats, pies, sausages, bacon, poultry, rabbits and cheese—all hygienically packed.

5—Meat is served from Sainsbury's special refrigerated counters. Or you can serve yourself from the cabinets.

6—Pay as you go out. The assistant puts what you have bought into your own basket and gives you a receipt.

A NEW PRICING POLICY

In 1964 there came a development that transformed retailing and enabled the supermarkets to prosper. Before then there had been Resale Price Maintenance, a law that controlled the prices of certain goods by allowing manufacturers to set shop prices, in effect stifling competition. Shops were able to get around this legislation to a certain extent, but in the late 1950s and early 1960s, retailers who favoured aggressive price-cutting, such as Jack Cohen of Tesco, campaigned for a change to the law. In 1964 the law was abolished and the way to more cut-throat competition on price was opened up. Even after the law was changed, some manufacturers tried to get around it. They sought legal backing to register their products as exempt from the new law, but Cohen challenged them in the courts and won. A new era had begun, in which competition was king and large companies like Tesco could defeat smaller rivals by buying in massive bulk and selling cheaply. After the change in the law smaller self-service shops were more likely to flourish outside the large towns where Tesco and Sainsbury's had stores.

A NEW KIND OF SHOPPING

Self-service stores made it easier to shop around because they broke the bond between shopkeeper and customer. Unlike a traditional shop, where customers and retailer had frequent conversations and built up a personal relationship, in a supermarket the only interaction was at the checkout. Any conversation with the

Overleaf By 1967 Sainsbury's had established the policy of stacking sweets and other tempting offerings near the busy checkouts to encourage impulse purchases.

Below A customer takes a wire basket and admires the goods on display at a self-service food store in London's Westbourne Grove.

SELF-SERVICE

THE PROS AND CONS

Many grocers took their first steps in self-service in the 1950s and, especially, the 1960s, installing checkouts and handing a wire basket to each customer as they entered the shop. The new breed of self-service shopkeepers were taking advantage of the fact that virtually all groceries were now available ready packaged and that if you were ready to invest in refrigerated cabinets you could sell a range of meat, dairy produce and other perishables. So, even if the local self-service grocers could not compete on range or price with a big-city supermarket, there was plenty to attract both regular shoppers and casual customers.

But the shopkeeper had to woo some of the more traditional customers over. Some, especially older people, resented the fact that the shopkeeper no longer offered such a personal service, that the pre-packaged goods were similar to those in other shops and that the groceries were no longer delivered to their door. It took a lot of sweet talking and some special offers to keep customers happy. It was worth it for the store owner in the long run. Self-service allowed quick turn-round of stock, and staff did not have to be highly skilled – they did not even have to be good at mental arithmetic because the till did all the adding up for them. And once customers realised that queuing once at the checkout usually took less time than waiting at several different counters, they came round to the idea of self-service too.

Not all shoppers preferred self-service. Some still valued the personal service provided by a traditional grocer and were willing to pay the price premium for the grocer's more friendly approach. Many shoppers liked the relationship they built up with traditional shopkeepers and found self-service impersonal. As one shopper put it: 'Well, I think it is very cold and there is not much conversation goes on, and it's not so cheery as what the old shops were, you know, because folk haven't got time for you. You are getting shoved through and sometimes,

ABOVE *In the 1960s, before the era of the barcode, the checkout operator had to check the price of every item.*

at my age, I feel that I am not even getting time to put my change in my purse.' This comment, from an elderly respondent in an article on customer loyalty and how this was affected by supermarket shopping, is typical of how many felt about the effect of self-service on the shopping process. Discerning customers, and those wanting a slower, more human kind of shopping, stuck to smaller shops. But those on a tighter budget might compromise, going to the self-service store for basic groceries but buying meat from a traditional butcher and also going to the greengrocer and baker.

checkout assistant was unlikely to influence what the customers bought because they had already made their choices when they got there. Shopping had changed radically and for good.

Another major change in food shopping during the 1950s and 1960s was the way in which goods were advertised. 1955 saw the introduction of commercial television in Britain with the beginning of ITV, the country's second television channel. Suddenly, in a world in which cinema audiences were dwindling, there were new advertising opportunities for manufacturers. Many embraced TV advertising enthusiastically and already well-known brands such as Heinz kept their position at the top of the tree. So, by the 1960s, the self-service grocer was the first port of call for the weekly food-shopping trip. Such stores were expanding too, offering a wider range of food products, and many migrated to larger premises in the shopping malls that were being built in town centres across the country.

THE RISE OF TESCO

Tesco is among the most famous British supermarket chains and its story is an object lesson in the rise of a retailer. The company was the brainchild of Jack Cohen, son of a Polish Jewish couple who came to Britain to escape persecution in 1882. After serving in the Royal Flying Corps in the First World War, Cohen hired a barrow and sold ex-NAAFI foods, soon expanding his business to take in several market stalls. From the beginning he bought cheaply and sold cheaply, and his business did well. In 1924 he sealed a deal to buy tea from a merchant named T.E. Stockwell, and the new tea was sold in packets with the brand name Tesco, made up of Stockwell's initials and the first two letters of Cohen's name. The tea sold well and after success with other foodstuffs Cohen moved into indoor market stalls and opened his first shops. In 1931 Tesco Stores Limited was born. By 1934 Cohen had more than 40 shops and continued steadily to open new ones over the following few years. He bought other assets too, such as nurseries to supply the shops' vegetable counters. Interests in industries such as canning followed, and by the end of the Second World War Cohen led a business empire that was ready to lead the trend towards stores offering value and wide choice. With a mixture of new openings and acquisition of other companies, Tesco grew rapidly during the 1950s, owning several hundred self-service stores.

Then in 1961 Cohen opened a new store in Leicester that showed the way forward. A true supermarket, it had a restaurant and a filling station, together with stock embracing both food and 'Home and Wear' departments. This mix set the style for future Tesco stores. The rise of the company was accelerated when Resale Price Maintenance was abolished and the company could compete aggressively on price. The 1960s was the first great heyday of Tesco, with its portfolio of more than 800 stores (though some 200 were later sold off in the economic decline of the early 1970s), dedicated warehouses and millions of customers. More than any other company, Tesco brought the old, street-market-style retail philosophy of 'Pile 'em high and sell 'em cheap' to the High Street.

EVERY SHOP HAS ITS PRICE

The rush to cut prices but still make people spend more had an impact beyond the supermarkets. Many owners of department stores, for example, felt that they would be left behind if they too did not offer promotions and price cuts – especially with supermarkets like Tesco offering items for the home as well as food on their shelves. So some department stores, such as Harrods in the 1950s, reduced their prices and as a result increased their volume of sales. If they were not in close competition with the supermarkets, department stores increasingly faced pressure from middle-market stores such as Marks & Spencer.

Marks & Spencer plc saw itself as more and more like a department store, buying up larger premises. The chain had suffered badly in the war, losing some 16 stores to enemy bombing, so first the company rebuilt these and then expanded many of its other stores. It went for a traditional, sophisticated look, giving the enlarged stores imposing neo-classical or neo-Georgian frontages, with the company name prominent above the window. The company's building programme continued through the 1960s, with 170 of its total of 245 shops

Above When it opened its store at Popes Road, Brixton, in 1966, Tesco claimed that it was the largest supermarket in Britain. This image shows its staff gathered for the opening.

TRADING STAMPS

Trading stamps provided a way in which a retailer could in effect offer a discount at the same time as encouraging customer loyalty. When a customer made a purchase, the retailer gave them some trading stamps, and the more valuable the purchase the more stamps were given. The customer stuck the stamps in a special book, and when they had accumulated enough books of stamps, these could be taken or sent to the trading stamp company and exchanged for goods. The advantage for the shopkeeper was that the customer would keep returning to the same shop, or another in the chain, to accumulate more stamps, so that customer loyalty would be built up.

The idea of trading stamps originated in the USA in the late 19th century, when they were issued only to customers who paid in cash. They caught on widely with the growth of chain stores in the USA in the 1920s, but were taken up in Britain with the rise of the supermarkets in the late 1950s. The prominent trading stamp brands in Britain were Green Shield Stamps, introduced by Richard Tompkins in 1958, and Pink Stamps, the British version of the American Sperry & Hutchinson (S&H) stamps. The Fine Fare chain gave Pink Stamps, while the Pricerite and Tesco chains gave Green Shield Stamps. There were also several other trading stamp schemes, but they had short lives and minimal impact compared with these two, which had the backing of major retailers.

Other retailers – not just food retailers but also outlets such as filling stations – also gave trading stamps, with Green Shield the most common brand. Customers got used to spotting signs proclaiming 'We give Green Shield Stamps'

before making purchases, and collecting the stamps became popular. In effect they were a way of saving, and customers redeemed them to collect all kinds of consumer goods. The accompanying 'feel-good' factor helped win people over to collecting the stamps – because no money changed hands the items you got in exchange for your stamps felt 'free' and were spoken of as 'gifts'. During the 1960s trading stamps certainly encouraged people to stay loyal to the shops that issued them.

A huge range of gifts was available, from small items such as cutlery to high-value consumer durables like televisions and food mixers. But saving enough stamps required plenty of determination and loyalty – to collect just one book of stamps you had to spend £32, and that one book would get you just a small 'gift', such as a set of six beer glasses. A 19-inch television needed 88 books. To save this many stamps you would have had to spend £2,816 (much more than most people earned in a year) on food and petrol. So most people exchanged small numbers of books of stamps for relatively low-value items, and were happy to have something for their efforts.

Many retailers opposed trading stamps. Companies such as Sainsbury's, John Lewis, Boots and Marks & Spencer plc argued that it was more honest, and better value, to keep prices down and give the customer a good deal at the point of sale. They formed the Distributive Trades Alliance, winning their view plenty of publicity and steering Parliament towards regulating the trading stamps industry. In spite of their opposition, trading stamps remained popular with many consumers throughout the 1960s.

undergoing major works. The revamped stores had spacious sales floors on which there were, as well as the traditional counters, rows and rows of rails containing dresses, all clearly priced and marked with the company's 'St Michael' brand name. As well as the established range of clothes, many of these stores now sold food in self-service departments. So Marks & Spencer plc was competing with both department stores selling clothes and supermarkets selling food, in both areas emphasising the quality of the goods on offer, while also keeping prices keen.

THE POWER OF YOUTH

After the Second World War things changed for Britain's young people. For a start there were more educational opportunities after the Education Act of 1944. Day-release courses were available, more teenagers were staying on longer at school and higher education was expanding. In the 1950s

Above In the 1950s, Marks & Spencer's magazine advertisements highlighted the range of women's clothing, claiming that the shopper would find something new every time she visited the store.

there was still National Service, but this ended in the early 1960s. So, many had the chance to stay on in education, with the freedom this entailed, while for those in employment, wages were on the whole rising faster than prices. All this gave young people more freedom and made it possible for a flourishing youth culture to develop – one born of a potent mixture of leisure, music and ideas. Art colleges were melting pots of this culture – young people from different classes met there, and the kind of work they did, in informal studio environments rather than quiet university libraries, encouraged interaction and the exchange of ideas and jokes. Bands flourished at art schools, and a host of meeting places for the young, from simple cafés to skiffle joints and rock and roll venues, grew up. From here the influence spread outwards and this, at a time when young working people's disposable income was increasing, encouraged the growth of eating and drinking places, as well as record and clothes shops, on the High Street.

But there was no single 'youth culture' in the 1950s and 1960s. Music and tastes were changing rapidly, and there were rival cultures and tastes. If many older people felt intimidated by groups of Teddy Boys, or their successors the mods and rockers, there were plenty of young people who were more docile. They soon became known as 'teenagers', an American term that spread to Britain in the 1940s and became popular in the 1950s. Soon canny retailers were thinking in terms of a 'teenage market', and youth culture, which had seemed threatening to some, was seen as an opportunity.

It was in the art schools that many of the new clothing fashions were tried out or even first developed. The new ideas of art students added to the successful rag trade in the capital made London a hotbed of new fashion ideas. If Paris was still the centre of high fashion, the place where the establishment designers ruled the roost, London had something new to offer – a direct line into youth culture. Here it led the world, as Mary Quant commented: 'London led the way in the changing focus of fashion from the establishment to the young. As a country we were aware of the great potential of this change long before the Americans or the French. We were one step ahead from the start . . .'

So, while the music and the very word 'teenager' came from America, the idea of a commercial youth culture expressed through clothes was a British invention. For a few years Britain, and especially London, was at the centre of youth culture, and British music and fashion were aped all over the western world. Even on a provincial High Street the influence trickled down, and young people pored over magazine articles about Mary Quant's clothes or rushed to the rare local gig of a new band.

Mary Quant's designs were just one symptom of the wider choice in the post-war era. After the narrow choice of wartime, even in the 1950s there was much more variety. This was clearest in London, where the various different shopping areas catered to different social classes with varying preferences. As one account pointed out, there was a huge difference between the clothes on offer to the masses in the department stores of Oxford Street and those sold in the exclusive shops of Mayfair:

> Here, on the pavements, are the dresses – in Oxford Street wishy-washy prints on pale backgrounds; in Regent Street better prints on darker backgrounds; in Knightsbridge natural shantungs and plain dark silks; in Kensington High Street so many blouse and skirt 'separates' that out-and-out divorce would seem a wise choice. And then, in Mayfair, to make up for everything, the sudden vision of a dazzlingly pure white dress, this season's highest compliment to ideal womanhood.

That account from the early 1950s shows that London's shopping areas were still very much targeted at specific social and economic groups, even though the range of clothes on offer embraced everything from cheap prints to luxurious silks. On the High Streets of smaller cities and towns, the range would be narrower, but as the period went on there would be an increasing variety for each group of shoppers to choose from. In addition there would be shops, small boutiques mainly, aimed at the young, many of which had their heyday towards the end of the 1960s but lasted well into the following decade.

Café culture

With the growth of youth culture in the 1950s, more and more young people were looking for somewhere to 'hang out'. The choice during the post-war years was limited. Pubs were where adults gathered to drink alcohol: they were not an option for the young. Restaurants were for formal meals and would not welcome teenagers who wanted to sit and talk but consume little. In some places there were working men's clubs and institutes, but these catered either for adult men or for families. That left High Street cafés. Again, not every café owner welcomed a group of teenagers who sat around all day talking and drinking a single coffee or a soft drink. But a few proprietors saw the potential of the youth market, installed a jukebox and put some teenage-friendly posters on the walls. It was Britain's first inkling of a fact that would become increasingly clear: young people not only had money to spend, they would come to have a huge influence on culture, especially in fashion and music.

In some towns, particularly seaside towns but some others too, the place to hang out was the ice-cream parlour. Often run by Italian families, these cafés came into their own in the 1950s and 1960s, when people had

Below Teenage girls gather at a Milk Bar in 1954, where milkshakes had become a popular drink.

THE POST-WAR CAFÉ

A GOOD ESPRESSO

If we appreciate good coffee today, this is not because of the host of modern chain coffee shops on the High Street, but because of countless small café owners who took the trouble to make good coffee in the 1950s and 1960s. They succeeded if they combined tasting skills with the ability to make concentrated, Italian-style coffee – in other words, the espresso.

An espresso machine works by forcing very hot water and steam through ground coffee in order to extract all the flavour. The secret of how to do this effectively was discovered just before the Second World War, with espresso machines incorporating a pump to force the water through the coffee. After the war the Italian company Gaggia began to produce machines using this kind of pump, and the modern espresso was born.

But making good espresso was about much more than the machine. The café owner had first of all to know all about coffee. The taste of his coffee would depend on the blend of beans he used, and one could buy a suitable blend from a wholesaler, or buy various beans and make a special blend.

Most people would choose the darkest beans for espresso, but this wasn't vital: all except the palest beans would do and the important thing was the taste. The café owner would also know that coffee is best used within a couple of weeks of roasting, but that, for espresso, it is best to let the beans rest for a day or two before first using them. And it is also important to grind the coffee beans properly, because the average size of the ground particles and the mix of coarse and fine particles affect the taste, and the person doing the grinding would learn the best approach by experience.

So anyone running a café in the 1950s and offering Italian-style coffee needed lots of practice in grinding the beans and using the espresso machine. But just as important was an appreciation of good coffee and its varying taste. This entailed, as it still does, a good nose and palette, and the enthusiasm and curiosity to try different beans and blends, and to keep sampling. Just like the best baristas today, the main qualification of post-war café proprietors was pride in their work.

more leisure time and wanted entertainment rather than nourishment from a café. Ice-cream parlours often had an up-to-date feeling about them – even the pastel shades of the ice cream went with the cream and *eau-de-nil* décor fashionable in the 1950s. What was attractive about these places was not just the ice cream but the whole ambiance. One resident of South Shields, Durham, remembers: 'Meeting at Porretas ice cream parlour in Frederick Street was the high spot of the weekend. We sat on the high stools, in little cubicles with long thin shelves, and ate ice cream with strawberry sauce and nuts. If we had the money we would play music on the jukebox.'

The jukebox was the key – that and a sympathetic proprietor who would let you stay for ages. 'A cup of coffee would last you all night,' as another memory puts it, and perhaps it is only a slight exaggeration. The trickle of money from the jukebox would have been welcome with such stingy customers, and cafés like this must have been businesses with a low turnover. But many also had low outgoings, being staffed by family members on minimal pay who most probably lived upstairs.

MILK BARS

One company that saw the youth market's potential was the National Milk Bar chain of cafés. These began in Wales between the wars when R.W. ('Willie') Griffiths opened the first Milk Bar in Colwyn Bay in 1933. Griffiths was a dairy farmer and started his Milk Bars as a way of providing a new market for his milk and cream – not to mention bacon, eggs, sausages and vegetables, the preferred ingredients of the classic British 'fry-up' breakfast or lunch. Milk Bars caught on, and Griffiths opened many branches across Wales and North-West England. They all had a similar décor: chrome fittings, black and white chequered floors and bar stools. By the 1950s and 1960s they were the places where young people wanted to be seen and other proprietors started similar ventures in other parts of the country. When the Beatles were seen frequenting a Milk Bar in Liverpool, Milk Bars were the places to be seen. What most teenagers drank in a Milk Bar

Below Showy, sometimes dandyish clothes typified the Teddy Boys of the 1950s. This group of Teds gather around a jukebox – no doubt to listen to some American rock 'n' roll.

was, naturally enough, a milk shake. The chain developed a wide choice of flavours, and signs on early Milk Bars proclaimed: 'Icy cold or steaming milk shakes. 47 different varieties.' And at a few pence a time they were within most teenagers' budgets.

The original business model for the National Milk Bars was based on food from the Griffiths' family farm being sold direct to the customer without a middleman taking a share of the profits. It worked for Griffiths, but not everyone liked milk shakes, and the cafés of the 1950s and 1960s also served coffee – proper Italian-style espresso and cappuccino, not the ersatz stuff that Britons had got used to before the Second World War. Kathy Headington, in a collection of memories of Maidenhead, Berkshire, recalls Good's Milk Bar in the centre of town: 'It was a great place socially. We all used to meet up there. It had a restaurant at the back, and at the front they did all the expresso [sic] coffees and such like.' British people in the early 21st century tend to think that coffee chains such as Starbucks brought good coffee to Britain. But in the post-war period there were many Milk Bars and Italian-run cafés that served a well-made espresso or cappuccino.

Above After the muted colours of wartime, designers of shops and cafés went for bright colours such as the vibrant red used in the Milk Bar.

WHOSE CAFÉ IS IT ANYWAY?

Like local pubs with their fixed casts of regulars, cafés too had their own dedicated customers. It could be important to know who went where, because parts of youth culture became highly tribal in the mid-1960s. This was the era of mods and rockers. The mods, neatly dressed, with short hair, rode scooters, while the motorcycle-riding rockers favoured leather jackets and long hair. Both rode around in gangs and made a beeline for coastal towns at the weekend, hoping for a fight. All those who wanted to avoid trouble steered clear of the haunts of these gangs. Jenny Stacey, in a collection of memories from Bletchley, Buckinghamshire, recalls one café she was not allowed to visit: 'We weren't allowed in Greenways café, it was a rough one. The rockers went in there – their motorbikes were the best bit about them. I liked their style, the way they dressed. They were threatening, I suppose.' This reminiscence perfectly captures the fascination of the rockers to an outsider, and also the danger, which of course is part of the fascination. Territorial issues like this dominated a young person's choice of place to hang out; they probably always do, although the mods and rockers, with their violent clashes, are an extreme example.

BEAUTY MEANS BUSINESS

The end of the Second World War meant a change of role for many women. Although women had been the mainstays of the Home Front – holding down demanding jobs, serving in the Women's Land Army and generally showing that they could do anything that a man could do – they were not encouraged to continue in these roles when the troops came home. Men who could not find better-paid work elsewhere wanted their old jobs back, and the government did not want these heroes who had put their lives on the line to be unemployed. So women were encouraged to return to traditional domestic roles. The government promoted the values of home-making, child-rearing and looking after the working husband. The result was a generation of women who stayed at home and a baby boom that went on from 1946 until the end of the 1960s.

Although opportunities in education and employment, bringing greater independence, slowly opened up for women, in the 1950s they still lived in a world of traditional values. Shopping – or window shopping – was promoted as a recreation and women felt pressure to look good because they would be judged above all by their appearance. They compared themselves with their favourite film stars and, as television ownership increased, television performers. They

Below The 1950s and 1960s were a time of elaborate hairstyles, and women spent a lot of time 'under the dryer' at every visit to the hairdresser's.

looked at women's magazines which featured the latest fashions. Clothes shops had more, and more diverse, stock to catch the eyes of the window shopper. Hairdressers themselves showed them the latest styles. Against this background, the hairdresser was an important person in most women's lives, and a vital presence on the High Street. Many hairdressers themselves were women and they took up the job because the skills were fairly easy to learn, it was a social job involving mixing with a variety of clients and, for those with ambition to own their own business, it involved minimal outlay on stock.

For customers, a weekly trip to the hairdresser was a social event at which they could catch up on gossip and perhaps meet friends. For many it was a welcome trip out of the house and a break from the drudgery of housework. It could replace the regular trips to the tea shop enjoyed by Edwardian women

PERM OR SET?

In the 1950s most women wanted their hair to curl, and if you had straight hair, hairdressers had the answer: the permanent wave. The 'perm' had been around for decades, but before the war the usual method of curling hair had been by using heat. There were no heated hair rollers for use in the home, so women had to go to the hairdresser's and sit for ages wired to an enormous contraption that heated each curl separately. But in the late 1930s a way of creating long-lasting curls by altering the chemistry of the hair was discovered.

The new 'cold' perms were highly effective, but originally took a very long time to do – some accounts tell of women sitting for six or more hours while the chemicals took effect. Later versions did not take quite so long but having a perm was still a lengthy process lasting a couple of hours – plus of course the initial discussion between the hairdresser and client about exactly how she wanted her hair to look. The hairdresser washed the customer's hair, curled it around rods or rollers and then applied a perming lotion. The customer then sat around for an hour or more and then the lotion was rinsed away and a further lotion was applied. The result, if the perm 'took' properly, was a wavy head of hair that could last for several months.

Hairdressers learned how to vary the effect, for example making the curls tight and small with thin rods, or more open and wavy with larger rods or rollers, so that the exact look required by the customer was achieved. But perms did not work for everyone. Hairdressers had to explain patiently that sometimes for people with very fine hair, or on certain medication, the hair would not curl. But for most, the permed look was the one to have, and women and hairdressers alike studied the fashion and film magazines to see exactly what sculpted effect was the flavour of the month.

LIFE IN ROLLERS

Between perms, or for a shorter-lasting restyling, women chose to 'set' the hair by applying setting lotion, putting the hair in rollers and drying it under a bonnet dryer. The use of chemicals on the hair, not to mention the heat of the dryer, was something that was potentially dangerous, but even so, many women in the post-war years set their own hair at home. There was a safer but very uncomfortable alternative: to put the hair in rollers overnight. Incredibly, many women did get used to sleeping with their hair in rollers, which, when fashions favoured big, bouncing curls, could be thicker than cotton reels. Many greeted the more natural looks of the hippy era with relief.

Towards the end of the 1950s a new style emerged which eclipsed the restrained waves of the first part of the decade: the beehive. To create a beehive, the hairdresser teased and lacquered the hair

LEFT *Audrey Hepburn is here pictured in Paris in 1964, three years after starring in the successful movie* Breakfast at Tiffany's, *which helped popularise this kind of hairstyle.*

into a tall, tapered dome shape that could add several inches to the wearer's height. Dramatically different, it spread throughout Britain, mainland Europe and the USA in the early 1960s, popularised by prominent film appearances – for example, Audrey Hepburn sported a beehive in the 1961 film *Breakfast at Tiffany's*.

The tendency in the later 1960s was towards a more natural look, with simpler styles. Hairsprays were used widely to keep the hair in place. The emphasis was on combining practicality and beauty, a combination that worked both at home and in the workplace in an era when more women were once more going out to work. Under the influence of the hippy movement, some women, especially the young, let their hair grow long, leaving it loose or tying it into a ponytail. Although these trends left little work for the hairdresser, many women still went to the salon regularly for restyling.

CREATE *Your Own Glamour* INSTANTLY

Thrill to the radiant beauty that can be yours the very first time you try "Pan-Cake," the famous glamour make-up . . . Instantly it gives you the smooth, flawless, lovely new complexion you have always wanted . . . and it will keep you looking irresistibly glamorous throughout all the daytime and evening hours . . .

PAN-CAKE
BRAND
MAKE-UP

VIRGINIA MAYO
in Samuel Goldwyns'
"THE BEST YEARS OF OUR LIVES "

MAX FACTOR · Cosmetics of the Stars' are obtainable from your local Chemist, Hairdresser & Store.

Max Factor ★
HOLLYWOOD & LONDON

The face of the future

...luminous, lovely—with Elizabeth Arden's new Illusion Foundation

A new look in faces—smooth, mysterious, lustrous—to make yesterday's make-up seem dated.
Soft though it feels, finely though it floats over your skin, Illusion gives magical cover and colour with a beautiful opalescent lustre. The look of the future is here to-day with Illusion, in nine natural shades, all at their loveliest with Elizabeth Arden's new Transparent Powder.

Elizabeth Arden

MICHAEL
General store worker

My favourite part of today was finding out that we've got a van – that van is really cool. We haven't had a van before. We had a push-bike, and that was it. Now we've gone up in the world. We've got a decent flat and we've got the van. The only problem is, we're not a butcher's we're a convenience store. But the convenience store is growing on me. It's a quick way of making money – there's a tin of beans, here's a quid, it will be like that. It's easy, but it's not what I'm used to at all. And I'll get to eat lots of sweets and drink lots of pop, so that will be all right.

......

We'll cope absolutely fine. We'll be able to sell lots and lots, but unless we get really busy, it could be quite boring. It's just handing over packaged products and there's no salesmanship really needed. But people go mad for the Green Shield Stamps. People want to buy as much as they can, to win the radio or the clock. Plus the fact that we deliver and give credit – that will help us sell too.

Previous page In the 1950s, make-up was promoted with images of sophistication and stardom. By the 1960s, a 'wilder', more futuristic look was the selling point.

– or could complement it if a woman could make time for a coffee after a perm or set. And in the 1950s a perm or set was what most women wanted. The fashion was for highly sculpted styles, with artificial waves and curls. Many women visited their hairdresser every week for a shampoo and set, and periodically for a permanent wave. Make-up tended towards the exaggerated too, with bright lipstick and heavy mascara contrasting with pale skin.

THE GLORY OF GADGETS

A striking change to the High Street in the post-war era was the increasing number of shops selling electrical goods. Mains electricity had come to Britain at the end of the 19th century, but at first spread slowly. Only 12 per cent of British homes had electric light in 1921, but in the 1920s and 1930s electrification spread more rapidly and by the start of the Second World War around two-thirds of British households had electric light. In the 1950s and 1960s there was therefore a large, and largely new, market for electrical gadgets such as cookers and fridges, fires and lamps, televisions and radios, irons and toasters. Many of these appliances replaced existing ones powered in some other way. Electric cookers, for example, were marketed as cleaner, more efficient and less smelly than gas cookers. Others helped reduce work around the house or provided home entertainment. Most people were experiencing these products for the first time, so dedicated electrical retailers had to dispense advice as well as stock, installing cookers, telling people which plug to use, giving advice on wiring, fuses and so on. Both small, locally owned specialists and growing national chains such as Curry's filled the bill. The modernity of the post-war age, typified by concrete buildings and increased car ownership, was summed up by the proliferation of electrical items that invaded even quite modest homes.

Both High Streets and homes in the post-war period saw themselves as entering a new, consciously modern, age. People looked optimistically to a future in which many would travel into space and most would own their own car, in which entertainment could be accessed at the flick of a TV switch and there would soon be robots doing the housework. Retailers grasped this vision of the future enthusiastically. The most successful shop owners embraced ideas such as self-service, or got in new stock, from three-piece suites to electrical gadgets. They set out to woo new markets, such as young people, and increasingly occupied bright, stylish premises courtesy of the major post-war rebuilding projects that spread across the country. They actively sought new opportunities, as any successful business needs to do, and rode on the wave of optimism that broke across Britain in defiance of the austerity that people endured after the war.

Below Fridges attracted a lot of interest in the Household Goods department of Selfridges in London.

Overleaf From cereals to sundaes: a variety of images that sum up the colour, vibrancy and fun of the post-war High Street.

AT CLIENT'S RISK ONLY

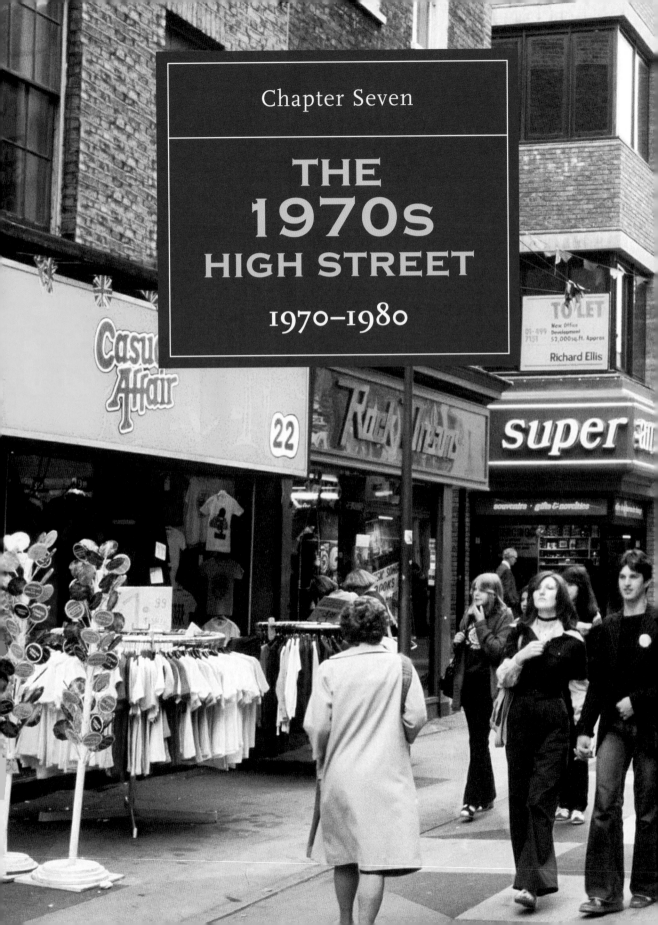

Chapter Seven

THE
1970s
HIGH STREET

1970–1980

THE 1970s SAW BRITAIN truly embrace the idea of self-service shopping: regular visits to the supermarket became the norm and sometimes this meant a weekly visit to an out-of-town shopping mall. Trips to the supermarket made shopping easier – and it was easier still when decimal currency at last replaced the old pounds, shillings and pence in 1971. But the 1970s were not all about the future. People also valued the old High Street names – whether famous chains such as Boots or trusted local shops – which provided continuity in a time of economic hardship for many and change for all.

By the early 1970s much of the optimism that had marked the 1960s had ebbed away. Britain faced inflation, bitter disputes between unions and employers and, in 1973–4, a crippling economic crisis and fuel shortages that saw many industries reduce their working week to three days. The terrible effects of the 'Troubles' in Northern Ireland – including disasters such as 'Bloody Sunday', in which 13 civilians were shot dead by British troops – made matters worse. The first few years of the decade had a sombre hue. At the same time the country's manufacturing industry – for so long a vital source of wealth and jobs – was in decline, a trend summed up for many in unpopular car models like the Austin Allegro and Morris Marina. As a result of this decline, unemployment was rising. And as the countries of the former British empire became independent they no longer provided captive markets for British goods.

1970
The Conservative Party wins the general election and Edward Heath becomes Prime Minister.

1971
Britain adopts decimal currency.

1971
British Leyland launches the Morris Marina to replace the Morris Minor and compete with the Ford Cortina.

1972
Thirteen demonstrators in Belfast are shot dead by British troops, an event that becomes known as 'Bloody Sunday'.

1972
The dictatorial ruler of Uganda, Idi Amin, expels the country's Asian population. Many of them settle in Britain.

As in previous eras, Britain's retail sector provided some relief from the gloom, and some business to help gee up the economy. Big retailers expanded and cut costs as much as they could – by using self-service or finding cheaper locations, for example. A greater variety of consumer goods came on the market, from food mixers to new formats for recorded music. And another key historical development set the stage for the future: in 1973 Britain became a member of what was then the European Economic Community (known as the Common Market), opening up the possibility of better trading links with Europe. So if times were hard, and neither the Conservative government of the first part of the decade nor the Labour one of the second part could lift the country fully out of its problems, retailing gave Britons one answer.

THE NEW CONSUMERS

Histories of the 1970s remember the strikes, fuel shortages and economic depression, and for some people this led to unemployment and hardship. Joblessness rose, with 2.6 per cent of the working population unemployed in 1970 and 6.1 per cent in 1978. But for those in work things were better. Wages had risen steadily during the late 1950s and 1960s, and a manual worker on the equivalent of £31 a week in 1951 took home £54 in 1975. Home ownership had also increased, and by 1979 over half of all families owned their own home.

Britons spent a lot of this extra income on consumer items. Most families already had a television and a refrigerator. In the 1970s many bought a freezer – only a handful had their own in the 1960s but by the end of the 1970s over 40 per cent of households had one. Many acquired music centres, too, as well as washing machines and other kitchen appliances. A lot of homes had central heating installed for the first time, in most cases fuelled by the North Sea gas that was being piped into homes.

1973
Britain joins the European Economic Community.

1973
The school-leaving age is raised to 16.

1974
As a result of fuel shortages and an economic slump, Prime Minister Edward Heath introduces a three-day working week.

1974
After a general election produces a hung parliament, Harold Wilson becomes the leader of a minority Labour government.

1974
The first Universal Product Codes, or barcodes, are introduced in the USA.

With the growth in home ownership another consumer trend emerged: do-it-yourself. Many people became almost addicted to DIY, inspired partly by popular television programmes on the subject. With home ownership increasing – many people moved house about every five years – the activity became more popular still. According to one estimate, Britons hung around a million kilometres of wallpaper in 1978 alone. An Englishman's home is his castle, and then as now people spent a lot of time and money on their homes. But Britons also looked further afield for interest and entertainment. They were more likely in the 1970s to take overseas holidays and try different cuisines. At home, people were increasingly likely to drink wine with their meals, even though the choice available was far narrower than it is now and tastes were unsophisticated – sweet white wine was a popular choice.

THE NEW BRITONS

The response of the country to overseas influence felt very different if you were a member of Britain's immigrant population. Immigrants had been arriving from the Commonwealth – especially from the West Indies, India and Pakistan – since the 1950s. Officially they were welcomed; in reality they felt like outsiders. As one West Indian described the attitude he met: 'You are unwanted. You are here because some higher order official let you stay, not because I want you . . . You only create problems. You want my job, you want my food, you want to live in my home, you want to use my school, my hospital, my stores.'

Often it was worse than this. Black people felt themselves the target of a prejudiced police force, who suspected them of crime and harassed them. A minority on the political far right (represented by the National Front and other extremist groups) campaigned for a stop to immigration and for repatriation. The disagreements between the racists and those campaigning against them

1975	**1975**	**1976**	**1976**	**1977**
The Sex Pistols perform in public for the first time.	The Sex Discrimination Act is passed, protecting people in areas such as education and employment.	Prime Minister Harold Wilson resigns and James Callaghan assumes the premiership.	The Anglo-French supersonic aircraft Concorde makes its first commercial flights.	Queen Elizabeth II's Silver Jubilee is widely celebrated.

could erupt into violence, as on the tragic occasion when the National Front provocatively held a meeting in Southall, West London, with its large Asian community. There was a large protest against the National Front, a huge police contingent was sent in and Blair Peach, a white teacher who was one of the protesters, was killed, probably as a result of action by a police officer.

In spite of such tragedies, most immigrants stayed and some prospered. Often they did so on the High Street, where many South Asian families started Indian restaurants or ran corner shops. Here they became key people in their communities, not only working long hours to provide vital services, but also introducing the British to the pleasures of Indian cooking. It was probably at this time that chicken tikka masala was properly introduced to Britain and began its rise to become the country's most popular restaurant dish – its 'true national dish' as politician Robin Cook called it. Behind the Asian restaurants and shops was a whole network of cooks, wholesalers, drivers and others, employing these new British citizens to ensure that the whole country got these new kinds of food, which it still enjoys to this day.

A BETTER LIFE?

The 1970s was a time of change for many. Women held few positions of power, but were more likely to have a job and so had more buying power. For people in work, household incomes were higher, holidays were longer, and working hours were often shorter. Young people were better off too – many bought consumer goods such as radios or hi-fis, and more had access to a car, even if it was one they borrowed from their parents. Of course, not everyone enjoyed these benefits. There was still a big gap between rich and poor. But although the 1970s was a grim decade for some, increased prosperity helped make life better for shop owners, shop workers, and some shoppers too.

1977	1978	1978	1978	1979
Star Wars is screened in Britain for the first time.	The 'Winter of Discontent' begins when several strikes by local-authority workers coincide with a pay freeze.	Louise Brown, the first baby to be conceived by IVF, is born.	The May Day bank holiday is introduced in Britain.	The Conservative leader Margaret Thatcher becomes Britain's first woman Prime Minister.

The Common Market

B y the end of the 1960s shopping played a greater part in people's lives than ever before. There was simply more to buy: after the wage increases of the late 1950s and 1960s the volume of goods sold by retailers had increased by around 2.5 per cent per year. This extra spending was partly in areas such as food and clothes, where there was more choice, but people were also spending more on consumer durables, especially electric appliances. By 1970 most households had a television, a refrigerator, a washing machine and more than one radio. In the 1970s the quality and sophistication of these goods was increasing – for example, colour television broadcasting had begun in Britain in 1967, and many viewers were trading up to a colour TV. So for many it was a decade of consumerism, of trying new gadgets and enjoying a bit more luxury.

On the High Street, this consumerism meant the arrival or expansion of some shops. There were more electrical retailers, of course, furniture shops did well and retailers of DIY and home-decorating items were on the increase. But the traditional big High Street names were also still strong: in a town of any size there would be a Boots selling medicines, toiletries and a range of household items; WH Smith offering its winning mix of newspapers, magazines, stationery and books; and Marks & Spencer, with its reputation for good value and sound quality in clothing. The supermarkets were a strong presence too, although today's famous names were more regionally based than now. Tesco and Sainsbury's still had most of their stores in the southern half of England; in the North the market was dominated by regional chains such as Morrisons. Big cities had their small

Opposite Chocolate bars and packets of sweets make an attractive display at the general store.

Above In the 1970s, more shoppers stocked up for the whole week in one go and the supermarket trolley was a common sight at stores like this branch of Tesco.

chains of clothing stores or grocers, and the Co-op was still organised regionally.

Retailing was also more efficient than ever before. Self-service had spread widely, and this way of selling enabled retailers to reduce staff numbers and also to employ less-skilled staff at lower wages. As sales increased too, this proved a winning formula at the start of the 1970s. But the economic crisis of the middle of the decade led proprietors to be cautious. For the larger retailers, this meant taking a more strategic approach, expanding, taking as much control as possible over distribution, stressing own-brand products that were cheaper to produce and generally taking advantage of the economies of scale. So Tesco, for example, concentrated on large stores. In 1972 the chain owned 518 stores of less than 5,000 square feet, but in 1981 it had only 131 stores of this size, while its handful of superstores (of over 25,000 square feet) had expanded to 66 by the start of the 1980s.

For firms like Tesco and Sainsbury's branding was key. One strategy was to put a huge emphasis on the retailer's own brand. Another approach, explored to begin with by the more specialised chains, was to develop several brands, each pitched at a target group. This was especially effective in clothes retailing, where, since the explosion of youth culture in the 1950s and 1960s, the market has been very fragmented. Young people do not want to buy the clothes their parents wear and do not want to be seen in the shops their parents visit.

For smaller, local retailers, coming to terms with these new market realities was harder. The traditional route would have been to stress service and quality, in the hope that consumers would find it worth paying a premium for these. But in the economic slump of the mid-1970s this worked only in the most affluent areas. The corner shop or small local supermarket in a small town had to pull out all the stops – offer the best possible value, stay open all hours and stock what local people wanted. If they could do this they had the chance of surviving to take advantage of the more prosperous times that came at the end of the decade and in the 1980s.

IT'S NOT JUST ABOUT SHOPS

Increasingly, the High Street became the home of all kinds of businesses that weren't shops at all, but were connected in various ways to the service industries. This trend reflected a wider change in the British economy, away from manufacturing and towards services, and it has continued to the present. So the High Street became more and more the place where people went to book a holiday, arrange a loan or find somewhere to live.

A lot of these new businesses were in the financial services sector. As well as the banks, many of which had been on the High Street since the 19th century, there were more and more branches of building societies and insurance companies. When house prices rose sharply, as they did in the late 1970s and the early 1980s, they were joined by more and more estate agents. Then there were a host of businesses offering personal services, from opticians to beauticians, hairdressers to dance studios and keep-fit classes. Add to the mix restaurants in increasing numbers and business services, from printers to employment agencies (some occupying first-floor offices, but more and more wanting the publicity afforded by a proper shop front), and the High Street was more varied than ever before.

With all these new businesses muscling in on the High Street, the total number of ordinary shops dropped. The decrease in High Street space was partly made up by new town-centre developments – shopping centres and malls. But overall in the

Below One advantage of vinyl LPs was that their large covers were decorated with distinctive artwork. This was not only attractive to music buyers but also a boon for retailers creating enticing shop window displays.

1970s there were fewer shops. One old name that saw a decline in numbers was the Co-op: between 1966 and 1975 the total number of its stores fell by about half. However, although shop numbers fell, sales went up, the number of people employed in retailing rose slightly and the stores tended to be bigger. These bigger stores were most often owned by the multiples, and one of the most common complaints about High Streets in the 1970s and the following decades

was that they increasingly all looked the same, with branches of multiples, both old names like Woolworth's and newer ones such as TopShop, dominating the scene.

Even where new products appeared and lines diversified, existing stores often expanded to create new counters or whole new departments. Ranges of cosmetics, for example, expanded rapidly, but the result was not new beauty shops, but larger branches of Boots. The vinyl record remained popular throughout the 1970s, but in many towns people bought their records from WH Smith or Woolworth's rather than from a specialist retailer. But things were slightly different in smaller towns. Here the market was not always large enough to attract a multiple retailer, and a town might have an independent chemist rather than a Boots, for example. In such an atmosphere of independent trading, a keen local entrepreneur could begin a new business, opening, say, a record shop and making it work because he was knowledgeable about music and keen to get to know the tastes of customers.

Above This branch of Woolworth's in Barnsley opened in 1971 and is a typical design of the early 1970s, featuring lots of concrete. Praised as 'ultra-modern' in the 1970s, this was a style that soon fell out of favour.

STORES IN DECLINE

Department stores as a whole did not do well in the 1970s. A combination of the recession of the beginning of the decade and high rents in town-centre locations put many of them out of business. In central London, for example, where the rents were the highest of all, a number of department stores closed. Whiteley's in Bayswater, Derry & Toms in Kensington, Gamage's in Holborn, Swan & Edgar at Piccadilly Circus and Bourne & Hollingsworth in Oxford Street all closed. Other stores changed hands, Oxford Street's DH Evans becoming a branch of House of Fraser, for example. One reason why so many department stores went to the wall is that since the 1960s retailing had been changing too rapidly for these big enterprises to keep up. Smaller shops, by contrast, could reinvent themselves more easily, whether this meant a change of stock to reflect new fashions or a complete revamp of the building. As they did so, the old department stores looked out-of-date and stuck in their ways.

Shoppers' attitudes had changed too. The novelist Marghanita Laski, in an article in *Vogue*, described the kind of customer loyalty, based on social class and attitudes learned from the previous generation, that lay behind shopping in the 1950s: 'our relationships with our favourite stores are indissoluble. For most of us, the choice is made, not by exercise of free will, but by factors as inevitable and remorseless as the processes of birth or history.' In such an atmosphere, shop assistants became 'teachers and mentors' who had a huge influence over what people thought and bought.

But by the 1970s, people, especially the young, were challenging these old ideas. Thanks to the social changes of the 1960s – the revolution in taste that affected music, clothes and food in particular – young people had become consumers, confident in their own choices and unwilling to follow the advice of shop assistants or the older generation. They wanted somewhere modern to buy their clothes and their records, or to eat, somewhere responsive to their own tastes.

Not all department stores were unchanging dinosaurs. The big shops did their best to respond to new demands, aiming their stock more deliberately at working-class customers to take advantage of their increasing affluence in the 1970s. And some store companies, such as the John Lewis Partnership, even had their own research staff, which investigated new sources of stock and did market research too. But most department-store proprietors wanted to be different from the chains like Marks & Spencer and Woolworth's, and this meant maintaining their middle-class, rather old-fashioned atmosphere.

Clothing stores like the middle-of-the-road Peter Robinson, with its flagship store at Oxford Circus and branches around the country, were especially affected by the rise of youth culture. They shed lines and whole departments designed to appeal to more mature customers, placing more and more stress on youth until the chain was rebranded as TopShop and aimed fairly and squarely at young women and girls. TopMan targeted the young male market in the same way. Meanwhile the older women who had shopped at Peter Robinson mostly looked to stores, such as Marks & Spencer, which stayed more traditional in their outlook, stressing quality as much as style. More than ever there was a generation gap on the High Street, with conservative-minded mothers perpetuating an urban myth about the poor workmanship in clothes bought at the youth-oriented stores. 'They told us that dresses and skirts bought at shops like that would fall apart,' one 1970s teenager recalls. But such advice went unheeded, and chains like TopShop continued to do well.

Since the 1970s the stress on youth marketing has continued, with clothing chains aimed specifically at young people increasingly common on the High Street. But the chains have not forsaken older consumers. Businesses such as the Burton Group operate a range of different stores, each aimed at a specific area of the market. So Burton operates Principles, TopShop, Evans and Dorothy Perkins for women, and a parallel series of men's shops, covering altogether a broad range of consumers, ages and tastes.

THE CHANGING GENERAL STORE

The general store in a small town that also had a supermarket – or was near a larger town with a supermarket – was often a marginal business. People would do their large shops at the supermarket and only go to the general store when they ran out of something, for impulse buys or when the other retailers were closed. So general stores did a lot of their business during odd hours, late at night or early in the morning, for example, when the other shops were not open. They also benefited from the custom of elderly people who were not so mobile, and those too poor to run a car, which they would probably need to get to the supermarket and do a large shop. Such customers were unlikely to spend a lot of money.

Of all the problems facing small general stores in their competition with the large supermarkets, the biggest was pricing. Companies like Tesco and Sainsbury's are vast, and buy their goods in huge quantities. They can negotiate rock-bottom prices and pass these on to customers, both in the form of special offers and generally low prices across the store. The supermarkets were especially keen to get the price of certain key items as low as possible. These were the 'Known Value Items' (KVIs) that shoppers bought regularly – things like tea, sugar and baked beans. When the supermarkets introduced own-brand goods, these were usually KVIs, but bought-in KVIs would also be very keenly priced. This way, shoppers familiar with the prices would be able to see instantly that they were getting a bargain.

Below Food, confectionery, and novelty items were the mainstays of the 1970s general store. Another income stream came from delivering newspapers to customers in the surrounding area.

The small shopkeeper, on the other hand, bought most of his goods from a local cash-and-carry. If the business was a general store, the owner might have to deal with several different cash-and-carries, perhaps one for general foods, one for sweets and another for meat. The buying side of the business was important and the shopkeeper needed a van and the time to go around and collect and pay for the goods. In the wholesale outlets, there was little flexibility on the price of KVIs or other goods, so the shop owner had little scope to discount. The value-conscious shopper would leave these items in the shop and put them on the list for the next visit to the supermarket.

On the other hand, a way in which the small shop could score over a supermarket was to operate as a family business, keeping wage costs low. While one family member did the buying, another could serve in the shop, with the 'buyer' coming back to help serve at busy times. Younger members of the family might also help out when the parents had to go off and prepare meals or attend to other duties. A part of the community that was especially good at this kind of working were Asian immigrants, many of whom came to Britain in the 1960s and early 1970s. Immigration from Britain's former colonies had begun on a large scale with the arrival of the *Empire Windrush* from Jamaica in 1948. The 1950s and 1960s had seen many people arrive from the Caribbean and some from India and Pakistan.

Above In London's Brick Lane, this general store of the late 1970s was packed to the ceiling with stock, including an impressive range of fresh produce. It would have been a regular port of call for people both living and working in this part of East London.

The Asian people who came to Britain in the post-war period went into many different jobs. Some took up menial positions in everything from textile mills in the north of England to hospitals in the Midlands. But many were more ambitious. They might already have had a British-style education in their country of origin, and saw Britain not only as their natural second home but also as a place where there were opportunities. This group included many people of South Asian origin – not just those from India and Pakistan, but also the new influx that began in 1972 when many ethnic Asians fled Uganda to escape the oppressive regime of Idi Amin.

Many of the new arrivals took to shop work, and many began their own businesses. Like most shopkeepers, they started small, often using contacts in their own communities to begin door-to-door selling, later perhaps graduating to a market stall and building up the skills and the capital to open a shop. In northern cities such as Newcastle they did this against a background of high unemployment – opting for self-employment was for many a way of avoiding the dole. But many brought a combination of hard work and entrepreneurial flair to their new role in retailing, establishing businesses that were to last decades. Typically, they opened for long hours every day and crammed their shops with a vast range of stock designed to appeal to members of the immigrant community and indigenous people alike.

These new business people combined their strong work ethic with the kind of extended family structures that lent themselves to running a family shop. As a result the 1970s was the decade in which Asian-owned general stores became a valued presence on Britain's High Streets. In many families the shop passed seamlessly from the older generation to the next, and such general stores have been around ever since.

Voluntary societies

One way in which a small general store could improve its chances was to join up with one of the 'voluntary groups' such as Spar or APT. These offered a range of facilities that could increase trade. If you joined Spar, for example, you got a Spar signboard for your shop, so that it looked as if you were a branch of a large grocery chain. You could sell the group's own-brand goods, and there was also the benefit of national advertising and special offers, with their own proper printed posters and flyers. Geoff Bonnett, a shopkeeper in Market Harborough, remembers deciding to join Spar just after taking over his shop in 1976:

I'd done quite a bit of homework before I actually took over the shop and decided that belonging to a voluntary group was a good idea. It gave an image to the shop, it gave you a respected own-label, an alternative to the brand name in the shop. It had certain advantages for me in that I didn't have to go to cash-and-carry, the orders were delivered to the shop, far less hassle, and for many years it worked extremely well.

The fact that belonging to a voluntary group like Spar cut down the work and simplified things for the retailer was a major advantage. A general-store manager or owner had a wide range of goods and these could come from many different sources. As well as journeys to the wholesaler there could be visits from a host of different reps and salespeople, and seeing them all took time.

Even for shops selling a restricted range of goods, seeing reps could be time-consuming. For example, Alice Burton recalled her time running a sweet shop in Stamford, Lincolnshire. She carried a wide stock, from jars of boiled sweets to bull's eyes, from children's favourites like jelly babies to high-class chocolates. At one stage as many as 25 different reps were calling at the shop to try to sell her sweets. Each visit could be lengthy, and each time a rep called, the shopkeeper had to negotiate prices and arrange for deliveries. There was no voluntary group like Spar that catered just for sweet shops, so someone running this kind of business had to deal directly with the companies, with all the work this entailed. For sweet shops the situation became slightly easier towards the end of the decade, when the number of dedicated confectionery wholesalers grew. But these wholesalers were never that widespread, so the shop owner might have to make a long journey to visit them – again, more work and extra petrol to pay for.

Below Spar was a familiar brand in the 1970s. Customers learned to expect a combination of value and good service from grocers who became members of Spar.

THE GROWING SUPERMARKETS

With the new freedom of pricing that had followed the abolition of Resale Price Maintenance in 1964, both multiples and supermarkets could flourish. They could exploit the benefits of buying in bulk, and could promote their stores with special offers. There was more choice on price and shoppers increasingly looked to the supermarkets for their weekly shop. Supermarket pioneers such as Alan Sainsbury were very clear that they wanted to offer good value, and that it was worth trading the old ways of personal service for keener prices: 'It has always struck me as socially unjustifiable and economically unsound that a customer who gets credit, home delivery, plus personal service should pay the same as a customer who goes into a shop, pays cash on the nail and takes the particular article away with her.'

For Sainsbury, competition was a good thing, and his outlook, like that of other supermarket pioneers, was a breath of fresh air on the High Street after years of control and austerity. The attitude of customers changed too. People were less loyal to specific retailers and shopped around more. The development

BEST BEFORE

Today supermarkets have sophisticated computer systems to help them keep tabs on their stock. As soon as an item is scanned, the checkout sends information about the sale to the warehouse, and the shop need never be out of stock. In the 1970s there was nothing like this. Supermarket managers had to watch their stock like hawks, to make sure new goods were ordered before any line ran too low. They also had to make sure that the older stock was sold first – but not, in the case of food, if it was going off. Back in the 1950s Marks & Spencer plc's management devised a series of printed codes on packaging to help them keep tabs on stock. Other stores used similar systems. Date codes helped warehouse and shop staff know when an item of food was no longer fresh, or when to reduce it for a quick sale.

Many customers were unaware of these date codes, but in the 1970s consumer journalists publicised them and complained that stores sometimes sold 'out of date' goods. As a result, food retailers adopted a more transparent system, with dates readable by customers. This was much easier to understand, and still helped managers and shopkeepers control their stock. But customers sometimes got confused about the different kinds of labelling used:

- Sell-by dates are intended to show the retailer how long an item can be kept in stock; they are intended to guide the staff, not the customer.
- Use-by dates are to tell the customer when an item is safe to eat; these dates are important safety indicators.
- Best-before dates indicate when a food will be at its best to eat, and are not indications of food safety.

In the early days of product dating, the owners of small independent supermarkets and grocers often removed 'out-of-date' stock and used it themselves. Today managers follow stringent rules about the disposal of food that is 'past its date', which has led to widespread criticism of waste.

had already started in the late 1950s. According to one study, in 1957 50 per cent of shoppers said that they invariably shopped at the same grocer's. Just three years later the figure had dropped to 25 per cent. With Resale Price Maintenance gone, this tendency increased.

So the supermarket chains expanded rapidly. After a period of vigorous expansion in the 1960s, Tesco continued to grow in the 1970s and to diversify too. In 1974 the company opened its first petrol station and by the end of the decade Tesco's annual sales had reached £1 billion, and £2 billion in 1982. This growth came in spite of the fact that Britain hit an economic recession in the early 1970s, when Tesco actually closed a large number of stores before trade picked up again towards the end of the decade.

The other supermarket chains were growing too. Morrisons was expanding in its northern heartland – the company began in Bradford – with a policy of offering both value and good service. Like Tesco, Sainsbury's began selling petrol in 1974 and, also like their rivals, began to stock a wider range of goods. It also began to open stores away from the High Street, seeking out sites on the edges of towns for big new stores with ample parking in front of them. These new sites also provided more space for trolleys, which were needed now as weekly shops expanded, and the adjacent parking meant that shoppers could take their trolley straight to the car.

The reason that the supermarkets burgeoned in the 1970s was not just their price competitiveness. They were valued for their sheer convenience, which allowed a busy home-maker to buy everything for the week in a single shop. This appealed especially to the growing number of women who were holding down a full-time job while also doing the lion's share of the shopping and the housework. This trend began in the post-war years and grew through the 1960s and, especially, 1970s. One woman surveyed about shopping in the 1960s put it particularly well, and her comment could just as easily apply to the experience of many in the following decade. The emphasis is on quick shopping and convenience foods:

> But when I did go back to work, that was when the supermarket was really handy. 'Cos I just didn't have time to do the cooking, because everything had to be made . . . everything had to be done right from scratch. And you accepted it, that was what homemaking was about. But when you were at work you thought 'can I have something quick'.

Checkout our shirts and ties

For most occasions, the traditional shirt and tie is still the most appropriate way to dress. And these days, buying smart clothes can be expensive.
But not at your Tesco Home 'n' Wear!
We've a super selection of colours and patterns all in easy-care polyester/cotton, with fashionable ties and belts to match.

So if it's value and range you want, Checkout Tesco.

Printed Polyester/Cotton Shirts £2.99
100% Polyester Ties Plain 99p
Fancy ..... £1.25 & £1.99
Offers subject to availability.

The "Delamare" trademark is the Tesco sign of Quality. If you look for it on every garment you buy at any Tesco store, you'll be assured of great value at low, low prices. (✔Delamare)

Checkout everything at ✪ TESCO

Prices that help keep the cost of living in check

Above Tesco were well known in the 1970s for their 'Home 'n' Wear' departments, which contained the kind of low-cost, easy-care clothing shown in this magazine advertisement.

Overleaf The Silver Jubilee of Queen Elizabeth II was celebrated in 1977. Communities all over the country held street parties on 7 June, with parades, bunting, and festive food for all.

This convenience, especially when combined with mass car ownership, helped drive another nail into the coffin of the traditional grocer. When most customers have their own car, home delivery becomes increasingly irrelevant, and home deliveries were generally phased out by the 1970s. Retailing had adapted to serve the affluent society.

With big supermarkets selling a vast range of food, butchers, bakers and other traditional specialist shops went into decline. In most towns the number of butchers and greengrocers began to fall through the 1970s as the supermarkets spread. Some bakers were casualties too, although more survived through the old expedient of opening a café or simply because people preferred their bread fresh. Fishmongers were another casualty, partly because of the British love of convenience products such as fish fingers and fishcakes, and partly because more and more people had freezers and bought frozen fish from the supermarket. So the 1970s was when many consumers left behind the traditional world of greengrocers with their poorly spelled price tickets, of fishmongers with their produce brought fresh from the coast each day, or of butchers with their ready advice on how to cook the various cuts of meat.

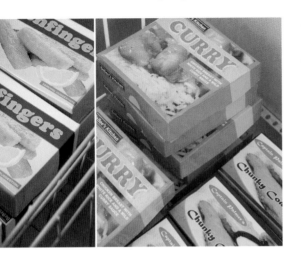

Above In supermarket freezers, familiar foods like fish fingers were joined in the 1970s by dishes such as curry. For some customers this was their first chance to taste Indian food.

The expanding supermarkets also affected other businesses. In the 1970s most British supermarkets had not begun to turn themselves into hypermarkets on the American model, selling everything from clothes to televisions, garden equipment to medicines. Tesco opened a hypermarket in Irlam, Greater Manchester, in 1976, but it was not successful and the company did not invest in more such superstores until the very end of the decade. But supermarkets were expanding and many sold non-food items such as clothes and kitchen utensils – an area that Morrisons referred to as 'lifestyle', a word that became increasingly familiar. This side of the business had its effect on clothes and other specialist shops, but not to the extent that it does today. People still saw the supermarket as above all the place to do the weekly food shop.

THE MOVE OUT OF TOWN

The 1970s saw the beginning of the trend that has changed shopping most in the last few decades: the move to large out-of-town, car-friendly developments. Out-of-town malls began in the USA. The first examples appeared there as long ago as the 1920s, though more were built from the 1950s onwards. In Britain shopping moved towards the edges of towns with supermarkets in the 1970s.

Retailing adapted to suit its new edge-of-town settings, although designing a building for a large out-of-town supermarket posed a challenge to architects and planners. What should this relatively new building type look like? Modernist designers favoured the simple factory-like 'shed' with flat roof, steel girders and plain walls. But towards the end of the decade ASDA's architects came up with a different idea. Why not make a supermarket like a barn, with sweeping tiled roofs, big gables and brick walls? One of the first examples was the ASDA in South Woodham Ferrers, Essex, and this kind of supermarket became known among architects as the 'Essex barn'. Because they represented a sort of fake vernacular architecture, many were snooty about 'Essex barns', especially when they sprang up in parts of the country with quite different local architecture, from Gloucestershire to Yorkshire. But these huge buildings were inoffensive to most customers, and acceptable to most council planning departments. The 'barn-style' supermarket was here to stay.

Below The large Brent Cross Shopping Centre changed the retail landscape for many shoppers in North London when it opened in 1976.

And not all supermarkets had forsaken the High Street. The big chains kept many of their town-centre stores and some chains, such as Marks & Spencer plc, stuck faithfully to their old buildings in such locations. It was still possible to shop 'the old-fashioned way' by using a mix of traditional food shops and multiples, all within walking distance of each other in the centre of town. But as more and more women took up paid work, learned to drive and even bought their own cars, this time-consuming kind of shopping seemed irrelevant to many.

Soon the food retailers were joined by a different group, companies selling electrical goods, furniture and DIY products, which set up warehouse-style retail outlets in industrial estates. Those early experiments in edge-of-town shopping proved successful. The non-food stores in these new locations also had only a small impact on the High Street because the DIY market grew from builders' merchants who were not High Street businesses, while the electrical-goods sector was largely an expansion, representing the new swathe of inexpensive consumer electronics. It was perhaps only the big furniture sellers who took much business away from the town centres.

But at the same time a very different development in out-of-town shopping began: the out-of-town mall. One of the first was the Weston Favell Shopping Centre, which opened in 1975 close to new housing developments east of Northampton. This was placed to attract both shoppers from the new houses and customers who would come from further afield in their cars. Clean-looking and white, with its shops sited above a covered car park and linked to nearby residential areas by pedestrian bridges, the Weston Favell Shopping Centre looked futuristic. It was soon followed by other large malls, most notably North-West London's Brent Cross, which was completed in 1976. Near the edge of London but not far from the suburban High Street of Golders Green, Brent Cross set the style for future out-of-town developments. With a large store at either end and a connecting section with lots of smaller shops, it had a glass dome that brought natural light to the main space. There was plenty of car-parking and the mall was carefully sited close to the North Circular Road.

Similar developments followed on the edges of many British cities, but only Brent Cross was anywhere near in size to the vast malls that opened in the 1980s and 1990s around major cities such as Birmingham, Newcastle, Sheffield, Leeds, Manchester and Bristol. Weston Favell and Brent Cross pointed to the future, and the impact of out-of-town malls on Britain's High Streets was felt most strongly towards the end of the 20th century.

EATING OUT, NEW-STYLE AND OLD-STYLE

Britain in the 1970s was more adventurous when it came to food than the 'meat and two veg' nation of the post-war period. There were several reasons for this. In books such as *French Provincial Cooking*, first published in 1960, Elizabeth David had introduced the middle classes to the joys of European cuisine. In the 1970s David's readers were more likely to holiday in France or Italy, so the culinary horizons of the middle classes were broadening further and French and Italian restaurants were opening in larger or more prosperous towns.

The influx of immigrants from Asia also added to the culinary mix and both Chinese and Indian restaurants and takeaways became common. Many British people got their first taste of foreign cooking from an Asian takeaway, and Indian and Chinese food have been popular in Britain ever since. But in the 1970s there was still a widespread resistance to 'foreign food' and many a Chinese restaurant also offered one or two British items on the menu, while Chinese takeaway outlets often served chips, sausages and other British staples. There was a similar reaction against trends such as health foods, wholefoods and vegetarianism – none of them new ideas but all gaining ground in the period.

What many British people still wanted was a plate of fish and chips – or egg and chips, or pie and chips, or anything else and chips. The old-fashioned 'greasy spoon', beloved not just of lorry drivers and market workers, but of nearly everyone, would not go away. So, many café owners kept their deep-fat fryer along with a freezer and the latest cooking technology – a microwave oven –

THE MICROWAVE

The microwave oven was invented as a by-product of research into radar and was patented in the USA in the 1950s. It works by firing microwave radiation at the food, which makes certain molecules – notably water molecules – in the food move rapidly, making them heat up. Large, unwieldy microwaves were initially developed for the catering business. Early models were over 5 feet (1.5 m) tall and weighed some 750 pounds (340 kg). Like most new technologies, they were also cripplingly expensive – around $3,000 for an early model in the USA, where they were first manufactured. So it took a while for the microwave to be accepted, but in the following years both sizes and prices came down, and by the end of the 1960s the first compact models were produced for use in cafés and smaller restaurants and in the home.

Because it dramatically reduced cooking times, the microwave was popular with owners of small eating places who did not have the staff to cook lots of different meals at once. With a microwave you could extend the range of your menu – by having one dish on the go in the microwave

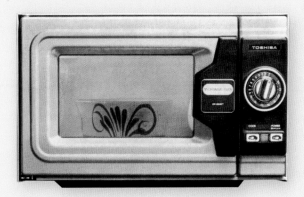

while cooking other food at a deep-fat fryer or in a conventional oven – and serve food quickly. And people soon found all kinds of ways of exploiting the microwave's fast-heating ability, using it to dry potato chips, for example, or to defrost frozen food, or warm up sauces or heat milk in a matter of seconds. They also discovered that, although they were fast and efficient, microwaves also have limitations – food does not go brown when microwaved, for example – making them unsuitable for some dishes. So microwaves did not become popular with high-class chefs, but they did have a role where speed was of the essence. And people liked the fact that, because they worked so quickly, they saved electricity too. Microwaves soon became popular with both café proprietors and their customers, once everyone had worked out which kinds of foods worked best with them, and how to avoid exploding Scotch eggs and similar disasters.

which gave them the scope both to cook food quickly and to extend the menu. Not that extending the range of the menu meant being especially adventurous. Most British people were still quite conservative in the 1970s: the traditional diet of chips with everything was favoured by the mass of the population and the microwave might be used mainly for cooking baked potatoes. But there were a few signs of new developments. The British taste for savoury snacks interacted with the influence of the Asian community to make samosas, bhajis and pakoras popular, for example.

INDIAN SNACKS

On the streets of India, fast-food snacks are made and served by cooks called 'chaat wallahs'. Britain's South Asian immigrants brought this tradition of street food with them from their homeland, and Indian snacks, often adapted to suit British tastes, are now a popular staple, available everywhere in fish and chip shops, general stores and even filling stations. Several from the wide range have proved especially popular in Britain, either as accompaniments to full Indian meals or as quick but filling snacks.

ABOVE AND LEFT *After chopping the vegetables – which include onions, potatoes and peas – and frying them with spices, the ingredients are mixed thoroughly together to make a tasty filling ready for the pastry.*

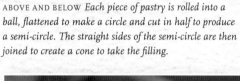
ABOVE AND BELOW *Each piece of pastry is rolled into a ball, flattened to make a circle and cut in half to produce a semi-circle. The straight sides of the semi-circle are then joined to create a cone to take the filling.*

■ **Samosas** Patties, usually made in a pyramid shape, fried, and stuffed with various ingredients, including potatoes, peas, or lentils, flavoured with spices. One of the most popular and versatile of all Indian snacks.

■ **Pakoras** Snack made by dipping the basic ingredient in a batter made from gram flour, then deep-frying. The most popular are soft cheese (paneer pakora), onion (pyaz pakora) and potato (aloo pakora). The bhaji is usually similar to a pakora.

■ **Ragda patties** Patties made from potato, with a variety of spiced fillings.

■ **Vada** Disc-shaped savoury made from dal, lentils or potatoes, traditionally served in a bun or between two slices of bread, when it is known as vada pav.

■ **Chivda** Crunchy snack made from beaten rice flakes mixed with peanuts and spices; in some versions the ingredients are deep-fried, in others microwaved or shallow-fried.

■ **Naan** The familiar leavened flatbread, which can be prepared plain or made with a variety of spices and stuffings.

NEW IDEAS IN DESIGN

Above Most boutique owners rented their premises so could not rebuild the entire shop front. But a striking sign and a good window display was usually enough to bring customers in.

Every shopkeeper wants to get people inside the shop and since the Georgian period the shop window had been the way to attract people with an enticing display. The shop window had another function too, to lead customers towards the shop entrance. So the twin bow windows of a typical Georgian shop front led the eye towards the central door, and the deep lobby of an interwar Art Deco store encouraged people to come ever closer to the door until they were 'sucked in'. The Holy Grail of shop-front design was to do away with the door completely, so that no barrier at all faced potential customers.

In the late 1960s retailers found this Holy Grail in the form of a new invention: the air curtain. An air curtain blows warm air down through a grille in the ceiling above the entrance; the air circulates through another grille in the floor and is filtered and passed up to the ceiling so that it can make the circuit again. It has the effect of keeping cold air out of the shop, meaning that the entrance can remain open all the time. Air curtains were first installed in shops within shopping centres at locations such as Birmingham's 1960s Bull Ring. By the 1970s they had spread to High Street shops as owners realised that they were worth the cost of installation and higher electricity bills. As time went on, more and more shops installed air curtains and entrances got wider too, and still more inviting. Combined with large sheets of tough plate glass, the air curtain enabled shop designers to reduce the shop front to its basics – window, entrance and fascia showing the retailer's name or logo. The important thing, once customers had identified the shop's name, was to draw their eyes to the stock inside, and this is how many retailers enticed customers in.

MUSIC IN THE HOME

Back in the 1960s the market for recorded music had exploded. Stereo sound became commercially available and vinyl records were the way to listen to music in the home. Both cheap 'singles', containing one song on each side, and albums, or LPs, were available, and there were many different units on which to play them. Most popular were simple, compact record players, with a single speaker and a turntable, and larger radiograms and stereograms, which had a radio, record player and one or two speakers built into a large wooden cabinet that looked like a piece of furniture.

In the 1970s miniaturisation revolutionised home entertainment. The use of transistors meant that the electronic innards of radios, record players and tape recorders could be made smaller. The first devices to benefit from this were radios, and transistor radios, some as small as a paperback book, had become popular in the 1960s. Both cheap and tiny, they brought personal listening to millions, including children and teenagers.

Miniaturisation came to recorded music in the form of the music centre. This was made up of three boxes – a pair of speakers and a central unit containing record deck, radio and a tape-cassette deck. With a music centre, you could not only listen to records and tapes, but also record music directly from vinyl, making duplicates and compilation tapes possible. The separate speakers also gave a better stereo effect than the old one-piece stereograms, although the sound quality of music systems varied – some, with very basic electronics, sounded tinny or muffled, others approached hi-fi quality. For those with more money who wanted better sound, there were also hi-fi separates, in which each part of the system – amplifier, turntable, speakers and so on – was in a different box, each built with sound quality in mind. But for most people the music centre, compact, easy to use and inexpensive, was the choice.

The popularity of music centres and hi-fi was based on a burgeoning market in

Below Japanese company Sansui made their name with hi-fi. This combination of separates – record deck, tuner, cassette deck, and amplifier – was designed to sit together in a cabinet, minimising unsightly connecting cables.

Sansui High Rise Hi-Fi

Way above the common or garden system.

If you want the performance of separate hi-fi without the tiring wiring, raise your sights. To Sansui High Rise Hi-Fi.

It's as neat as a music centre, but it's pure hi-fi from top to bottom. With Sansui High Rise, you can enjoy records, radio, or tapes—and we do mean enjoy.

A pulsing light indicates radio signal strength. Two large meters tell you when your recording levels are spot-on. There's even a cunning little 'traffic light' which first monitors peak reception, then locks in the station for you.

The cassette deck is Dolby* of course — and there's a press-button selector to get the best performance from different types of tape.

Now the best feature: prices for the range of Sansui High Rise systems start from around £300 complete with speakers. Get the lowdown on High Rise Hi-Fi. Post the coupon.

Sansui

Even the name makes music

Dolby is a trade mark of Dolby labs inc.

THE 1970s HIGH STREET

VINYL FORMATS

The 1970s was the golden age of the vinyl record, because there was a vast range of recorded music on the market, young people had more money to spend on music and there were plenty of places to buy it. Buyers had a choice of formats. For many, especially the young, the way to buy music was as 7-inch 'singles'. This was how most bands released their individual songs and people would hear new singles on the radio and rush out to buy them. They played at 45 rpm and you got the bonus of another, less highly promoted track on the 'B' side.

Music lovers also bought albums of tracks, usually including hit singles, which were played at 33 rpm. When they first appeared these long-players, or LPs, were seen as expensive items, aimed at older consumers with more disposable income than the buyers of singles. But in the 1970s everyone collected LPs. Rock and pop bands increasingly saw the album as a total work of art, often containing songs that were related or covered a similar theme. LPs were also the format of choice for classical music, where longer playing times were important, and for anyone looking for a compilation of an artist's

best songs or hits. The size of the 12-inch LP made the front of the album cover an important feature and often the notes on the back were read avidly, and the whole package became a collectable object. For all these reasons, albums became increasingly popular in the 1970s.

ABOVE AND TOP *Customers could look through selections of LP covers and, when they found a disc they wanted to sample, they could take it to a record deck fitted with headphones, for a quiet spin.*

There were also 'extended play' records, or EPs, halfway houses that had a longer playing time than a single but were shorter than an LP. Some of these were mini-albums, gathering together three or four previously issued tracks to give the music extra sales. Others included original material that had not been issued previously. Or EPs provided a format for extra-long tracks, such as the extended jam 'Voodoo Chile' (1971) by Jimi Hendrix. The EP was not a format: it could be a 7-inch disc, played at 45 rpm, that simply contained more music than a single; or it could be a 10- or 12-inch disc, played at 33 rpm. In addition, 12-inch vinyl singles began to appear in 1977, providing still more choice for the record buyer.

ABOVE, LEFT AND BELOW *LPs were kept in enticing 'browser' stacks. Customers could thumb through these but if they could not find what they wanted, the proprietor was always ready to advise.*

vinyl – both singles and albums were selling well. Although singles were mostly limited to the pop market, there were plenty of LPs across all genres, from pop, through jazz and 'easy listening', to classical. Many towns had a record shop with a large selection, while other kinds of shops, including music stores and chains such as WH Smith, also sold recorded music on both vinyl and cassette.

Record stores were popular places for teenagers to hang out. There would always be music playing, and if you ran a record shop you kept a close eye on the pop charts to see what was selling. Most record shops had listening booths where customers could sample a record before buying. Inevitably, young customers liked to sample a lot of music, often without intending to buy anything, but most shop owners tolerated this. Like today's Internet retailers, they knew that sometimes it's hard to resist buying something once you have heard it. In addition, a shop that was full of customers was good for trade, and the sight of people enjoying themselves would attract more customers through the door.

FASHION HIGH AND LOW

If there were fewer food shops on the High Street during the 1970s, the number of clothes shops was on the increase, especially after the economic difficulties of the early part of the decade were less in evidence. Clothes retailers continued to grow, as they had in the 1960s, in response to fast-changing youth cultures, and, as young people had more and more money in their pockets, wearing the right clothes became increasingly important, a part of being attractive and cool. As in the 1960s, it was the small, young businesses that took the lead here. This was even more true when the economy took its downturn, as small boutique-style shops could adapt, keep costs low and in some cases survive the worst the recession could throw at them. Most were run on the cheap, with the proprietor designing and often making the clothes, and sometimes working in the shop too. Locations were up side-streets, to avoid expensive High Street rents, but this did not matter, because part of the buzz of visiting one of these shops was that it was off the beaten track.

The young customers who visited these boutiques knew about them by word of mouth, and if a shop took off, it became one of the places to be seen. Shop owners soon

Below The boutique owner shows off an example of her stock from the fast-changing and varied fashion scene of the 1970s.

Above This group of punks, caught on camera in the early 1970s, are showing off many of their favourite fashions – leather, zippers, badges, military-style caps and jackets, and of course loud hair colours.

became friendly with regular customers, sharing their tastes in clothes and music, and the experience of visiting a shop like this was the polar opposite of shopping in a department store, with its rigid hierarchies and its sometimes intimidating staff. So these fashionable little shops didn't need an impressive window display, or even a very big window. As Marnie Fogg puts it in her book *Boutique*, 'Boutiques in obscure back streets and side alleys had little use of a window display. Passing trade was insignificant in the context of word of mouth and the grapevine.'

In many ways the boutique turned traditional retailing upside down. The window display was not important, the interiors were often rather dark compared with the usual 'see everything' approach of most shops and there was often loud music. Low-volume piped music was by now common in many stores and there was a whole science of choosing the best music to relax customers and put them in the mood for purchasing. But boutique music was often much more dominating – the beat pulsated throughout the shop and some owners claimed that the higher they turned up the volume the more clothes they sold.

What was actually sold in these shops changed rapidly. The youth scene did not respect the traditional cycles of fashion, with its seasons and responses to what was being shown on catwalks in Paris. Inspiration came instead from television, films and that week's *Top of the Pops*. George Melly caught the mood in his book *Revolt Into Style*. He was writing at the beginning of the 1970s about the previous decade, but his description summed up an effect that continued:

GILL COCKWELL
Boutique owner

I've been pleasantly surprised. I had this funny image of the 1970s being really tacky and nylon-y and synthetic but actually my boutique is super-stylish and I love it! I've sold some really beautiful dresses and they looked absolutely great on the girls who bought them. It's been ever so easy to sell stuff because I've got some great stock. They're all one-off pieces and all the dresses are good quality. And everyone has commented on how good they think the shop looks. I've got a new sign which people really like and I've had some good feedback about the shop's name.

It's been a very good day, I've taken a lot more money in this era than in the previous periods, but I feel exhausted. It might be because I'm used to dealing with customers one-on-one rather than a whole shop full of people all asking questions at the same time. So I've found it difficult to concentrate at times. But I'm still absolutely loving it.

'TV programmes such as "Ready Steady Go!" made pop work on a truly national scale. It plugged in direct to the centre of the scene and only a week later transmitted information as to clothes, dances, gestures, even slang to the whole British teenage Isles.'

Everyone now had access to the mass media, and youth fashions changed fast. Hippy looks left over from the late 1960s vied with flared trousers and platform shoes just as the followers of progressive rock vied with devotees of pub rock. By the mid-1970s the big development in youth culture was punk – urban, aggressive and in your face. If the music was discordant, loud and iconoclastic, so were the clothes. Punk revelled in torn fabrics, zippers in odd places, safety pins and chains. From big Doc Marten boots to razor-blade pendants, punk was in a way anti-fashion. But not so anti-fashion that it could not be sold and marketed, as Vivienne Westwood found when she opened her shop on the Kings Road, London, with Malcolm McLaren. The shop, at first called Sex (it was later Seditionaries, and later still, when Westwood embraced other styles, World's End), sold clothes to the Sex Pistols and other punk bands, and soon the style was being copied, and sold, more widely.

A year or so after punk began, its ideas were being translated off the streets into the mainstream, with international designers adopting many of the motifs and the 'distressed' or torn look. Youth fashion, though, moved on, endlessly changing and dividing into a mosaic of subcultures – from gothic and post-punk to mod revival – all of which needed clothing from small, side-street shops where young people went because they were the place to go.

By the end of the 1970s Britain's shopping habits had changed radically. Most households owned a car and had a freezer at home, so their preferred method of food shopping was to drive to a big supermarket on the edge of town and load up with at least a week's groceries. They might also buy furniture or electrical goods from an out-of-town site too. The big shopping chains had responded to this trend – not only with more out-of-town stores but also with marketing ploys that lured more and more customers their way: own-brand promotions, bigger, more seductive shops and additional ranges. Developments such as the vast Brent Cross shopping centre showed the way forward. Yet the city centres and High Streets still offered plenty of choice. Old-style butchers and fishmongers might have been dwindling, but plenty of retailers, from chains like Boots to clothes shops, were doing well.

Below By the late 1970s Habitat had 27 stores and a lavish catalogue. The cover sums up some of the company's key selling points – simple, good-quality style in a range of colours for every decorative scheme.

So the 1970s were a time of transition in retailing. The seeds of the big shift out of town were sown, but most companies had not made the move. Supermarkets were everywhere, but there were still a few traditional grocers. There were hints of the growing restaurant and café culture, but most people still liked traditional food. Terence Conran's Habitat stores, founded in 1964, were popularising good design, but there were still many traditional furniture and hardware shops too. And the time-honoured corner shop was still serving local communities by adapting to new fashions and needs.

As the trend away from small, traditional shops continued into the 1980s, the retail sector as a whole did well in the economic boom. And in the early years of the 21st century many retailers built on their success as the sector became more and more important to the economy with the decline in manufacturing and the increasing focus on the service industries. But in many towns the High Street itself suffered as out-of-town shopping increased in popularity. At the same time, many people believe that British High Streets have become less characterful and more dominated by a small number of big firms.

So, as the High Street faces the aftermath of the global financial crisis, retailing needs all the adaptability it showed in previous eras, especially that of the 1970s. The decade's mixture of hard-nosed business sense, expansion and innovation on the one hand, matched with respect for traditional values on the other, has much to offer to retailers today, whether they sell goods in a vast shopping mall or in an old-fashioned shop on the High Street itself.

Overleaf Images from the 1970s High Street, featuring up-to-date equipment such as the electronic till and the pricing gun, and traditional products from vinyl LPs to stylish dresses.

Chapter Eight

The Future of the High Street

Since the end of the 1970s British retailing has changed a great deal, although many of the changes have grown from seeds sown 30 years ago. Developments from the shopping mall to the Internet have posed huge challenges to conventional businesses on the High Street. But there are also more recent trends, from the increasing move towards ethical shopping to the preservation of historic town centres, that are giving some retailers a new lease of life.

Retailing as big business

A key development then was the move to out-of-town developments that started in the late 1970s. This has continued, not just with the vast shopping centres on the edges of major cities, but also with retail 'parks' and centres near virtually every sizeable town. Out-of-town shopping is big business, and, like the rest of British retailing, it is dominated by the multiples – one study puts the market share of independent retailers at under 10 per cent. From food to fashion, the chains are big businesses, and they dominate both the out-of-town centres and the High Street.

Part of the power of the chains comes from technology. Computerised stock control allows retailers to keep a constant electronic eye on what they buy and sell. Retailers also keep an eye on consumers, using loyalty cards to gather data about who buys what, so that they can target advertising and offers. The information superhighway can also make the whole supply chain shrink dramatically. A fashion designer can produce a design for a garment, get it approved and ordered by a retailer, have it produced in bulk in the Far East and have it in the shops in just a few weeks.

Consumers like this rapid-response technology, too, hence the rise of online shopping. Where Amazon led the way, a host of others have followed, selling music, holidays, financial services, groceries and almost everything else via the Internet. Even items such as clothes, which many people like to try on before they buy, are now widely bought online. The combination of value and home delivery is a big draw for millions of customers.

Opposite With some 330 stores and parking for 13,000 cars, Bluewater in Kent is Britain's second largest out-of-town shopping mall.

THE ETHICAL REACTION

Above Westfield, a vast shopping centre in London's Shepherds Bush, was opened in 2008. Its roster of around 250 stores is impressive, but there are fears that it will take business away from traditional High Streets in West London.

Both online shopping and the bricks-and-mortar multiples have brought prices tumbling. All kinds of goods, especially food and clothes, are cheaper now in real terms than they were 20 years ago. This has happened because of the enormous power of big retailers to buy in huge bulk and to dictate the terms at which they buy. And the implications for the producers, when a supermarket chain can offer two pairs of jeans for £5, are huge. There have been many accusations of sweatshop factories in Asia, and, as Jane Shepherdson, former boss of TopShop, has said, 'If something is very, very cheap, then someone, somewhere down the line is paying.' Many consumers feel uncomfortable with the buying power of the big supermarkets and other chains, but at the same time Britain has bought into this price revolution: good value is popular.

The idea of ethical shopping is a corrective to the unquestioning acceptance of cheap goods instantly delivered. The ethics of retailing is now a huge concern for many who no longer simply accept cheap mass-produced food or clothes without at least asking how it was produced, how the production process has affected the environment and whether the workers who produced it were properly treated. A concern for the environment has attracted people to organic foods; commitment to animal welfare leads some to seek out ethically farmed beef and millions to buy free-range eggs. The move towards farmers' markets in many places is part of this tendency – a desire to be reconnected with the food producer, to learn how the food is produced, to try different items from a range of sources and to keep food local. And when it comes to imported goods, the Fairtrade movement is now enormous, embracing a trading system that works for better trading conditions and sustainable development, and that encourages people to think about the conditions under which their goods are produced, bought and sold.

ON THE STREET

All these changes have made a huge difference to Britain's town centres. The move out of town left its scars, and some towns have High Streets with little but empty shops, pound stores and charity shops. The global economic crisis has done nothing to improve matters – several familiar names have disappeared, including shoe retailer Dolcis, home-entertainment chain Zavvi and of course Woolworth's. In addition, many independent businesses have gone, often as a result of competition from online merchants. Small booksellers, independent travel agents, insurance brokers, music shops and others are all now thin on the ground. The desolate High Streets that result confirm some of the criticism of many British towns in books such as *Crap Towns: The Fifty Worst Places to Live in the UK* and its sequel, *Crap Towns II: The Nation Decides*. Although such books are light-hearted, and booming cities such as Bath are included in the second volume, they are a symptom of the anxiety people feel about our towns and their centres in times of change and difficulty.

In the current economic climate it is often difficult for small independent retailers to take advantage of the empty units in town centres. This is because, even during an economic depression, it costs a lot to have a presence on the High Street, because both leases and business rates are expensive. Modern planning practice does not always make it easy for the shopkeeper either. Kevin Hawkins, director of the British Retail Consortium, summed it up in a 2007 *New*

Below Originally home to a street market, Briggate in Leeds is now pedestrianised. Shoppers enjoy a range of shops dating back to Edwardian, Victorian, and earlier times. Access to several of the city's famous arcades is also from this street.

Statesman report on the state of Britain's shops: 'If you ask independent retailers where their main difficulties lie, they do not cite competition from the multiples. They talk about high rent and rates, parking restrictions and overzealous traffic wardens keeping people away.'

It is not all about empty shops, though. The multiples, committed as they are to big shopping centres, have also returned to the High Street. The supermarkets spearheaded the move, with their small local stores, designed to combine the role of High Street grocer and convenience store. Other chains that do well out of town, such as Next, have also stayed on the High Street or returned. And Boots and Marks & Spencer, now with many stores in retail parks, have never left the town centres. These chains have filled some of the gaps. But at a price – consumer choice reduces, and, from Newcastle to Newquay, the nation's High Streets have all started to look the same.

HOPE FOR THE FUTURE

So how can a town plan for the future to make its High Street successful? There are some pointers in towns that have become popular shopping centres, and often the answer seems to be to offer things that the out-of-town malls cannot provide. What is actually offered varies a lot from place to place, but there are some patterns.

One solution is to specialise. For many people shopping is a major recreation and they will travel to find good specialist shops. A town that can make a name for itself in a particular area stands a chance of prospering. A famous, though off-the-wall, example is Hay-on-Wye, a town completely dominated by shops selling secondhand books. In the time of the Internet, with its vigorous global secondhand book market, it should not work, but this little Welsh town survives and most of its booksellers are well established – many sell online as well. In addition, Hay had created one of the most successful literary festivals, to which thousands flock every year to hear authors talk about their latest books: 'The Woodstock of the mind,' Bill Clinton called it. Ludlow is another town that thrives on specialist retailing, this time in the more widely appealing area of food. This small town in the heart of the Shropshire countryside has no fewer than five butchers and four bakers, plus a mouth-watering array of delis, cheese shops and organic food shops – plus a market that sells food several days each week. Add to that an impressive roster of excellent restaurants and you have a popular destination and one of the most vibrant High Streets anywhere.

Both Hay and Ludlow are historic market towns and this makes them attractive places to visit and shop in. A number of other places have benefited still more strongly from their heritage to attract visitors who also come to shop. York, home of the famous Shambles, one of the country's most ancient shopping streets, is a case in point. Chester, with its famous Rows, late-Medieval elevated shops, is another. Few towns have such stunning historic buildings that actually house shops, but many cities could do nearly as well. And conservation bodies such as English Heritage are very supportive. They point out that old shops, with their irregular layouts and unusually shaped rooms, are often more fun to shop in than uniform modern retail units. Buildings like the old shops of cathedral cities from Durham to Salisbury create an atmosphere that is pleasant and fun; people want to be there, and want to shop there too. Planners are now well attuned to the 'history effect' and are introducing 'heritage' street furniture and opening up views of old buildings between shops to make town centres more attractive. Exeter is a particularly successful example.

Another strategy involves emphasising the quality and diversity of local shops, often in conjunction with an attractive or historical environment. Star examples here are places such as Bath or Cheltenham, where Georgian or Regency architecture complements a mixture of multiple and upmarket shops, drawing visitors in. The combination of handsome classical architecture and aspirational shops works, and both these towns are home to many successful retailers.

For smaller, more countrified places, the answer can be for the town to underline its connection to the surrounding agricultural area, holding farmers' markets, hosting shops stocking locally grown produce and creating links with local growers and farmers. If there are also good footpaths, nature reserves or similar facilities nearby, these too can help attract visitors.

All these solutions rely in one way or another on creating attractive places that are distinctive and different from the typical 'clone' shopping centre. They are also about pulling in visitors, to bring in extra revenue. But the High Street is also for the locals, and if a town is to be a useful local centre it must not turn into a theme park or a designer shopping village. So towns have to find ways of accommodating both upmarket shops and retailers offering value.

As shoppers from the Victorian period to the 1970s also knew, the High Street also needs good shopkeepers. The qualities demonstrated by retailers in the past – a commitment to service, adaptability in both good times and bad, knowledge about the stock, a flair for promotion and an instinct for what customers want – will also be needed in the future. When all these qualities come together in vibrant town centres, we'll have buzzing, successful High Streets that we can be proud of.

Above This butcher's, one of many specialist food shops in Ludlow, offers local produce, meat from rare breeds and prize-winning sausages. This is the kind of traditional retailing that has brought back life to some High Streets in Britain.

Chapter Nine

YOUR HIGH STREET'S STORY

Researching the history of your own High Street can provide fascinating insight into local history. To find out about your High Street's past, it is best to begin with a visit to your library's local-studies department. This should provide plenty of information about the history of your town or region, and may well include items, such as local documents or maps, that are not available elsewhere. Your local museum should be able to help too. You may then want to widen your search to encompass national and other archives.

Using a combination of directories, census records, old maps and photographs and local histories, you should be able to build up a picture of how your High Street has changed over the past 100 years or more. Information on some of the most important sources, including archives, websites and books, is given on the following pages.

LOCAL COLLECTIONS

County and city record offices and local reference libraries are rich sources of both published and manuscript material about the local area. Main libraries often have a local-studies section that contains material such as census records, registers of electors and all kinds of books about local history. Libraries like this are a good place to start researching to get a broad picture of a particular town or area.

Local museums are also rich sources. Most have objects, documents, old photographs and maps relating to their area. Remember that most museums only display a fraction of the objects they have, so it is worth asking a staff member about your museum's collection to find out what 'hidden' items there may be. Museum staff may also know about other collections and other researchers who might be working in the same area as you.

Opposite The historic centre of Shepton Mallet, Somerset, scene of the BBC TV series *Turn Back Time . . . The High Street*, with its small shops and ancient market cross.

More detail is contained in city and county record offices. These contain a host of resources, many of which will not be available anywhere else, such as letters, personal documents and records connected to local landholders and estates. As well as these documents, the material held by county record offices is likely to include all or most of those listed below. Many of them are held on microfiche or on hard disk, and you will probably be allowed to buy printouts of this material. Because of the large amount of material available it is worth telephoning beforehand to make initial enquiries about what the office holds, and to get information about opening hours, regulations (many archives ban pens, so you will need to come equipped with a pencil for note-taking) and other arrangements (you may have to book a microfiche reader). When you begin, consult the archive's place-name indexes to find documents relating to your town or village.

PARISH REGISTERS

These contain records of baptisms, marriages and burials which can tell you where specific families were living. Some registers also give people's occupations. Poor relief was organised by parishes between the 17th and 19th centuries, and parish records give details of the money and other support given in this way to the poor.

CENSUS RETURNS

From 1801 onwards, ten-yearly censuses have been taken in Britain, but the full enumerators' returns only exist from 1841 onwards. Enumerators' returns give some personal information about the respondents, for example, people's age, birthplace and occupation – though not all of these are recorded in the older returns. Because access to census material is restricted for 100 years, the most recent returns available are those from 1901 (and 1911 from 2011 onwards). Returns for some years are also available online, and the 1901 online returns are fully searchable, including a facility to search by street. The census provides a mine of information, but it is not always perfect – the enumerators relied upon what people told them, and occupations, for example, may give only part of the picture when someone did two jobs.

PROPERTY RECORDS

These are very useful for researching the history of shops and other businesses as they include not only deeds but also records such as planning applications, which may show how the use of a particular building has changed from one period to another.

COUNCIL RECORDS

In addition to records dealing with local taxes, council archives may also record registrations of businesses and evidence of any dealings that the council has had with specific businesses.

NATIONAL ARCHIVES

The following are the contact details of the official British national archive collections. They contain records going back to the Middle Ages, covering everything from charters and information about markets to records of wills, taxpayers, tithes, etc.

NATIONAL ARCHIVES
The official record office for England and Wales.
Ruskin Avenue, Kew, Surrey TW9 4DU
www.nationalarchives.gov.uk

NATIONAL ARCHIVES OF SCOTLAND
HM General Register House, 2 Princes Street, Edinburgh EH1 3YY
www.nas.gov.uk

PUBLIC RECORD OFFICE OF NORTHERN IRELAND
66 Balmoral Avenue, Belfast BT9 6NY
www.proni.nics.gov.uk

MAPS AND PLANS

Local archives will have many maps of their area – both original maps drawn for local reasons connected with planning or rebuilding and printed maps produced by the Ordnance Survey (OS).

Some of the most informative early maps are tithe maps, individually drawn in the mid-19th century to enable the tithe (the tax representing one-tenth of a person's income, originally paid directly to the church in kind) to be collected. Tithe maps list the owners and those occupying every property in the parish that they cover. Three copies of each tithe map were made – one will usually be in the local record office, one in the National Archives and one in church archives.

OS maps began in the late 18th century, and the OS created its first 1 inch to 1 mile general maps (the Old Series) in the early 19th century. Later came the New Series, consisting of larger-scale maps (6 inches to 1 mile and 25 inches to 1 mile), which were produced in the second half of the 19th century. The larger-scale maps contain a huge amount of detail, with individual properties marked and sometimes named.

LOCAL PUBLICATIONS

For around 200 years local newspapers were the main way a community circulated information about itself – its people, businesses, events, leisure activities, crimes and special achievements. In addition, local listings publications – directories and gazetteers – offer lots of information about the names, sites and owners of local businesses.

NEWSPAPERS

Old newspapers are fascinating sources for local history. Local reference libraries usually have back copies of newspapers going back years; the British Library's newspaper collection, based in Colindale, North London, has back copies of all the newspapers published in Britain. Libraries usually keep their back copies on microfilm.

Most newspapers are printed to a set format – for example, many modern newspapers put the news on the front pages, the sport at the back and advertisements somewhere in between. This arrangement varies from one publication to another and changes over time, so it is worth familiarising yourself with the way a newspaper is laid out by looking through a few issues quickly. Information about local shops can be found all over the newspaper, but an important area is the advertisements, which tell you which shops were where, who was selling what, what the prices were like and all sorts of fascinating detail about fashions, new gadgets, foods and other items that were on sale.

DIRECTORIES

Trade directories list the businesses and tradesmen in a particular town or district – and some include text on the character and history of the town or locality and its most prominent citizens. Some also cover subjects such as local government, as well as locations of railway stations and times of coaches. The first directories appeared in major cities in the 18th century, and by the 1830s there were directories for many smaller towns, and also a number of publications covering entire counties.

The most famous series of directories was published by Kelly's. The company's directories first came out in the 1840s, and continued to appear until the 1970s. By this time much of the information Kelly's directories contained was also available in telephone directories and the Yellow Pages, but they listed much more than the title 'directory' implies, including street-by-street sections that gave the name of the family living at each house.

Local directories were published regularly, often annually, and runs of Kelly's and other directories can be found in reference and local-studies libraries. It is often revealing to look at how a street is covered across a whole run of local directories. Comparing the names and businesses at a particular address, it is often possible to find out when a shop first began in business and to chart how it was passed down from one generation to the next or changed ownership. It is also possible to see how businesses changed over the years, an ironmonger's becoming a bazaar, for example, or a draper's turning into a clothes shop.

LIVERY COMPANIES

The City livery companies grew out of the Medieval craft guilds, organisations that had originally regulated different trades, controlling wages, quality of goods, prices and so on. Many of them have deposited their archives, which include records of apprentices, at the Guildhall Library in London. Among the many livery companies, the following are relevant to the story of retailing and shopping:

Bakers, Harp Lane, London EC1
Butchers, 87 Bartholomew Close, London EC1
Drapers, Throgmorton Street, London EC2
Fishmongers, Fishmongers Hall, London Bridge, London EC4
Fruiterers, 1 Serjeants Inn, London EC4
Grocers, Princes Street, London EC2
Haberdashers, Staining Lane, London EC2
Ironmongers, Aldersgate Street, London EC2
Leathersellers, St Helens Place, London EC3
Mercers, Ironmonger Lane, London EC2
Merchant Taylors, 30 Threadneedle Street, London EC2
Salters, Fore Street, London EC2
Stationers and Newspaper Makers, Stationers Hall, Ave Maria Lane, London EC4
Tallow Chandlers, 4 Dowgate Hill, London EC4
Vintners, Upper Thames Street, London EC4

ORAL HISTORY

Tapping into people's memories can yield all kinds of information about communities, towns, shops and businesses in the past. Oral history is now a growing field, and many local groups spend time with older residents recording memories. The resulting conversations contain all kinds of information, from simple lists of the locations of shops on the High Street to in-depth memories of how particular businesses were run and fascinating and sometimes amusing recollections. Records of oral history work are often kept in university libraries and local-studies centres. They are also sometimes published, and it is worth scouring your local library for books that include the words 'memories' or 'voices' in the title.

VISUAL EVIDENCE

Your eyes can tell you a lot about the history of your neighbourhood and its High Street, A huge amount of evidence survives in old photographs – postcards, images in books on local history and photographs that local people have collected. In addition, you can tell a surprising amount about the history of your local shops by looking closely at the buildings themselves.

OLD PHOTOGRAPHS AND POSTCARDS

Photography was invented in the 1840s and by the end of the 19th century professional photographers were taking pictures of both people and landscapes. But photography really caught on at the beginning of the 20th century, both with the invention of cheap, simple cameras like the Kodak Box Brownie and with the increase in professional photographers, many of whom were producing postcards.

Early postcards provide all kinds of evidence about how the High Street developed. General town views often include High Street shops, although names of businesses are usually only legible in the foreground. The more different images you can find the better, both alternative views of the same scene and cards dating from different periods.

Look out for postcards at antiques fairs and in shops selling antiques or secondhand books. Many are available on eBay and there is also a Postcard Traders' Association. There are also many published collections, including entire series such as *Britain in Old Photographs* (published by Sutton) and *Images of England* (published by Tempus).

Photographs can be difficult to date unless they have an inscription on the back, but it is possible to make an educated guess at the date of many photographs by looking at people's clothes, the cars on the street and similar period details. Many postcards are franked with the date.

ARCHITECTURAL EVIDENCE

Throughout this book there are pictures of shop fronts from different periods which show how shop design changed from one period to another. The vast majority of old shop fronts have disappeared because retailers are always upgrading their premises in the latest fashion. But a few old shop fronts survive. Often, even if the main front has been altered, some old details remain. Sometimes a historic shop name has been kept. Look out for ghost signs, partly faded signs painted on side or upper walls that may advertise a local business. And small details may survive a revamp. Examine the floor near the shop's entrance, as sometimes an old shop name survives embedded in the tiles or mosaic. And don't ignore details such as rainwater pipes and fittings. Some retailers had these specially made – some WH Smith shops had the initials 'W H S' stamped on the tops of the downpipes.

INTERNET RESOURCES

These websites provide information about local history. Most have many links to other online resources.

BRITISH ASSOCIATION
FOR LOCAL HISTORY
General information for local historians; links to national organisations, local history societies, etc.
www.balh.co.uk

CENSUS
Census returns online.
www.nationalarchives.gov.uk/census

GENUKI
Large family history site.
www.genuki.org.uk

HISTORICAL DIRECTORIES
Digital library of local and trade directories for England and Wales, 1750 to 1919.
www.historicaldirectories.org

LOCAL ARCHIVES
Comprehensive list of local archives.
www.nationalarchives.gov.uk/archon

LOCAL HISTORY ONLINE
Major resource for local historians, with links to societies, courses, speakers and events, created in conjunction with *Local History Magazine*.
www.local-history.co.uk

OLD MAPS
High-resolution scans of Ordnance Survey maps from about 1870 onwards.
www.old-maps.co.uk

OLD PHOTOGRAPHS
The Francis Frith Collection: commercial site selling prints of old photographs.
www.francisfrith.com/uk/

VICTORIA COUNTY HISTORY
Project to create scholarly histories of all the English counties.
www.victoriacountyhistory.ac.uk

YOUR MEMORIES
Archive of memories, plus heritage-related information.
www.yourmemories.co.uk

FURTHER READING

The following books and articles have been consulted during the production of this book and provide useful background reading to the commercial, social, architectural and oral history of shops and shopping:

Alison Adburgham, *Shopping in Style* (Thames and Hudson, 1979)

Alison Adburgham, *Shops and Shopping 1800–1914* (George Allen and Unwin, 1964)

Peter Ashley, *Open For Business* (Everyman Publishers, 2002)

Sonia Ashmore, 'Extinction and Evolution: Department Stores in London's West End, 1945–1982', *The London Journal*, Vol. 31 no. 1, June 2006

Maurice Baren, *How It All Began Up The High Street* (Michael O'Mara, 1996)

Maurice Baren, *How Household Names Began* (Michael O'Mara, 1997)

John Benson and Gareth Shaw, *The Retailing Industry*, 3 vols (I.B. Tauris, 1999)

Rachel Bowlby, *Carried Away: The Invention of Modern Shopping* (Faber, 2000)

John Burnett (ed.), *Useful Toil: Autobiographies of Working People from the 1820s to the 1920s* (Penguin, 1984)

David Buxton, *Devizes Voices* (History Press, 1996)

Margaret Llewelyn Davies (ed.), *Life As We Have Known It: By Co-operative Working Women* (Woolf, 1931)

Dorothy Davis, *A History of Shopping* (Routledge, 1966)

John Dawson, 'Retail Change in Britain During 30 Years: The strategic use of economies of scale and scope', http://www.retaildawson.com/papers/Strategies.pdf, (retrieved 27 April 2010)

Marnie Fogg, *Boutique* (Octopus, 2003)

Marjorie Gardiner, *The Other Side of the Counter* (QueenSpark, 1985)

Jean Gumbrell, *Voices of Saffron Walden* (Chalford, 1998)

Jane Hamlett et al., 'Regulating UK Supermarkets: An Oral History Perspective', *History & Policy*, Policy Paper 70, April 2008 (http://www.historyandpolicy.org/papers/policy-paper-70.html#S3, retrieved 23 April 2010)

Susan Higlett, *Business and Trade in High Street Hounslow 1803 to 1982* (Hounslow and District Historical Society, 1982)

P.C. Hoffman, *They Also Serve: The Story of a Shop Worker* (Porcupine Press, 1949)

Pamela Horn, *Behind the Counter* (Sutton, 2006)

Christopher P. Hosgood, 'The "Pigmies of Commerce" and the Working-Class Community: Small Shopkeepers in England, 1870–1914', *Journal of Social History*, Vol. 22 no. 3, 1989

John W. Howes and A.D. Law, *Shoppers' Paradise* (on Walthamstow) (Walthamstow Historical Society, 1991)

James B. Jefferys, *Retailing Trading in Britain 1850–1950* (Cambridge, 1954)

M. Jeune, 'The Ethics of Shopping', *Fortnightly Review*, Vol. 63, January 1895

David Kynaston, *Austerity Britain* (Bloomsbury, 2007)

John Land, *Bishop Auckland and West Auckland Voices* (Tempus, 1998)

Ian MacLaurin, *Tiger by the Tail: A Life in Business from Tesco to Test Cricket* (Pan Macmillan, 2000)

John Marchant, Bryan Reuben and Joan Alcock, *Bread: A Slice of History* (History Press, 2008)

Cecil A. Meadows, *The Victorian Ironmonger*, booklet (Shire, 1978)

Raynes Minns, *Bombers and Mash* (Virago, 1980)

Chris Morris, *Dairy Farming in Gloucestershire* (Gloucester Folk Museum, 1983)

Kathryn A. Morrison, *English Shops and Shopping* (Yale University Press, 2003)

H.G. Muller, *Baking and Bakeries*, booklet (Shire, 1986)

Sam Mullins and David Stockdale (eds), *Talking Shop* (on Market Harborough) (Sutton, 1994)

New Statesman, The Future of the High Street (October 2007)

David Newton, *Trademarked: A History of Well-Known Brands from Aertex to Wright's Coal Tar* (Sutton, 2008)

William Paine, *Shop Slavery and Emancipation* (P.S. King & Son, 1912)

Mollie Panter-Downes, *Good Evening, Mrs Craven* (Persephone, 1999)

Maud Pember Reeves, *Round About a Pound a Week* (Virago)

Sefryn Penrose and contributors, *Images of Change* (English Heritage, 2007)

Nikolaus Pevsner, *A History of Building Types* (Thames and Hudson, 1976)

Humphrey Phelps, *Forest Voices* (Amberley, 2008)

Erika D. Rappaport, '"The Halls of Temptation": Gender, Politics, and the Construction of the Department Store in Late Victorian London', *Journal of British Studies*, Vol. 35 no. 1, 1996

John Richardson, *The Local Historian's Encyclopedia* (Historical Publications, 1986)

Elizabeth Roberts, *A Woman's Place: An Oral History of Working-Class Women* (Blackwell, 1985)

Desmond C. Whyman, *Shoulder of Mutton Field: The Retail Butcher's Trade in Camden* (Meathist Publications, 2005)

B. Williams, *The Best Butter in the World: A History of Sainsbury's* (Ebury, 1994)

Michael J. Winstanley, *The Shopkeeper's World* (Manchester University Press, 1983)

THE SHOPKEEPERS

The families who took part in *Turn Back Time . . . The High Street* all run modern-day businesses as butchers, bakers, caterers and shopkeepers. Over six weeks they left their modern lives and livelihoods behind to set up shop in the market town of Shepton Mallet where four High Street shops were taken back in time.

Andrew

Michael

Simon

BUTCHERS & GENERAL STORE OWNERS

IRONMONGER, BAZAAR, TOY SHOP & HARDWARE STORE OWNER

Nigel

Caroline

Jack

BAKERS, TEA SHOP, BRITISH RESTAURANT & MILK BAR PROPRIETORS

Raif

Saffron

Chloe

Karl

Debbie

Harry

Saffron

GROCERS & SUPERMARKET MANAGERS

Sunder

Pam

Gill

DRESSMAKER, HAIR SALON & FASHION BOUTIQUE OWNER

Karina

Josh

David

1970s GENERAL STORE OWNERS

RECORD SHOP OWNER

INDEX

Page numbers in *italics* denotes an illustration

A

Adulteration of Food, Drink,
    and Drugs Act (1872) 52–3
advertising
    post-war years 196
    Victorian era *32, 33, 34–5*
Aerated Bread Company (ABCs) 91
Aero 123
air curtain 240
apprenticeship 86–7
Art Deco 104, 133, *133*, 137
Art Nouveau 65, 69, 71
Arts and Crafts movement 25, 65
ASDA 235
Asian immigrants 227–8, 236, 238
Associated British Cinemas 104

B

backslang 57
bacon 157
bakers
    interwar years 111, 112, 114–17,
      114, 116
    1970s 234
    opening of cafés 91–2, 116–17
    Second World War 171
    Victorian era 48–53, *48, 49*
bananas 165
banks 223
bazaars *see* penny bazaars
BBC (British Broadcasting
    Corporation) 136, 179
Beeton, Mrs 51
bicycles 81
Bird's 122, 164
biscuit-making 53
black market 156, *156*
Bloomer, Amelia 81
Bluewater 250
Bobby and Company 74
Bonnett, Geoff 228
Booth, Charles 66, 83
Booth, William 66
Boots 75, *75*, 113, 221, 224, 254
boutiques 244–6, *244*
Bovril 105
Brandenberger, Jacques E. 120
bread
    adulterated 50, *50*, 52–3
    interwar era 114, *114*, 116
    introduction of sliced 114
    Second World War 171–3
    Victorian era 48–9, *49*, 51
bread-baking competitions (1930s)
    114, 116
Brent Cross Shopping Centre 235,
    236, 247

Burlington Arcade (London) 67
Burton, Alice 229
Burton Group 225
butchers 18, 255
    decline in 1970s 234
    differences between town and
      village 122
    Edwardian era 74–5, 84–6, *84, 85*
    interwar years 111, 117–22, *117*
    post-war years 189
    Second World War 148, 157, 160,
      161–2
    Victorian 54–7, *56, 57*
butter, making of 30

C

Cadbury's 123
cafés
    Edwardian era 90, 91, 94
    interwar years 116–17
    post-war years 201–3, *201*, 204
cakes 53
    baking without fresh eggs during
      Second World War 164
    Edwardian 92, *92–3*
    interwar years 116, *116*
Campion, Sidney 87
candle-making 44–5, *44–5*
Cellophane 120
Chance Brothers of Birmingham 36
cheese, making of 30
chemists, chains of in Edwardian
    era 75
Chester 254
chicken coops 162
Chinese restaurants 236
chocolates 123
Churchill, Winston 178
cinema 104
Civilian Clothing (1941) 171
Clark and Son, Thomas 47
class divisions 17–18, 28, 64, 65–6,
    188
Clifton, Charlie 83

clothes/clothes shops
    Edwardian era 94
    interwar years 130–2, *130*, *131*, **132**
    1970s 225, 244–5, *244*, 246–7
    post-war years 200
    Second World War 170–1, *170*
Co-op 77, 78–9, *79*, 122, 189, 191,
    222, 223
Co-operative Wholesale Society (CWS)
    78
Cockaynes department store
    (Sheffield) 71

Cockwell, Gill 96, 246
coffee 202
Cohen, Jack 192, 196
convenience foods 105, 122
corned beef 160
Corner Houses 91
craftsmen, early 13
Cramer, Philip 118
Crawley 113, *186*
credit 83, 87, 107
currency, Victorian era 33, *33*
Curry's 211
'customer is always right' motto 132
cycling 81

D

dairy products
    and Victorian grocer 30
date codes, for food 230
David, Elizabeth 236
Day, William 75
Debenham & Freebody 73
decimal currency 216
deliveries, interwar years 110, 111, 112,
    112–13, *113*, 117, *117*, 118
department stores
    Edwardian 64, 70–1, 72–3
    interwar years 183
    1970s 224–5
    post-war years 197
design and display
    early shops 16
    Edwardian era 69
    interwar years 132–3, *133*, 136
    1970s 240–1
    post-war years 184–5
    Second World War 165
    Victorian era 36–7, *36, 37*,
      46–7, *47*
    see also shop window displays/
      design
Deutsch, Otto 104
Devlin, Nigel 52
Dewhurst 75
DH Evans 73
Dickens, Charles
    Sketches by Boz 36–7
Dig for Victory campaign 152–3, *155*
Distributive Trades Alliance 198
do-it-yourself (DIY) 218, 235
domestic appliances 43, 103, 180, 217
dough mixers 53, 114
dressmakers
    Edwardian era 94–6, *95*
    interwar years *131*
dried eggs 163–4, *164*
dried milk 167

E

economic crisis (2009) 253
Edward VII, King 64, 65–6
Edwardian era (1901–17) 8, 62–99
    bazaars 64, 69, 75–7, 76, 77
    butchers 74–5, 84–6, 84, 85
    cake-making 92, 92–3
    class distinctions 64, 65–6
    credit 83, 87
    cycling 81
    decline in apprenticeship 86–7
    department stores 64, 70–1, 72–3
    dressmakers 94–6, 95
    First World War 65, 67, 85, 97, 102, 105, 134
    grocers 68, 82, 83, 86
    importance of service 80–1
    increase in size of shops 70–2
    measures taken to help the poor 66–7
    personal approach and shopkeeper-customer relationship 83, 84
    rise of multiples 74–5
    tea shops and cafés 90, 91, 91, 94
    timeline 64–7
    and traditional values 77, 80
electrical gadgets 210–11, 221
electrical retailers 107
Elizabeth II, Queen 179
    coronation (1953) 179
    Silver Jubilee 231, 232–3
English Heritage 255
EPs 243
espresso coffee 202
Essex barn 235
ethical shopping 252
European Economic Community (EEC) 217

F

fairs, early 13
Fairtrade movement 252
farmers' markets 252, 255
fashion see clothes/clothes shops
Fenton, Roger 59
financial services sector, 1970s 223
Fine Fare chain 198
First World War 65, 67, 85, 97, 102, 105, 134
fishmongers 14, 234
Fogg, Marnie
    Boutique 245
food adulteration 24, 32, 50
    bread 50, 50, 52–3
    government action against 52–3
food inspectors, Victorian 53
founderies/foundrymen 40–1, 42

G

garages 107
Gardiner, Marjorie
    The Other Side of the Counter 131
gas appliances, first appearance of 43
Gaumont 104
general store 187, 226–8, 227
General Strike (1926) 102
Gothic architecture 25, 46
Great Depression 102
Great Exhibition (1851) 19, 36
Great Fire of London (1666) 15
Green Shield Stamps 198
Griffiths, R.W. ('Willie') 203, 204
Griffiths, Winifred 97
grocers
    Edwardian 68, 82, 83, 86
    interwar years 105, 109, 122, 124, 127
    1970s 234
    post-war years 188, 193
    Second World War 163–5, 163, 173
    Victorian era 28–33, 28, 29

H

Habitat 247, 247
hairdressers 182, 205–7, 205, 207, 210
hairstyles, post-war 206–7
Hancock, Peggy 107–8
Harrods 67, 70–1, 183, 197
Hassall, Arthur Hill 50
hat shops 131–2
Hawkins, Kevin 253–4
Hay-on-Wye 254
Headington, Kathy 204
Heinz 196
Hepburn, Audrey 206
Hepworth's 74, 94
High Street
    early history 10–19
    future of 251–5
Higlett, Susan 107
Hills, Frederick and Ada 84
historic market towns 254
Hoffman, Philip Charles 73, 80, 81
Home and Colonial 163
Home Guard 144
Hooper, Alfred and Louise 77, 80
Horn, Pamela
    Behind the Counter 150
Hornby, Frank 134
Hornby trains 134–5
Hounslow High Street 107
houses
    post-war era 180
    Victorian 43
Hovis 114
Huntley & Palmers 53, 53
hypermarkets 234

I

ice-cream parlours 201, 203
immigrants, 1970s 218–19, 227
Indian restaurants/snacks 219, 236, 238–9, 238–9
Industrial Revolution 17, 22, 29
International Stores 163, 189, 191
Internet, shopping online 251
interwar years (1918–39) 8, 100–39
    bakers 111, 112, 114–17, 114, 116
    butchers 111, 117–22, 117
    challenges for retailing and shopkeepers 107–8, 109
    and cinema 104
    delivery of goods 110, 111, 112, 112–13, 113, 117, 117, 118
    design and display 132–3, 133, 136
    difficulties in 137
    economy 102
    food fashions 105
    grocers 105, 109, 122, 124, 127
    impact of Great Depression 103
    Post Office 127, 127, 136
    radios 136–7, 136, 137
    rationing 108
    recovery after depression 103
    sweet shop 123, 123
    timeline 102–5
    toy shops 134–5, 134
    unemployment 102, 103, 132
    women working in retailing 108–9
    women's clothes 130–1, 130, 131
    working conditions in shops 108, 109
ironmongers
    Second World War 167
    Victorian 26, 27, 38–47, 38, 39, 42, 46, 47

J

jam, making own during war 166
jazz 104
John Lewis Partnership 225

K

Kendal Milne 183
Kilner Brothers 38
Kit Kat 123

L

Laski, Marghanita 225
Leeds Model Company 134
lighting, Victorian era 44
Lipton's 32–3, 163
livery companies 260–1
livestock fair 87, 88–9

London 14, 15, 70
    Booth's survey of 66, 83
    department stores 70–1, 224
    early shops 16
    psychedelic shop front 184, *185*
    shopping areas 200
Lord John *185*
LPs 242, *242, 243,* 244
Ludlow 15, 254
Lyons & Co, J. *90,* 91

M

McLaren, Malcolm 246
Macmillan, Harold 180
macon 157
Madame shops 130
make-up 208–9, *210*
malls, out-of-town 234, *235,* 236,
    250
markets
    early 11, *12–13*
    Victorian era 27–8
Marks & Spencer 64, 75, *76,* 130, 197,
    199, *199,* 221, 225, 235, 254
Marks, Michael 75
Mars Bar 123
Mars, Forrest 123
meat 54, 56–7
    Edwardian era 84–5
    post-war years 189
    shortages and managing of in
        Second World War 157–62
    Victorian era 54, 56–7
    see also butchers
meat auctions 119
Meccano *133,* 134
Melly, George
    Revolt Into Style 245–6
metalwork *42, 43*
microwave 236–7
Middle Ages 11–14, 15
milk 30
    delivering of during Victorian era
        30, *30,* 31
    Second World War 166–7
Milk Bars 203–4
Milky Way 123
Minns, Raynes 163
    Bombers and Mash 161
mock foods *160*
modernist architecture *132–3,* 184
mods and rockers 204
Morrisons 221, 231
multiples 251
    interwar years 122
    post-war years 189–90
    return to High Street 254
    rise of in Edwardian era 74–5
mushrooms 166

music, 1970s 241–4
music systems 241, *241*

N

National Front 218, 219
National Loaf 171–2, *172*
Nelson & Sons, James 75
Next 254
1970s 9, 214–49
    clothes/clothes shops 225, 244–5,
        244, 246–7
    consumerism 221
    decline of traditional specialist
        shops 234
    decrease in number of shops 223
    department stores 224–5
    design and display 240–1
    eating out 236–7
    economic problems 216, 222
    financial services sector 223
    general store 226–8, *227*
    immigrants and Asian
        shopkeepers 218–19, 228
    music 241–4
    other businesses on High Street
        223
    out-of-town shopping 234–6, *235*
    supermarkets 216, 221, 226,
        230–1, 234, 235, 247
    timeline 216–19
    unemployment 216, 217
    voluntary societies 228–9

O

Odeon cinemas 104
Old Age Pensions Act 66
online shopping 251, *252*
Opie, Robert 190
out-of-town shopping 234–6, *235,* 251
ovens, Victorian bakery *48, 49*
Owen, Robert 78, *78*

PQ

Pearce's Beef Steak Puddings 54
pedestrianisation 186, *186*
penny bazaars 64, 69, 75–6, 77, 80
Pepys, Samuel 15
perms 206
Peter Robinson 225
photographer, Victorian 58–9, *59*
pig breeds 54
pig clubs 158, *158*
pigs, Second World War 157–8
Pink Stamps 198
poor
    and bread 114
    measures to help in Edwardian
        era 66–7
    and shopping 28, 29, 31, 64, 67, 77

Popular Café (London) *90*
pork 54
Post Office 127, *127,* 136
post-war years (1945–69) 176–213
    advertising *196*
    butchers 189
    cafés 201–3, *201, 204*
    department stores 197
    electrical gadgets 210–11
    grocers 188, 193
    hairdressers 205–7, *205, 207,* 210
    milk bars 203–4, *204*
    pedestrianisation 186, *186*
    pricing policy 192
    rationing 183
    rebuilding town centres 185–7
    rise of Tesco 196
    self-service 181, *184,* 188, 189–93,
        189, 190, 191, 192
    supermarkets 191
    timeline 178–81
    trading stamps 198
    traditional food shopping 188–9
        and women 205
    youth culture 199–200
pricing policy 192
Pritchard, Jack 111
processed foods 31, 105
punk 245, 246–7
Pure Food Acts 24

Quant, Mary 183, 200

R

rabbit pie 159
radios 136–7, *136, 137,* 241
railways 23–4
rationing
    interwar years 108
    post-war years 183
    Second World War 142–3, 147–8,
        149, 150–1, *150, 152*
record shops 223, 224, 244
Reeves, Maud Pember 87
refrigerators 119
Reith, John 136
Resale Price Maintenance, abolition
    of 192, 196, 230
retail parks 251
rickets 50
River Plate Fresh Meat Company
    74–5
Rouquet, André 16
Rowntree's of York *112*
royal icing 92, *92*

S

Sainsbury, Alan 230
Sainsbury, John 32, *32,* 33, 36

Sainsbury's 157, 181, 191, *191*, *192*, *194–5*, 221, 226, 231
Salisbury 15
sausages 55, *55*, 160
Sayers, Dorothy L.
    Busman's Honeymoon 110
Second World War (1939–45) 8, 140–75, 178
    bakers 171
    black market 156, *156*
    bombing 142, 148
    bread 171–3
    butchers 148, 157, 160, 161–2
    clothes 170–1, *170*
    Dig for Victory campaign 152–3, *155*
    foraging for wild food 166, *168–9*
    grocers 163–5, *163*, 173
    increase in social mobility 145
    ironmongers 167
    Make Do and Mend campaign 167, 170, *171*
    meat shortages and ways of managing 157–62
    milk 166–7
    phoney war 143
    preparing for potential invasion 144
    problems faced by shopkeepers 148–9, 173
    shortages and rationing 142–3, 147–8, 149, 150–1, *150*, 152
    timeline 142–5
    and women 144–5
self-service
    1970s 222
    post-war years 181, 184, *188*, 189, *189–93*, *190*, *191*, *192*
Selfridges 71, *71*, *211*
Sergison, Debbie 165
Sergison, Saffron 126
Sex (shop) 246
shambles 12, 14, 15
Sharp, Michael 210
Sheperdson, Jane 252
Shepton Mallet (Somerset) 12, *256*
shoe shops *132*, 174
shop opening hours 90, 108
shop signs 184
shop window displays/design
    interwar years 132–3
    1970s 240, *240*
    post-war years 184
    Second World War 165
    Victorian 36
shop windows 15–16, 36–7
shop workers
    conditions in interwar dress shops 131–2
    hours worked 90

    living in 72–3, *72*
    working conditions in interwar years 108, 109
shopkeeper–customer relationship
    breaking of bond by self-service 192, *193*, 196
    Second World War 162
    Edwardian era 83, 84
    post-war years 188
    Victorian era 31, 57
shopping centres 181, 186
Shops Act (1911) 90
Small Pig Keepers' Council 157
spam 160–1, *161*
Spar 228, *229*
specialist retailing 254
Spencer, Tom 75
Stacey, Jenny 204
Starley, John Kemp 81
Stevens, Ebenezer 53
Stow, John
    A Survey of London 14
supermarkets 181, 190
    1970s 216, 221, 226, 230–1, 234, 235, 247
    post-war years 191
    and pricing in 1970s 226
sweatshops 252
sweet shops 123, *123*, 126, 229
sweets 122, 123, *123*, 126
    home-made 124, *124*, *125*

T

tailors 74
tallymen 87
tea shops 91, *91*, 94
Teddy Boys *203*
television 179–80, 196, 221
Tesco 181, 191, 192, 196, *197*, *198*, 221, 222, *222*, 226, 231, *231*
tinned foods 105
TopShop 225
toy shops 134–5, *134*
Traders' Defence Associations 78
trading stamps 198
transport, Victorian era 23–4
Turner, W.F. 90

U

unemployment
    interwar years 102, 103, 132
    1970s 216, 217

V

Verrall, Marie 160
Victorian era (1870–1901) 8, 19, 20–59
    advertising 32, 33, *34–5*
    bakers 48–53, *48*, *49*
    breaking down of class distinctions

    in shopping 28
    butchers 54–7, *56*, *57*
    candle-making 44–5, *44–5*
    currency 33, *33*
    design and display 36–7, *36*, *37*, *46–7*, *47*
    fashion and taste 25
    food adulteration 24, 32, 50
    grocers 28–33, *28*, *29*
    homes 43
    impact of industrial activity and trade links on shops 22–3
    ironmonger 26, 27, 38–47, *38*, *39*, *46*, *47*
    markets 27–8
    quality and marketing 32–3
    timeline 22–5
    transport revolution 23–4
vinyl records 241, 242–3, *242*
voluntary societies 228–9

W

Wall Street Crash (1929) 102, 103
Westfield *252*
Weston Favell Shopping Centre 236
Westwood, Vivienne 246
WH Smith 221, 224, 244
Whiteley, William 71
Wholesale Meat Supply Associations 157
Wilkinson's 38
William the Conqueror 11
wireless *see* radios
women
    cycling in Edwardian era 81
    First World War 105
    money management 87
    in 1970s 219
    post-war years 205
    Second World War 144–5
    vote campaign 66
    working in retailing during interwar years 108–9
Women's Land Army 144, 149, 205
Wonder Bread 114
Woolf, Virginia 91
Woolton, Lord 157
Woolworth, Frank Winfield 75–6
Woolworth's 64, 69, 76, 77, 97, 130, 224, *224*, 253
workshops 13
Wren, Sir Christopher 15
Wyatt and Son, George 46

YZ

York 15, 254
youth culture
    1970s 222, 225, 245, 246
    post-war years 199–200

Quercus Publishing Plc
21 Bloomsbury Square
London
WC1A 2NS

First published in 2010

PROGRAMME AND FORMAT
© Wall to Wall Media Limited
EXECUTIVE PRODUCER: Leanne Klein
SERIES PRODUCER: Cate Hall
PRODUCER: Tom St John Gray

TEXT AND PHOTOS
© Quercus Publishing plc
TEXT: Philip Wilkinson
DESIGN: Austin Taylor
PHOTOGRAPHY: Mark Winwood
PICTURE RESEARCH: Emma O'Neill

Philip Wilkinson would like to thank
Zoë Brooks for her invaluable help with
research; also Peter Ashley, Ann Kramer,
and Margaret Wilkinson for answering
queries. The publishers would like to
thank Cate Hall and Tom St John Gray
for their invaluable assistance
throughout the making of this book.

A catalogue record of this book is
available from the British Library

ISBN: 978 1 84916 420 7

Printed and bound in Germany

10 9 8 7 6 5 4 3 2 1

PICTURE CREDITS

All images in this book were photographed by Mark Winwood with the exception of the following:

2 Mary Evans Picture Library/The Francis Frith Collection; 20-21 Mary Evans Picture Library/The Francis Frith Collection; 22 left Mary Evans Picture Library; 22 right Getty Images/SSPL; 23 left Mary Evans Picture Library; 23 right Getty Images/Hulton Archive; 24 left Mary Evans Picture Library; 24 right Getty Images/Hulton Archive; 25 left & right Mary Evans Picture Library; 29 Mary Evans Picture Library; 30 top TopFoto/HIP/Museum of London; 30 centre & bottom TopFoto; 31 Getty Images/Hulton Archive; 32 The Advertising Archives; 33 Courtesy of Tony Clayton; 34 Mary Evans Picture Library; 35 top left The Advertising Archives; 35 top right, bottom left & right Mary Evans Picture Library; 37 ©English Heritage.NMR; 39 top Mary Evans Picture Library; 40-41 TopFoto/HIP/English Heritage; 42 Mary Evans Picture Library; 44 left Mary Evans Picture Library; 46 Mary Evans Picture Library; 47 fotoLIBRA.com/Sharon Poole; 48 Corbis/Jennifer Kennard; 49 Oxfordshire County Council Photographic Archive; 50 Mary Evans Picture Library; 53 Mary Evans Picture Library; 54 TopFoto/HIP/The National Archives; 56 Mary Evans Picture Library; 59 top Getty Images/SSPL; 62-63 Mary Evans Picture Library/Francis Frith Collection; 64 left Getty Images/SSPL; 64 right Getty Images/New York Daily News Archive; 65 left Shell Brands International AG; 66 left Getty Images/Rischgitz; 66 centre The Advertising Archives; 66 right Getty Images/Popperfoto/Bob Thomas; 67 left Mary Evans Picture Library/Robert Hunt Library; 67 right Mary Evans Picture Library/Illustrated London News; 70 Mary Evans Picture Library; 71 TopFoto/HIP/National Motor Museum; 72 Mary Evans Picture Library; 75 TopFoto/HIP/Print Collector; 76 Getty Images/Popperfoto; 78 Getty Images/Hulton Archive; 79 top & bottom Mary Evans Picture Library; 81 Mary Evans Picture Library; 84 TopFoto; 87 Getty Images/Topical Press Agency; 88-89 Mary Evans Picture Library/The Francis Frith Collection; 90 ©English Heritage.NMR; 92 TopFoto; 97 Getty Images/Fox Photos; 100-101 Mary Evans Picture Library/The Francis Frith Collection; 102 left TopFoto/The Granger Collection; 102 right Getty Images/SSPL; 103 left Mary Evans Picture Library/Illustrated London News; 103 right Mary Evans Picture Library; 104 left TopFoto/HIP/Print Collector; 104 right TopFoto/Topham Picturepoint; 105 left Mary Evans Picture Library/Illustrated London News; 105 right Mary Evans Picture Library/Interfoto Agentur; 110 TopFoto/HIP/University of York; 112 TopFoto/HIP/University of York; 113 top Mary Evans Picture Library; 113 bottom TopFoto; 114 Mary Evans Picture Library; 116 Alamy/Mirrorpix/Trinity Mirror; 118-119 Getty Images/Hulton Archive/Fred Ramage; 121 Getty Images/Popperfoto/Bob Thomas; 124 Mary Evans Picture Library; 127 Getty Images/Popperfoto/Bob Thomas; 128-129 The Advertising Archives; 132 Mary Evans Picture Library; 133 RIBA Library Photographs Collection/Architectural Press; 134 Mary Evans Picture Library; 135 top left & right The Advertising Archives; 136 TopFoto/The Granger Collection; 137 Mary Evans Picture Library; 140-141 Getty Images/Hulton Archive/George W. Hales; 142 left The Advertising Archives; 142 centre Getty Images/Hulton Archive; 143 left Mary Evans Picture Library/Robert Hunt Library; 143 right Getty Images/Hulton Archive/Fred Morley; 144 left Getty Images/Hulton Archive; 144 right TopFoto/HIP/Land Lost Content; 145 left Mary Evans Picture Library/Robert Hunt Library/Imperial War Museum; 145 right Getty Images/Hulton Archive/Picture Post; 150 TopFoto/Topham Picturepoint; 154 top The Advertising Archives; 154 bottom left TopFoto/HIP/Public Record Office; 154 bottom right The Advertising Archives; 155 TopFoto/HIP/Public Record Office; 156 Getty Images/Hulton Archive/George Konig; 157 Mary Evans Picture Library/Onslow Auctions Limited; 158 Getty Images/Hulton Archive/Harry Todd; 161 The Advertising Archives; 164 Corbis/Bettmann; 167 Mary Evans Picture Library/Robert Hunt Library; 168-169 Getty Images/Hulton Archive/Reg Speller; 172 Getty Images/Popperfoto; 176-177 TopFoto/HIP/Museum of London; 178 left Getty Images/Hulton Archive/Douglas Miller; 178 right Mary Evans Picture Library/Chris Coupland; 179 left Mary Evans Picture Library/Rue des Archives/PVDF; 179 right Mirrorpix; 180 left Getty Images/Hulton Archive/Evening Standard; 180 right The Advertising Archives; 181 left Getty Images/Hulton Archive/Henry Kreuger; 181 right Getty Images/Hulton Archive/RDA; 185 TopFoto/Topham Picturepoint; 186 Mary Evans Picture Library/The Francis Frith Collection; 191 ©The Sainsbury Archive, Museum of London Docklands; 192 Getty Images/Hulton Archive/John Chillingworth; 194-195 Mirrorpix; 197 Rex Features/Daily Mail; 199 The Advertising Archives; 201 Getty Images/Hulton Archive/Topical Press Agency; 203 Getty Images/Popperfoto; 206 Getty Images/Roger Viollet; 208 Mary Evans Picture Library/National Magazines; 209 The Advertising Archives; 211 Getty Images/Hulton Archive/John Murray; 214-215 Rex Features/Chris Capstick; 216 left Getty Images/Popperfoto; 216 right The Advertising Archives; 217 left Getty Images/Hulton Archive/Keystone; 217 right Getty Images/Hulton Archive/Wesley; 218 left Rex Features/Ray Stevenson; 218 centre Mary Evans Picture Library; 218 right Mary Evans Picture Library/Illustrated London News; 219 left Getty Images/New York Daily News Archive; 219 right Getty Images/Tim Graham Photo Library; 222 TopFoto/Topham Picturepoint; 224 TopFoto/HIP/Walters Industrial Archive; 227 Getty Images/Hulton Archive/Evening Standard; 229 Rex Features/Daily Mail/Little; 230 The Marks & Spencer Company Archive; 231 The Advertising Archives; 232-233 TopFoto/Topham/Colin James; 235 TopFoto; 237 top & bottom The Advertising Archives; 241 The Advertising Archives; 242 top Getty Images/Hulton Archive/Angela Deane-Drummond; 242 bottom Rex Features/Lehtikuva Oy; 245 Getty Images/Redferns/Virginia Turbett; 247 Alamy/M&N; 250 Corbis/Construction Photography; 252 M&S Westfield (Corbis/Jane Sweeney); 253 Corbis/Richard Klune; 255 Corbis/Andrew Fox; 256 Mike Barnsley/commissioned by www.no21.com.